Writing Processes and Structures

AN AMERICAN LANGUAGE TEXT

Brian Altano
BERGEN COMMUNITY COLLEGE

ANN ARBOR
THE UNIVERSITY OF MICHIGAN PRESS

Copyright © The University of Michigan 2004

All rights reserved
ISBN 0-472-08939-0

Published in the United States of America by The University of Michigan Press
Manufactured in the United States of America
2007 2006 2005 2004   1 2 3 4

Grateful acknowledgement is made to the following authors, publishers, and journals for permission to reprint previously published material.

Brian Altano for Lloyd's Center in Portland, Bergen County, Accommodations, Here Comes the Bride, The Basket of Cabbages, Doctors Tie Male Mentality to Shorter Life Span, Baseball and Football, Dr. Kevorkian Sentenced, Cats and Dogs, Living in Miami and Hallendale, Personal Ads, A Night in Chicago, Recipe: Tortellini All'Altano, Yakitori, and Honey Boy.

Associated Press for "Run DMC DJ Gunned Down," © 2002 and for "51 Drug Traffickers Executed in China," © 1995. Reprinted with permission.

Elizabeth Barnett, literary executor, for "Lament" by Edna St. Vincent Millay. From *Collected Poems,* HarperCollins. Copyright 1921, 1948 by Edna St. Vincent Millay. All rights reserved. Reprinted by permission.

Carcanet Press for "To a Poor Old Woman" by William Carlos Williams, from *Collected Poems: Volume 1,* edited by Walton Litz and Christopher McGowan, © 1987 by Carcanet Press Ltd. Reprinted by permission of Carcanet Press Ltd.

Defense Visual Information Center for the photograph of Abraham Lincoln (HD-SN-99-01776).

The Franklin Delano Roosevelt Presidential Museum for photograph of FDR's inaugural speech, 1933.

Library of Congress prints and photographs division for Benjamin Franklin: The statesman and Philosopher LC-USZ62-28235, Frederick Douglass LC-USZ62-94490, and The Tomb of Kosciusko: West Point LC-USZ62-51102.

Miami Downtown Development Authority for the photograph "Key Biscayne and the Miami Skyline."

New Directions for "To a Poor Old Woman" by William Carlos Williams, from *Collected Poems: 1909–1939, Volume 1,* © 1938 by New Directions Publishing Corp. Reprinted with permission of New Directions Publishing Corp.

The New York Times for "Titanic: A Spectacle as Sweeping as the Sea" by Janet Maslin © 1997.

Psychology Today for "The Truth about Lying" by Allison Kornet, May/June 1997. Reprinted with permission from *Psychology Today* magazine, © 1997 Sussex Publishers, Inc.

Random House Group Limited for "In Another Country" from *The First 49 Stories* by Ernest Hemingway published by Jonathan Cape. Used by permission of the Random House Group Limited (U.K.).

Simon & Schuster for "In Another Country" by Ernest Hemingway. Reprinted with permission of Scribner, an imprint of Simon & Schuster Adult Publishing Group, from *The Short Stories of Ernest Hemingway.* Copyright by Charles Scribner's Sons. Copyright renewed 1955 by Ernest Hemingway.

United States Army Signal Corps/John Fitzgerald Kennedy Library, Boston for JFK's inaugural speech photograph.

The University of Michigan Photo Services for the baseball and football photographs.

The Vail Daily for "Fine Dining Meets Rocky Mountain Eclectic" by Stephen Lloyd Wood, © 2000.

To the following students who allowed their material to appear in this book: Claudio Aponte, Gladys Arguello, Andrej Dombrowski, Roberto Fracaviglia, Sojita Ghanshyman, Hanna Huang, Makiko Imai, Hanna Jawinska, Jae Won Lee, Rebecca Lee, Olga Levit, Giuliana Maraini, Manuel Morales, Juan Murillo, Patrick Onwubu, Usha Patel, Doris Pava-Ruiz, Frida Pertonceli, Manuala Rojao, Tatiana Runjka, Tipavan Sinisgalesh, Jadwiga Stefinska, Iryna Tsyvova, Alyssa Wai, and Yoojin Yoon.

Every effort has been made to contact the copyright holders for permission to reprint borrowed material. We regret any oversights that may have occurred and will rectify them in future printings of this book.

ACKNOWLEDGMENTS

To Isabelle, the inspiration for so many creative ideas, who gave me the time to write this book.

To Brian, whose talent is surpassed only by his generous and spontaneous nature.

Special thanks to Dr. Al McDowell and Dr. Steve Ryan for their close analysis of the text, and to Professors Bob Freud, Carol Miele, Milena Christov, Margarita Lopez-Bernstein, Chuck Zisa, Lisa Glick, Admer Gouryh, Don Martini, Ru Ru Rusmin, Hillary Sweig, Sonya Rimokh, Kathleen Maree, Tom Ihde, Kristina Nordstrom, Susana Lansangan Sabangan, Beth Snyder, Hanna Prashker, Joe Klauber, Maria Montoya, Maria Kasparova, Macey Faiella, Gemma Figaro, Brian Quinn, Herb Pierson, Tony Cruz, Kathleen Maher, Burt Wexler, Pamela Stewart, Jamal Elborj, and Harold Kahn for utilizing this text in class and for offering their kind suggestions on its improvement. I would also like to thank the more than 3,000 Bergen Community College students in the American Language Program and the students at Raritan Valley Community College who have used the text in their writing courses. Their interest, enthusiasm, and intelligence have provided me with a great deal of encouragement.

My gratitude also to Bob Modelski at the Ridgewood Press for his prompt attention, professionalism, and patience these five years during the development of the book.

Art work, including that for the cover, was provided by Brian Joseph Altano.

All inquiries should be addressed to:
Brian Altano
c/o The University of Michigan Press
esladmin@umich.edu

CONTENTS

This section provides suggestions for the use of *Writing Processes and Structures: An American Language Text.* Of course, you should personalize any text used in class and choose topics and exercises that are of interest to you and that fit into the goals and objectives of the individual course. Since there are at least 10 writing assignments in each Part, and more than 75 in the book, use the following notes to help you decide which ones to use.

The Structure of the Book

This book is divided into seven Parts, an Appendix, and an Answer Key. The Parts represent rhetorical modes, or paragraph types: description, narration, process, comparison and contrast, persuasion, and the five-paragraph essay. The Appendix provides a summary of paragraph types, with the key words, the principal verb tenses, the structure, and the outline of each. There is an overview of the ten types of journals, with additional journal entry suggestions, as well as model paragraphs written by ESL students. The Answer Key supplies responses to the grammar, reading comprehension, and discussion questions, as well as answers to the Part Summary Sections.

Each Part is structured in the same way:

+ an introduction to the paragraph type

+ a vocabulary acquisition section

+ a section on grammatical structures

+ a writing skills segment

+ a journal description and activity

+ three units with specific writing assignments and activities

+ a Part summary page

+ a reflections page in which students will write their reactions to the Part

+ an assignment checklist so that students can record their progress

+ a journal summary

VOCABULARY DEVELOPMENT

As students progress to the advanced levels of English, vocabulary presents an increasing challenge to their writing. More and more language concepts are abstract, and students are often required to write on a wide variety of topics. This book approaches vocabulary development in several different ways: proficiency in the identification of parts of speech, writing a list of vocabulary words specific to topic (hotels, mall activities, self-improvement terms, literary terms, art terminology), telling the difference between *denotation* and *connotation* and *literal* and *figurative* meaning, using context clues to help identify the connotation and meaning of words, and establishing word clusters to improve comprehension.

Vocabulary building requires *active* interest and effort on the part of the student. Some instructors recommend that students keep a vocabulary journal or list in a separate notebook or a separate section of a larger notebook. Students certainly should be encouraged to write down new words and to establish glossaries for certain paragraph types and writing topics. Generally, writing topics tend to repeat themselves in other courses, so the time spent here may actually save time in the future. At any rate, the development of strong vocabulary acquisition skills is an important one in order to be a successful student.

SPECIFIC VOCABULARY

Vocabulary may pose a serious problem for students. When they are asked to write about a very specific topic—such as hotels, works of art, apartment hunting, dinner party etiquette, or mall activities—the lack of knowledge of precise words might hinder their writing and shift the focus away from writing techniques toward finding the correct word. It is a good idea to discuss as a class the vocabulary to be used in a particular piece or writing. Another way of approaching vocabulary is to have students compose their own lists of words for homework and share them with the class. For several assignments in the text, a glossary has been provided. Instructors might wish to make composing a specific vocabulary a routine activity in the writing process.

THE WRITING SKILLS SEGMENT

Each Part has a writing skills segment that introduces a different part of the writing process. This section should be closely covered by you and understood by students. The concepts presented include work on the structure of the paragraph, the topic sentence, revision techniques, outlining, proofreading, organization of support, brainstorming, symbolism, and figurative language.

GRAMMAR IN A WRITING CONTEXT

Students must be acutely aware of grammar in both the writing and editing process. Certain grammar points are specific to a particular type of paragraph. Thus, subject–verb agreement, the most common mistake on the sentence level, is important for description writing because the structures *there is/there are, am/is/are,* and *have/has* are very common. Students should analyze this grammatical concept and apply it **in isolation.** That is, in proofreading, they should underline all the verbs in the paragraph, and check them against the subject to make sure they are correct.

Other chapters treat thorny grammatical challenges such as punctuation, verb tenses, adjective clauses, sentence combining, run-on sentences, and noun clauses. The grammar exercises probably should be assigned for homework and may be corrected in class, in groups, or through the Answer Key; analyze specific problem areas suggested by students.

The focus of the writing method is not solely grammatical. It is the ***awareness*** of grammar points on the part of the students that is the goal. Students should closely analyze their paragraphs for potential mistakes. Especially in paragraphs written at home when they have extensive revision time, students should be very demanding, check each grammar point introduced in the book, and strive for improvement in writing and the application of grammar skills to the writing process. During the editing process, they should check each point *separately* and go through the paragraph several times. Students must recognize that they cannot simply write a paragraph and hand it in for correction and a grade. They must edit and revise the paragraph until they have checked it several times before they submit it.

WRITING IN CLASS VERSUS WRITING AT HOME

During the course of a semester, writing instructors might give approximately one assignment per week, aside from work that is self-corrected or peer-corrected. Students assignments for the semester should be divided equally between in-class and at-home work. The two occasions for writing actually have different goals, objectives, and scenarios. In-class writing provides the following data: how student write under pressure (a preparation for in-class essays in regular college courses), how they write without additional tools (spell-check and grammar-check on the computer; the assistance of more proficient family members, friends, and tutors), and how they manage their time. Grammar assumes primary importance during in-class assignments while spelling is less essential. In-class writing actually provides you with the only true means of evaluating student skills and improvement. A graded writing assignment is provided for Parts 2 through 7.

During at-home writing, students must seek perfection. Accept *no spelling mistakes* on at-home paragraphs. Students have extensive time for proof-reading and must look up *every* word in the dictionary if there is a doubt. They must also be instructed that errors in basic grammar concepts such as the ones highlighted in the book (subject–verb agreement, punctuation, verb tenses) should be corrected before they hand in their paragraphs. The quality of at-home writing should be higher. Since most of the writing that students will do in Freshman English / English Composition classes is done at home, they should be reassured that developing this demanding attitude toward their writing will reap not only present but also future benefits.

THE PART SUMMARY PAGE AND REFLECTIONS ON PROGRESS PAGE

Each Part concludes with a Part Summary page, which reviews the concepts introduced and requires students to demonstrate mastery. These questions take time, so they should probably be assigned as homework. They can be reviewed in class before the next Part is introduced. The Reflections on Your Progress page is more personal. There are no right or wrong answers, just reactions to the writing and journal topics, and considerations on progress made. Students should be assigned the Reflection on Your Progress page as homework in order to keep them updated in terms of their goals and objectives for the course.

Part One: The Basics

This Part provides the foundation for the book by introducing the terms and concepts that the students will need throughout the course. Many will do their writing on the computer, so a brief introduction to Microsoft Word is given. The transferability of Word is its strongest asset because it is found on computers in school labs and libraries as well as on all home and laptop computers. Since students will have to word process all work in college classes, it makes sense to have them begin (continue) to use Microsoft Word at this level.

PARTS OF SPEECH

The section on parts of speech provides a detailed introduction that students will use in all their writing. Since it is difficult to write anything without specific vocabulary, when students learn new words they should be aware of their part of speech and function. While the identification of parts of speech is both a writing and reading skill, the knowledge of what particular part of speech fits in a specific position in a sentence is essential in sentence development. Thus, it is advisable to focus on the second part of speech exercise (inserting a word in a sentence) and duplicate more of this type. As students move toward more sophisticated grammar structures (more complex sentences), part-of-speech work should be reinforced with an exercise every other week.

SENTENCE PATTERNS

In Part 1, five of the most common sentence patterns are introduced. These will probably suffice for most of the course. Students are taught here how to identify the types and are also asked to reproduce them. In every writing assignment they do, it is possible to have them analyze individual sentences. Especially when they make mistakes in punctuation, students should be directed to tell what type of sentences they have written and which grammar rules apply.

THE JOURNAL

Soccer players warm up before the game and have many practice sessions. Musicians practice again and again before they are able to perform. The same holds true with writing. The journal is an important part of the writing process. Because you should not grade them for mistakes and lacunae, journals represent nonthreatening writing. This concept should be stressed to students. Journals are for improvisation and creativity, reaction, and assertion. They should be interesting and fun. It is important for students to develop the *habit* of writing and to realize that it is an everyday activity. At the beginning of each Part, journal suggestions are given, according to the type of paragraph introduced. However, it should also be pointed out that students have free reign in choosing journal topics. I have found that students who keep journals assiduously make far greater improvement in their writing skills than those who don't. Journals should be collected regularly (once every three weeks, once per month, three times per semester, etc.) and read by you. The grades might be A (if all the work has been done), C (if several are missing), and F (if the journal is not kept). The grade is not according to the quality of the individual writing, but simply a reflection of the fact that the journal is complete. Students should be assigned a journal at least three to four times per week.

There are ten types of journals introduced in the book. They are presented in each Part and also summarized in the Appendix. The types are the personal journal, the creative listing journal, the dream journal, the double-entry journal, the four-entry journal, the memorandum journal, the essay as journal, the lying journal, the personal improvement journal, and the advice journal. The variety of journals is meant to encourage continued interest on the part of the student. Because diary writing (recounting the simple themes of our quotidian existence) can become repetitive and even boring, the expansion of the diary into a journal, and the use of ten different journals, should stimulate the students to continue their journal work throughout the semester.

PEER EVALUATION

It is a good idea to treat a writing course as a workshop in which all students participate and share their skills in order to improve their writing. While exchanging papers for peer evaluation might be difficult at first, especially given the cultural background of the students, it is an important part of the writing process. Theoretically and practically, students forge closer bonds when they realize that they are not alone in their struggles. Make sure that peer evaluation is as much about finding positive aspects as negative ones. Students should always begin by telling what they like about their partner's work. The recommendations for improvement should be specific, which is why point no. 4 ("the one change that would make the greatest improvement in this piece") is the most important one. They probably must be taught to do this in a very tactful manner.

PERSONAL INTRODUCTION AND ESTABLISHMENT OF GOALS AND OBJECTIVES

When we teach writing, we come to know many aspects of our students' lives. This involvement reveals that improving writing is a very personal process. I find that this must be reciprocal, which is why I distribute a brief autobiography to my students on the first day. After we read my piece, the students write their own personal introduction. Of course, this activity may be done in pairs, where students introduce themselves, interview each other, and write about their partner. At any rate, personal introductions reveal details of students' lives and also give an indication of the level of their proficiency on the first day of the semester, so that the instructor can better gauge baseline individual and class proficiency levels. Students should also establish personal goals and objectives and write them down. At the end of the semester, they can analyze their current situation and see if, in fact, they have achieved their goals.

Part 2: Description Paragraphs

There are three purposes to the Part on description. There are several *icebreakers* that help the students to get to know each other and to overcome any initial jitters. The atmosphere in a writing class must be relaxed, with a spirit of cooperation, involvement, and perhaps commiseration. Second, this Part gives students their first practice in the book in writing, developing, expanding, and perfecting a paragraph. Finally, it shows them how important organization is to effective writing.

The Face in the Mirror in Unit 2.1 on page 45 is supposed to be lighthearted. By stressing a negative aspect of their appearance, students should take this opportunity to laugh at themselves, realizing that everyone is created equal early in the morning. The *Personal Ad* activity on page 45 should be enjoyable, too. Depending on the mood and personality of the class, students can either write an ad about themselves (if they are outgoing and familiar with such ads) or about the characters drawn in the caricatures. They could also use family members and friends as subjects for the personal ad. In general, international students might be a bit reticent at first. On the other hand, when I did this activity in Composition I class with a predominance of American students, they were so familiar with this genre that they did not take the writing seriously. They produced wonderful verbal caricatures that had no relationship whatsoever with reality. (This might, in fact, be the case with most personal ads.)

In introducing the *National Hero* activity on page 48, it is essential to stress the difference between the citation of sources and plagiarism. Students might not understand this concept, so the instructor must make it very clear through specific examples. Utilizing research as the basis of writing implies understanding the rules of citation. It is best for students to learn this skill and these rules here, where the atmosphere is less threatening and more supportive, rather than on the final paper in a psychology course, where plagiarism might lead to a grade of F.

Students will be able to exercise their creativity in this Part by designing their own hotels and living spaces. The vocabulary work from the hotel reading passage and exercises should serve as the basis for this paragraph. The *Design a Living Space* activity in Unit 2.2 on page 54 is a practice in prepositional phrases (*in the corner, above the television,* etc.) and is important for students to practice. This is a good activity for peer correction, so that they can learn from each others' mistakes.

The *Description of Mall Activities at Lloyd's Center in Portland, Oregon* on page 58 offers practice in vocabulary, sentence structure, and verb forms and tenses. It also should make students realize the concept of *globalization.* Most malls have the same stores, no matter what region of the United States, and even in many countries around the world. Sears, J.C. Penneys, Bed Bath & Beyond, Macy's, the Yankee Candle Shop, Pier One Imports, and Linens & Things are ubiquitous, as are the restaurants in the food court. Perhaps you will want students to write about this concept: whether having identical malls with identical stores adds something or takes something away from local flavor.

The final activity in the Part, a graded writing assignment (page 62) that entails *Describing a Painting or Work of Art,* should also be an enjoyable communal experience that introduces students to the library. It is quite interesting to watch their reactions as they browse through the oversized books searching for an artist that they know and love. The conversations I have with them in the library bring us much closer because they take place outside the traditional classroom environment. For this assignment, stress the dual requirement in the paragraph—description and personal reaction. First, students should attempt to describe the work as they understand it artistically, in a detached and spatial fashion. Then they should react personally to the work and explain its significance to them.

Part 3: Narration Paragraphs

One of the goals of this Part is to make students understand the relationship between oral presentation and writing. Since "we live life in narration," as the introduction states, it is one of our most common rhetorical forms in conversation. The transition from a story narrated aloud several times to a written piece should be smooth and painless. Students should grasp that an organized oral narration is transformed into a seamless written one through a solid chronological outline and transition words.

The journal for this Part entails recalling and analyzing dreams, and students should relate well to this topic, especially after a pointed introduction to the theme by the instructor. Dreams and memories are common themes in narration, with the traditional "most embarrassing" (which may be changed to "scariest," "most enjoyable," "proudest") experience forming the basis. The *My First Memory* activity in Unit 3.1 on page 82 may be done about their own lives or about classmates, family members, friends, or coworkers. Interviews provide an excellent opportunity to combine oral and writing skills, so this approach might be encouraged.

"The Hyena of Zimbabwe" in Unit 3.2 on page 83 introduces the concept of folktale or beast fable, which is a common genre in every culture. Students should be asked to think back to their youth to recall their favorite story. The experience of listening should be vivid for them. *"The Tortoise and the Hare"* exercise on page 78 combines listening and speaking skills, as they listen to and narrate the tale again and again until it is absolutely clear in their mind. This should be their easiest piece of writing in the chapter and should show them how familiarity with a narrative and its organization almost guarantees clear writing.

"The Diamond Necklace" story on page 85 might be familiar to several students, so they must be warned not to reveal the surprise ending. Students should be given a week to read the story, answer the questions, and write the chronological outline. Then discuss the characters, plot, and themes of the story with the class. Finally, students are given the opportunity to write an ending to the story, which concludes with the climax. They should be encouraged to let their creativity run free, not to just fall back on a short and predictable happy ending.

The final writing activities in the chapter require students to complete narrations given only the first few sentences. Depending on the mood of the instructor and the class, one or the other might be chosen. *The Telephone Call* on page 93 is an optimistic story, one that starts with loneliness but ends happily. *A Night in Chicago* (page 98), on the other hand, begins in a beautiful setting but recalls a terrible incident when the narrator was a teenager.

Part 4: Process Paragraphs

The universal nature of process writing makes it very popular. Everyone loves to give advice, and it is one of the best-selling forms of writing. Send the students to a large local bookstore (a megastore such as Barnes and Noble or Borders) to see just how many books fit into this category. They will amazed and will probably return to class ready to perfect their skills in this type of writing.

The exercises in this Part should be tailored to the demographics of the class. If too many of the students do not cook and have no interest in kitchen activities (other than eating), then the exercise on writing a recipe will not work. On the other hand, in several semesters, this activity was so popular that students wrote, revised, and printed their recipes, and I collated them into a *Class Cookbook,* which was then distributed to all contributors. It was a great deal of fun. However, it will not work for every class. Similarly, the exercise on weddings in Unit 4.1 on page 119 works very well with people who are already married and those who are very familiar with the wedding customs of their country. On the other hand, very young people might not know enough or be interested enough about wedding practices to enjoy the assignment.

One activity that certainly works is **Making a Good Impression** on page 124. The essential step is to pair people from completely different geographical regions, if possible. Students are going to write about their partner's culture and will learn a great deal while they prepare the paragraph. Prepare them by introducing the proper behavior when someone is invited to a dinner in America. It is also important to make sure that the students study the vocabulary before they conduct the interviews.

The *Analytical Writing* section in this Part (Unit 4.2, page 128) has three group activities, any of which might be chosen for use in class. The *Anonymous Problems* activity on page 130 requires precision: the students must write a problem at home and bring the assignment to class, where they are exchanged. If students don't do the homework, the activity will not work. Once you have distributed the papers and students have written advice, the problems are to be discussed aloud. As long as the anonymity of the writer is maintained, the activity is safe and enjoyable. Many students share the same problems, and the responses might help more than one of them.

In the *Political Analysis* section (Unit 4.3, page 131), assign one of the three speeches for homework. Perhaps the class could choose which one to discuss. They should do some research on the Internet or in an encyclopedia to understand the times in which Kennedy, Roosevelt, and Lincoln lived and the important cultural and historical events occurring in the period.

Part 5: Comparison and Contrast Paragraphs

The concepts introduced in this Part should be among the most congenial for international students because many of them are already bicultural or are seeking to become so. There are two important aspects in teaching comparison and contrast. First, the points of comparison should come from a lively brainstorming session and should provide enough material for a rich and interesting paragraph. Second, the organizational structures for comparison, the direct and separated forms, will serve as the basis of much college writing. This is especially true in the case of direct comparisons, which should be used on all essay examinations requiring the comparison of two people, two concepts, or two historical events or eras. The ability to write a quick and effective outline and to follow that outline to write an organized paragraph or essay will increase the student's performance in regular college courses.

The four-entry journal on Dr. Kevorkian and euthanasia (page 168) should be of interest to students, and they also get a chance to develop a mastery of the courtroom vocabulary so necessary for watching American television (in which the discussion of crimes, court cases, and punishment predominate). The four-entry journal encourages a written debate, and students will move on to written preparation for oral debate in Parts 6 and 7, so this is a good introduction for them. Remind students that in the four-entry journal, if they don't agree, they should challenge the opinions. However, they should understand that they are attacking the ideas, not the person who wrote them.

The *Cultural Characteristics* activity in Unit 5.1 on page 174 introduces adjectives that force students to make generalizations about Americans, people from their country, and themselves. Of course, people vary *within* a country (from north to south, east to west, among various social levels), but students should ask whether there are combining elements that compose a particular culture. Of the 14 adjectives presented, the students should write about the *four* or *five* that differ most between cultures. The *Cats and Dogs* activity on page 170 might be difficult for them if they don't have pets or have never had them, but it is a good basis for discussion about the place of domestic animals in different cultures. Ask them if they think that Americans take their adoration of pets to an absurd degree. The idea that owners resemble their pets is amusing, but also possibly true.

I have found that international students react quite openly and positively to poetry and are likely to have studied it extensively in their native language. They should be encouraged to react personally to the poems in Unit 5.2 by Edna St. Vincent Milay, William Carlos Williams, and Walt Whitman. I have read wonderful students poems written in response to "To a Poor Old Woman" (page 178) in which they choose an everyday object and write a poem about it. Poetry is a global language and continues today quite strongly in pop and hip-hop lyrics, which sometimes tell interesting stories. In fact, it might be interesting to bring in the lyrics to a popular song, perhaps something by a popular rock, rap, or hip-hop artist.

The *Visions of the World* activity in Unit 5.3 on page 184 should make students feel very positive about their personal achievements. It is easy for them to lose sight of the progress they have made in their second language: they are on the verge of taking college courses in English after only a few years of instruction. Think of how long it would take you to become as proficient in Russian, Chinese, or Arabic after only a few semesters in the country. Students will probably see that their goals and aspirations are much broader than those of their grandparents. This is especially true for women, who probably have more sophisticated educational and career goals than their grandmothers.

Part 6: Persuasion Paragraphs

This Part is the first of two to deal with the transition to college courses. Some English Composition / Freshman English textbooks focus on literature as the basis for writing while others deal with analysis of cultural issues and social problems. The Part on persuasion paragraphs in this book provides an introduction to both concepts.

A great deal of work is done with the *"Honey Boy"* story in Unit 6.1 on page 204, so students should be given a week to read it and answer the comprehension and interpretation questions. "Honey Boy" introduces the concept of regionalism in America, perhaps a new concept for students. The setting of the story (Mississippi in the early 1930s) should be stressed, and students should discuss whether this setting is *unique* (it can only function at the particular place and time) or *transferable* (it can be moved almost anywhere at anytime). A moral discussion of the mother's actions could involve a delineation of *moral universality versus moral relativism,* that is, whether an action should be considered wrong under all circumstances or whether the individual situation dictates the judgment. For example, is stealing always wrong, or do mitigating circumstances (hunger, poverty, extreme want) mitigate the severity of the deed. Is stealing a diamond necklace the same as stealing a piece of bread? Is it the same when Wynona Ryder steals designer clothing as when a homeless person steals a quart of milk to feed an infant?

In the Cultural Issues and Personal Opinions Units on pages 210 and 214, respectively, students should understand that in the American academic system, instructors really want them to make a decision on these issues in order to participate in debates. It is considered a weakness if students "sit on the fence" on issues such as military service, capital punishment, drugs, and life expectancy. Introducing Machiavelli (Unit 6.3, page 214) depends on the level of the class and their prior preparation. While the reading may be somewhat difficult, the concepts of *inherent goodness* and *inherent evil* are more readily understood and form the basis for good classroom discussion. By this point in the semester, students should be able to write down their ideas in note form and then actively participate in debate, whether in pairs, groups, or with the whole class involved. The discussion of the *military draft* might require you to give a bit of background (it was abolished at the end of the Vietnam War in the early 1970s and is currently under debate for reinstitution). But it is a current issue, especially in light of America's intense involvement in conflicts abroad.

Finally, it is also important to stress the importance of *research* and *note-taking* as part of the persuasion process. Students should not speak "off the top of their heads" or "from the seat of their pants." Discussion should stem from study and analysis, which lead to a more detached and level-headed approach. Perhaps a heavy-handed approach is best taken here. If students have not researched the subject by reading articles in newspapers, magazines, or on the Internet, they might not be permitted to participate in the discussion. Instead, they can participate as silent observers and/or chroniclers. That should suffice to ensure that they do the work for the next assignment.

Part 7: The Essay

The purpose of the last Part in the book is to provide the transition from the paragraph to the essay, the form that will be used throughout the student's college career. Stress that the essay is simply an *expansion* of the paragraph, not a completely separate structure. By clearly defining the role and function of each of the five paragraphs, you can show the students that the work they have done in the course serves as the foundation for the essay.

The first section focuses on literature, with passages in Unit 7.1 from Edgar Allen Poe, O. Henry, and Ernest Hemingway. These writers will certainly reappear in the students' subsequent English courses, as will the method used here: read the passage, answer straightforward and interpretive comprehension questions, participate in a classroom discussion, and finally write an essay on one of the themes presented in the literary work. It is important to involve students personally in the literary text, for example, by having them judge whether the narrator of "The Tell-Tale Heart" is insane. Have them discern the relationship between the two friends in "After Twenty Years" or among the soldiers in "In Another Country."

The *Lying* activity in Unit 7.2 on page 256 should be both fun and meaningful. Like the Dream Journal from Part 3 and the Self-Improvement Plan from Part 7, it is a long-term activity that requires consistency and continuity. Students must read the article, understand the concepts and categories of lies, keep a lying journal, quantify and categorize their lies, fill out the final questionnaire, and write an essay on their experience. This activity employs almost all the skills learned in the course. They could also interview other people about their lying habits and write about whether they feel lying is necessary in today's society.

The *Problem-Solving Model* in Unit 7.3 on page 271 is a group activity that provides a preparation for business classes, which often employ similar methodology during in-class and at-home exercises. If the cafeteria that the students regularly attend is far above the norm, a substitute activity might be found involving an improvement in the school atmosphere, perhaps something dealing with the library, the student center, the computer center, or the parking/dormitory situation.

The Appendix

The Appendix is to be used for a general review in the last week of the course and may also serve as the basis for a final test. Provide blank charts with the paragraph type indicated and the headings included (keywords, verb tenses used, outline, and structure). Students must then fill in the boxes with as much information as possible.

The appendix may be used as a point of reference for students when they are taking regular college courses. The list of journal types may similarly form the basis for future writing.

Finally, the writing work of ESL students is also presented in the Appendix. These paragraphs should serve as models for students using the book and as an indication of successful strategies employed. You may analyze them with the class or simply assign them as reading material. Many treat the same topics assigned in the book. I have not changed or improved them, so they range from A to B- work.

If there are any questions or comments on the text, feel free to contact Brian Altano c/o The University of Michigan Press (esladmin@umich.edu).

Brian Altano
2004

PART 1

The Basics

A. Working with Microsoft Word

In college classes, most professors require that writing assignments be submitted in typewritten form. The benefit of using word processing on the computer is that you can not only make changes more easily but also check spelling and grammar. As a result, your writing should be more polished. If you are not familiar with word processing programs on the personal computer, this is a good time to start. Microsoft Word is the most commonly used word processing program, and it is probably installed on the computers around campus.

STARTING MICROSOFT WORD

1. Turn on the computer (press the on/off button on the computer and on the monitor).

2. Insert your diskette in the disk drive *after* you see the start-up screen.

3. Point the cursor at the **Start** button at the bottom left of the screen and click the left mouse button.

4. Point the cursor to **Programs** and click the left mouse button.

5. Point the cursor to **Microsoft Word** and click the left mouse button to open the program. (Note that Microsoft Word is often called MS Word or simply Word.)

EXPLORING THE MICROSOFT WORD DESKTOP

The Microsoft Word screen has several useful tools to help you create your documents.

- **Title Bar.** Find this at the top of the screen. As soon as you open a document, the title bar says, "Microsoft Word–Document1." After you save your document, the title bar will contain your new document name.

- **Menu Bar.** Find this on the second band at the top of the screen. It contains File, Edit, View, Insert, Format, Tools, Table, Window, and Help. If you click any of these words, a menu drops down with commands you can use to manage your work.

- **Standard Toolbar.** Find this on the third band at the top of the screen. It contains several pictures or "icons" that cause your computer to perform certain functions if you point to them with the cursor and click on the left mouse button. The following icons help you create documents such as papers for your classes.

  - **Page with turned corner** opens a new document.

  - **Open File Folder** opens a previously saved document.

  - **Floppy diskette** saves your document.

  - **Printer** prints your document.

  - **Page with magnifying glass** previews the document before printing.

  - **ABC** checks your spelling and grammar.

  - **Scissors** cuts a highlighted portion out of your document.

  - **Double pages** copies a highlighted portion of text.

  - **Clipboard with page** pastes a highlighted and cut portion of text in a new place.

  - **Left pointing curved arrow** undoes your last action.

- **Formatting Toolbar.** Find this on the fourth band from the top of the screen. It contains menus and buttons that will help you format your document.

  - **Style menu** allows you to choose from a variety of type settings.

  - **Font menu** allows you to choose from a variety of type faces.

  - **Size menu** allows you to choose from a variety of type sizes.

  - **Bold button** changes type to **bold** typeface.

  - **Italics button** changes type to *italics* typeface.

  - **Underline button** changes type to <u>underlined</u> typeface.

  - **Left alignment button** aligns text at the left margin.

  - **Centering button** centers text on your paper.

  - **Right alignment button** aligns text at the right margin.

  - **Justification button** aligns text to both margins.

- **Close Button.** This is the "X" in the upper right corner of a window. Click it to close the window, file, document, or program.

WRITING YOUR DOCUMENT

When you write in Microsoft Word, you only need to press **Enter** when you want to begin a new paragraph. Word will start a new line of typing automatically. However, the typing you do will be single-spaced, unless you provide a command to double-space your work. To do this, begin to type your essay. Type at least two lines of text. Then press the **Ctrl (Control)** key on your keyboard and the number **2,** and Word will double space. **Ctrl** and **1** will return to single spacing.

SAVING YOUR DOCUMENT

The first time you save a document, you must give it a name.

1. Open the File Menu.

2. Move the cursor to **Save as** and click: a dialog box appears.

3. In the window entitled **Save in,** click on the drop-down menu and highlight **Floppy A** so you can save the document on your own disk.

4. In the window entitled **File name,** type a brief title that describes the assignment, like "Essay1" or "Personal."

5. In the window entitled **Save as type,** be sure "Word Document" is entered (unless you need to save the document in a different word processing program to work on at home).

6. Click the **Save** button.

If you have previously saved your document, merely click the diskette icon on the standard toolbar to resave the document. Word will save the document with the same name. If you want to change the name of your document, choose the **Save As** function, retitle your document, and click **Save.**

OPENING A SAVED DOCUMENT

Once you save a document on your floppy disk and leave Word, you can find it again by clicking on the file folder icon on the task bar. A dialog box will appear; set the **Look in** box to **3½ Floppy (A:).** A list with all the files from your disk will appear. Highlight the file you wish to work on and press **Open.**

CHECKING YOUR SPELLING

1. On the Standard Toolbar, click on the **ABC** icon.

2. A dialog box appears, and the spell checker will automatically begin checking your document.

3. At the first word it does *not* recognize, the spell checker lists alternate spellings, if any. By clicking one of the suggestions, Word will automatically *change* the spelling or *ignore* the change and go on to the next unrecognized word.

4. Word will also highlight grammar and formatting errors. It will make suggestions for correction. Your can choose whether to *change* or *ignore* the suggestion.

PRINTING YOUR DOCUMENT

To print your document, open the File Menu, highlight **Print,** and click. A dialog box appears that allows you to determine the number of copies you wish and the pages you want to print.

CLOSING MICROSOFT WORD AND SHUTTING DOWN

Once your work is saved, close the Word Program by clicking the X in the upper right-hand corner of the screen. **Do not touch the power button!** Always click the **Start** button, highlight **Shut Down,** and click. The computer and monitor will shut off automatically.

B. Parts of Speech

Throughout the course we will be using grammatical terminology. It is a good idea to get to know the terms early in the semester. **Parts of speech** indicate the function of a word in a sentence.

VERBS

A **verb** shows action, a state of being, or functions as an auxiliary (helping) verb when paired with another verb in a sentence. A verb has **tense** (*time:* present, past, future; *tense:* simple, progressive, perfect, perfect progressive); **number** (singular/plural); and **voice** (active/passive/imperative).

Verbs	
Function	Examples
1. Action	I **ate** a large spider last night. He **ran** twenty-six miles from Marathon to Athens and then collapsed. She never **cries** when she **slices** onions.
2. State of being	He **is** the ex-president of the International Club. They **are** very tall for their age.
3. Passive voice	Lincoln **was assassinated** in 1865. The Golden Gate Bridge **was built** in 1937.
4. Auxiliary	My brother's wife's cousin **is sleeping** on her couch. He **has** had six cups of coffee so far today.
5. Imperative	**Leave** your shoes at the door, and **make** sure that your socks are new. Never **loosen** your tie while you are barbecuing steaks.

ADJECTIVES

An **adjective** describes a noun or a pronoun. It is usually placed right before the noun. It may be placed after a verb that shows a state of being (or a form of the *be* verb) (as in the second adjective in example 1 below).

1. The **long** movie that I saw last night was **fascinating**.

2. His **golden** hair looked like an **intricate** spider's nest.

3. The **loud** music at the Korn concert made the **tiny** hairs in my ears stand on end.

4. The **friendly** bear ate our **delicious** sandwiches in a **famished** mouthful.

5. Her **meticulous** professor required Maya to show all the work on the **difficult** math exam.

ADVERBS

An **adverb** modifies a verb, an adjective, or another adverb. Many adverbs end in **ly**. Adverbs indicate time (when?), manner (how?), place (where?), degree (that is, they describe other adjectives or adverbs), and frequency.

Adverbs	
Function	Examples
1. Time	He came **immediately** when he heard there was free coffee. She is talking on the phone with her lawyer **now**.
2. Manner	Mario dances **gracefully** and **smoothly** when he dances **alone**. My brother always speaks **softly** when he lies.
3. Place	I live **here** in this large tent. He was sent **there** to serve his time.
4. Describing an adjective	They were **very** happy with their **previously** owned vehicle. He felt **incredibly** lucky to have a mole on his foot.
5. Describing an adverb	He ran away **very quickly** when he saw the police. John spoke **extremely nervously** during his interview for the job.
6. Frequency	She **sometimes** files her nails in class, but she **never** combs her hair. Giovanni **frequently** tunes his guitar, but he **rarely** plays.

NOUNS

A **noun** is a person, place, thing, or a mood or attitude (abstract). A noun may serve as the **subject** or the **object** of the sentence. It may be common (such as *rice*), compound (such as *flight attendant*), collective (such as *the team*), or proper (such as *Juan*).

1. John looks like a **vampire** in that black **suit**.

2. London has beautiful **weather** if it doesn't rain.

3. Rice is very dry if you forget to turn off the **gas** after 20 **minutes**.

4. Honesty in a **politician** is as rare as **laziness** in a **child**.

5. I watched the lovely **sunset** in the polluted **skies** of **Akron**.

PREPOSITIONS

A **preposition** usually introduces a prepositional phrase that includes a preposition, an article, and a noun or pronoun.

1. He climbed **up** the stairs and then rode **down** the elevator.

2. The professor looked **out** the window **during** the examination.

3. I found the dog hiding **in** the corner, afraid **of** the cat.

4. He always sleeps **under** the bed, not **on** the bed.

5. She has a large statue of Stalin **in** the corner, and she often throws balls **at** it.

CONJUNCTIONS

A **conjunction** joins phrases and clauses.

1. He works in McDonald's on Tuesday **and** tends bar at night.

2. She will study more, **or** we will call her parents.

3. Marco has asked 42 women on dates, **but** he still goes to the movies by himself.

4. **Neither** the butcher **nor** the letter carrier has ever seen her before.

5. **Because** Maria has an import business, she got the nice Turkish rug at a good price.

PRONOUNS

A **pronoun** stands for a noun and may be as a subject, object, possessive, and relative clause.

Pronouns	
Function	Examples
1. Subject	**He** is a doctor's spouse, so he drives a Jaguar. **They** work until they have enough money to party.
2. Object	I saw **him** walking across Hollywood Boulevard last night. She talked to **them** about the Peruvian revolution until **they** fell asleep.
3. Possessive	What's **mine** is **mine**, and what's **yours** is **mine**, too. The stolen manuscript is **his.**
4. Relative	People **who** work all day and all night seldom see their friends. The dog **whose** hair is short and stubby is sleeping in the mud.

ARTICLES

An **article** is definite *(the)* or indefinite *(a, an)*. (The article *a* is used before a consonant sound, and ***an*** is used before a vowel sound.) The article is positioned before a noun.

1. The Gucci bag on **the** table belongs to Nabila.

2. I always drink **a** strong cup of coffee before listening to his long stories.

3. She wore **an** outrageous hat.

4. Jason attends **a** university. (The *u* in university has a consonant sound, so *a,* not *an,* is used.)

5. Her brother the lawyer has **an** honest face.

Parts of Speech and Their Functions				
Part of Speech	Form (Endings)	Function	Position in the Sentence	Notes
Noun	*-ity -ide -ude* *-logy -or -ess* *-er -ant -tion*	1. Subject 2. Object of a. verb b. preposition	1. Subject: Beginning of the sentence, before the verb 2. Object: After the verb or preposition	• Count or non-count nouns • Person, place, or thing • Abstract nouns • Collective nouns
Verb	*-ize -ate -fy*	1. Action 2. State of being 3. General fact	1. After the subject in a normal (declarative) sentence 2. Inverted order in a question (interrogative sentence) (**Are you** hungry?)	A verb shows: • **tense** (past, present, future, simple, perfect, progressive, perfect progressive) • **number** (singular or plural) • **voice** (mood) ▪ active ▪ passive ▪ imperative
Adjective	*-ous -cal -ful* *-less -ic*	Modifies a noun or a pronoun	1. Immediately before the noun it modifies 2. After a **be** verb	The tall man died. She is intelligent.

Parts of Speech and Their Functions *(continued)*

Part of Speech	Form (Endings)	Function	Position in the Sentence	Notes
Adverb	*-ly* (also **very**); answers the questions **how? when? where? how often?**	Modifies: 1. a verb 2. an adjective 3. an adverb	1. After a verb (John writes **carefully**.) 2. Before an adjective (Selma is **incredibly** lucky.) 3. Before an adverb (He spoke **very** slowly.)	Adverbs of **frequency** (*always, usually, often, sometimes, seldom, rarely, never*) usually **go before** the verb. Also, **here, there, yesterday, today, tomorrow** are adverbs.
Pronoun	*I you he she it we they me him her us them my your his her our their*	Stands for the noun: 1. Subject 2. Object 3. Possessive 4. Relative	1. Subject: Before the verb 2. Object: After the verb 3. Possessive: After the verb 4. Relative: After a noun	Relative pronouns introduce a new clause: • I know a woman **who** owns a taxi. • The man **whose** sister is in politics always wears a hat.
Article	*the a an*	Definite (the) and indefinite (a, an)	Placed before the noun	Use **a** before consonant sounds and **an** before vowel sounds.
Preposition	*in at on from between to for about*	Indicates position or direction	May begin a sentence, follow a verb, or be placed at the end of a sentence	Often introduces a **prepositional phrase** (Preposition + Article + Noun or Pronoun)
Conjunction	*and but so for yet because although or*	Transition word to another clause, phrase, or word	Usually after a clause and before the subject of the next clause	If **and, but, so,** and **yet** are preceded by **five** words, a comma is placed before it.

Exercise 1 In the following sentences, give the part of speech of each word. For verbs, indicate tense, number, and voice. For nouns, indicate function (subject or object).

1. In the soap opera, the doctor loves the shy nurse, but the nurse loves the doctor's wife.

2. I have never met a person from Colorado who did not like to ski and climb mountains.

3. My mysterious neighbor, who works the night shift, goes to sleep in the morning.

4. The man with the dreadlocks is drying himself with a colorful towel on the beach.

5. Sometimes Jimena drinks four cups of tea in order to be social.

6. People travel great distances to return home.

7. My paternal grandmother never flew in a four-seat plane, but my intrepid father has several times.

8. The Houston Astrodome, the first indoor baseball stadium, was built in 1963.

9. While she was reading the end of the fascinating novel, she did not stop to make coffee.

10. I saw several very beautiful shells on the beach on Marco Island, Florida.

11. The lovely child bit the hairy man on the cheek.

12. The mammoth soldier was very hungry, so he ate the cookies and the box.

Exercise 2 Insert a word in the blank, and indicate its part of speech.

1. The _____ student walked _____ out of the class-room when she found she had passed the test.

2. The sophisticated _____ whispered to the _____ writer.

3. The rock guitarist _____ a _____ song _____.

4. In the _____, the suntanned _____ analyzed the

_____ who were wearing very _____ shorts.

5. Because _____ the _____ weather, the _____ was

_____.

6. _____ tall engineer _____ with her brother and

_____.

7. Several days _____ the flood, the _____ were still covered with

_____ .

8. While the cardinal _____ a sweet song, the _____ watched it

_____ .

9. The _____ teachers _____ to the cafeteria for a _____

lunch, _____ they could not _____ because it was

_____ for renovations.

10. _____ I go shopping, I _____ buy a pair of _____ .

C. Sentence Types and Punctuation

SENTENCE PATTERNS

As your writing becomes more sophisticated, your sentences will grow and expand. When you first began to study English, you wrote simple sentences composed of one independent clause. You used four patterns: SV, SSV, SVV, and SSVV. During this course, though, you will concentrate on longer sentences composed of two or more clauses. Remember that a clause is a *group of words with a subject and a verb*. There are two types of clauses: an **independent** clause, which can stand on its own, and a **dependent** clause, which requires an independent clause to make a complete sentence.

The longer sentences that you will write this semester may be divided into two general groups: *compound sentences* (two independent clauses joined by a conjunction) and *complex sentences* (one independent and one dependent clause). The chart on page 14 is an introduction of the five most common sentence patterns for sentences using advanced grammar.

The Five Most Common Sentence Patterns Using Advanced Grammar

Sentence Pattern	Examples
1. D , I (comma between the two clauses) The **dependent** (D) clause begins with a conjunction. The clause is followed by a comma then an **independent** (I) clause, which is followed by a period.	Although he is rich, he has no friends. Because she is an excellent manager, she will go far in this company. When I first met him, I liked him a lot. While my brother was driving to the lake, he almost fell asleep at the wheel. If you pay close attention to his directions, you will understand how to get to his house.
2. I D (no punctuation between the clauses) This combination is the same as in Pattern 1, except that the sentence begins with the **independent** clause and ends with the **dependent** clause. No punctuation is used to link the two clauses.	I love you although you are often unkind to me. He is happy when he completes a task. I left after I cleaned the house. He ate all the food because he was starving. I will come right away if you need my help.
3. I, conjunction I (comma *before* the conjunction) The conjunctions used to connect two independent clauses using a comma are **and, but, so, yet,** and **or.**	My sister-in-law never tells the truth, so no one trusts her. I mowed the lawn all afternoon, and my cat slept soundly on the couch. I asked my uncle for help, but he was too busy. Aida has played all 60 minutes of the game so far, yet she doesn't appear to be tired. You will wash the dishes, or you will not watch your favorite show.
4. I . I (period between the two independent clauses) Two independent clauses with no conjunctions joining them must form two separate simple sentences.	He left. I stayed. The hungry man ate the burned chicken. He got heartburn. The teacher lectured. The students took notes.
5. I; conjunction, I (semicolon before the conjunction, comma after it) According to the type of relationship between the two clauses, the following conjunctions are used: **Adding information:** *in addition, moreover, furthermore* **Contrast:** *nevertheless, nonetheless, however* **Result:** *therefore, thus, hence, as a result, consequently*	I have never been to Buffalo; nevertheless, I plan to go there next year. Joanna has worked 52 hours so far this week; therefore, she must be exhausted. The handyman painted my house and cleaned out the basement; in addition, he fixed the doors. I have never liked Mr. Johnson personally; however, I do respect his work.

PUNCTUATION OF CLAUSES AND IDENTIFICATION OF SENTENCE PATTERN

Exercise 3 Insert periods, commas, semicolons, or leave the following clauses with no punctuation. Do <u>not</u> add any extra words. Begin new sentences with capital letters. Then identify the sentence pattern (pattern 1, 2, 3, 4, or 5). For example:

> **Admer has never been to South Africa nevertheless he has read two novels by Nadine Gorimer.**

> ___5___ **Admer has never been to South Africa; nevertheless, he has read two novels by Nadine Gorimer.**

In this sentence, we have two subjects *(Admer, he)* and two verbs *(has been, has read).* The conjunction *nevertheless* is used in sentence pattern 5. It requires a semicolon before it, and a comma after it.

_____ **1.** She is always angry but her brother is a calm guy.

_____ **2.** Because John is rich he always has many people in his dining room.

_____ **3.** I love her so much since she has a well-paying job.

_____ **4.** My brother cannot swim however he is not afraid to go on a small boat in the ocean.

_____ **5.** Although he never gives flowers to his mother she still loves him.

_____ **6.** John's face is disfigured in addition his teeth are not straight.

_____ **7.** My uncle and aunt sing duets they have no talent.

_____ **8.** I have never eaten food from Somalia nevertheless I have heard that it is excellent.

_____ **9.** The hungry man ate two cheeseburgers furthermore he ate two orders of fries.

_____ **10.** Because she is a skilled manager Maria has received two promotions this year.

_____ **11.** Professor Jackson speaks Chinese however she does not speak Russian.

_____ **12.** In the morning I always cook breakfast my kids seldom eat with me.

_____ **13.** Whenever I see a full moon I think of all my long-lost loves.

_____ **14.** In the winter snows falls in the summer the weather is warm and sunny.

_____ **15.** Before I ate dinner with my mother-in-law for the first time I drank a double martini.

Exercise 4 Insert periods, commas, semicolons, or leave the following clauses with no punctuation. Do *not* add any extra words. Begin new sentences with capital letters. Then identify the sentence pattern (pattern 1, 2, 3, 4, or 5).

_____ **1.** On July 4 my brother always has a big barbecue I bring the food and he cooks it.

_____ **2.** My mother made tv dinners every Thursday for ten years they were delicious.

_____ **3.** Since he came to the United States he has had six jobs.

_____ **4.** In the summer my sister sits in the backyard trying to get a tan I go to Aruba.

_____ **5.** She cried when her boyfriend lost $19,000 in Atlantic City.

_____ **6.** The bus driver fell asleep in the bus station so the bus was two hours late.

_____ **7.** My car is so old that I might have to buy a new one this year.

_____ **8.** While I was driving to Philadelphia I saw many polluted rivers.

_____ **9.** Last night a mouse walked into my bedroom my cat enjoyed it a great deal.

_____ **10.** Because you are so cheap no one ever invites you to go away for the weekend.

_____ **11.** Marco has a big mole on his nose and several long hairs come out of it.

_____ **12.** Mrs. Jackson hates Mr. Jackson she loves his money though.

_____ **13.** The professor doesn't understand his subject however he never stops talking.

_____ **14.** You smell as if you had been working in a fish store your whole life.

_____ **15.** If I had met you two years earlier we would be married now.

Exercise 5 Insert periods, commas, semicolons, or leave the following clauses with no punctuation. Do *not* add any extra words. Begin new sentences with capital letters. Then identify the sentence pattern (pattern 1, 2, 3, 4, or 5).

_____ **1.** I would marry you if you promised to stop smoking.

_____ **2.** She married her dance teacher now they go to clubs every Saturday night.

_____ **3.** After I saw her bank balance I immediately fell in love.

_____ **4.** He is such a dedicated worker that he never leaves before 11:00 P.M.

_____ **5.** His wife works the graveyard shift so she never sees her husband.

_____ **6.** Tomorrow after I get home I will write a letter to my brother in jail.

_____ **7.** Whenever she cooks I notify the fire department in advance.

_____ **8.** My mother is not Turkish but her coffee is very thick and strong.

_____ **9.** Olivia's sister works for an international company she is a programmer.

_____ **10.** The coach screamed at his players in addition he yelled at the referee.

_____ **11.** Although he yelled during the whole game the team still lost.

_____ **12.** I was cheering for Germany yet Brazil won the World Cup.

_____ **13.** Olga never loses anything she just misplaces things.

_____ **14.** Hae Soo makes excellent kimchi nevertheless some people call it too spicy.

_____ **15.** I did not fully understand the punctuation of clauses before however I think I do now.

D. Basic Definitions

THE PARAGRAPH

During this course you will be writing paragraphs. In the way that it is used in this book, a **paragraph** is a group of 10 to 12 sentences united by a common theme with a recognizable beginning, middle, and end. The word total should be between 100 and 150. As the semester progresses, the number of words in your paragraphs will increase as a result of your facility in writing complex sentences. By the end of the course, you will write approximately 200 words on a given topic. At that point, you are ready for the five-paragraph essay, which will be introduced in the last chapter. The essay is the principal writing structure used in Composition I or Freshman English class. Here is a common structure for the paragraph:

1. Topic Sentence (contains the controlling idea)

2. Point 1

    a. Support 1

    b. Support 2

3. Point 2

    a. Support 1

    b. Support 2

4. Point 3

    a. Support 1

    b. Support 2

5. Conclusion (restates the topic sentence and emphasizes it)

THE TOPIC

Students tend to write better in paragraphs that have a high interest level for them. For this reason, the journal portion of this text allows free writing on any topic within the particular paragraph structure being studied. The journal topics presented in the Contents of each chapter are merely *suggestions*. If none of them interests you, substitute something else. The goal in the journal is to write every day in order to practice processes and structures and improve your writing.

Although interest level is important, in most of your classes, you will not have control over the choice of the topic. For example, in history class a student may be required to compare the American and French revolutions. Even if this topic does not seem interesting, it must be discussed and analyzed. Similarly, many writing examinations (essay exams in college courses) present a topic to students, who then must mold it to their liking. While it is advisable to practice free writing, inventing topics and feeling liberated in approach, it is also essential to be able to write an excellent paragraph on a given topic.

THE JOURNAL

The word *journal* comes from the French word *jour,* which means *day.* It is highly recommended that journal writing become a **daily** activity for you.

Keep a separate notebook for your journal. A journal is a written record that documents your life, your impressions, feelings, thoughts, and reactions to everyday life and to specific issues. In fact, it is probably advisable to alternate in your journal between general descriptions of your life and daily occurrences and writing on specific issues.

Journal writing should become a **daily habit.** Improvement in writing is most noticeable when a journal is kept assiduously. Writing is the activity we perform the least (compared to speaking and reading). The only way that it can become natural is to do it as much as possible, so that the words that flow so easily from our brains to our mouths also find their way from our brains to our pens.

Journal writing should take **15 minutes** per day. Because you are trying to establish a habit, the time that you write should be consistent. For example, if you are fully functional in the morning (that is, if you are a morning person), it is best to write your journal before you leave your house for the day's activities. On the other hand, if you are more of a night person, it is advisable to write the journal at the end of the day. Consistency brings habit, so try to write in the journal at the same time each day.

If you find that your life is somewhat repetitive (all of our lives may be so), then you should mix some **reaction writing** into your journals. For example, read the newspaper, and write on some developments in the world. Watch the news, and analyze the features presented. Go to an interesting website, and write about what you have experienced. Write a description of your favorite sports star, your favorite singer, a movie that impressed you, etc.

Journals are non-threatening writing. Don't worry too much about grammar, spelling, or mistakes. Let the words flow. Don't stop to correct mistakes. No one will analyze your journal for errors. Be free in your thoughts. The following is the procedure for journal writing, an activity that you should continue throughout the semester and, hopefully, beyond.

PROCEDURE FOR JOURNAL WRITING

1. Use a separate notebook for your journal.

2. Each new entry should begin on a new page.

3. Each entry should be numbered and dated.

4. Try to write at the same time each day to better develop the habit.

5. Write continuously for 15 minutes.

6. Do not worry too much about grammar or spelling. Let the words flow.

7. After 15 minutes, stop. Re-read your entry. If you want to make a comment on your writing at this time or change anything you have written, do so now.

E. Journal Type 1: The Personal Journal

There are many possible topics for journal writing, but the most readily available ones come from descriptions, narrations, and reflections on our everyday life. In this sense, the personal journal closely approaches a **diary.** Diaries, however, are usually secret (many come equipped with a lock and key). The journal writing for Part 2, which concentrates on description, will be personal in nature. Perhaps you kept a diary when you were younger, and you recorded thoughts that you wanted to hide from others. The journal entry on page 21 was taken from *Narrative of the Life of Frederick Douglass.* Notice the way that Douglass describes his condition, presents a narrative of how he learned to read, and finally analyzes the wonderful power that reading gave him.

Frederick Douglass (1817–1895) was the son of a slave woman and a white father. For the first 21 years of his life he was a slave. In 1838 he escaped to the North, and a speech that he made during an antislavery rally made such a strong impression that he came to be in great demand as a speaker. He moved to England and made enough money in two years to return to the United States and buy his freedom. He published the newspaper *The North Star* for 17 years and later held several public offices after the Civil War.

In *Narrative of the Life of Frederick Douglass,* the simplicity of his writing style is in excellent balance to the power of his message. His ability to succeed in the face of terrible conditions and circumstances is an inspiration to everyone. This passage discusses his desire to learn to read. His master's wife had been teaching Douglass to read, something that was strongly discouraged and, at times, even prohibited in areas of the South in the 1800s. When his master found out, he immediately put an end to the lessons. However, this only gave Douglass more incentive to learn.

Narrative of the Life of Frederick Douglass

Frederick Douglass. Courtesy of The Library of Congress.

From that moment, I understood the pathway from slavery to freedom. It was just what I wanted, and I got it at a time when I the least expected it. While I was saddened by the thought of losing the aid of my kind mistress, I was gladdened by the invaluable instruction which, by the merest accident, I had gained from my master. Though conscious of the difficulty of learning without a teacher, I set out with high hope and a fixed purpose, at whatever cost or trouble, to learn how to read. The very decided manner with which he spoke, and strove to impress his wife with the evil consequences of giving me instruction, served to convince me that he was deeply sensible of the truths he was uttering. It gave me the best assurance that I might rely with the utmost confidence on the results which, he said, would flow from teaching me to read. What he most dreaded, that I most desired. . . . In learning to read, I owe almost as much to the bitter opposition of my master, as to the kindly aid of my mistress. I acknowledge the benefit of both.

Source: *Narrative of the Life of Frederick Douglass, An American Slave*

Journal Activity

The Most Important Thing I Have Learned in Life

Write a journal entry in which you describe the most important thing that you have ever learned in life. Why is it so important? Who or what taught you this lesson?

F. Peer Evaluation Form

During peer evaluation, you will exchange papers with a classmate so that you can read and evaluate each other's work. Using the form on page 23, your classmate will give an educated response to your work. This form may be used several times during the semester. Make a few photocopies of it before you use it for the first time.

Writing Assignment

Personal Introduction

You are in a new class and have a new professor. You probably do not know your classmates. During this first class, introduce yourself to your teacher and your classmates. Write a paragraph on a separate piece of paper in which you present all the information that you consider important to give a clear picture of your personality, your interests, and your background. Your professor might also give a personal introduction. After you write it, be prepared to introduce yourself to your classmates.

Writing Assignment

Goals and Objectives

The beginning of a new semester is a good occasion to set short-term goals and objectives. This is done by asking direct questions. Where do I want to be at the end of the semester? What skills do I have to improve to arrive at that point? Goals should be very specific. Obviously, one goal will be to do excellent work and get a good grade in writing class. What other goals do you have for this semester? For the rest of the year? Where do you see your-self one year from now? What courses will you be taking? What will your major be?

Write a paragraph on a separate piece of paper delineating your goals and objectives and the ways in which you will try to achieve them.

PEER EVALUATION FORM

Writer: _____   Evaluator: _____

1. What I like best about this piece of writing is:

   _____

   _____

   _____

2. These particular words and phrases were very strong:

   _____

   _____

   _____

3. Some things are not clear to me. These words or lines could be improved:

   _____

   _____

   _____

4. The one change that would make the greatest improvement in this piece is:

   _____

   _____

   _____

5. Your supporting points were (strong/weak/insufficient, etc.).

   _____

   _____

   _____

6. I was particularly impressed by one of the following points:

   _____

   _____

   _____

PART 2

Description Paragraphs

Suggested Journal Topics for Description Paragraphs

- Your best friend from the first grade

- Your best/worst high school teachers

- All the places you have visited on vacation

- The pets that you have had

- The houses in which you have lived

- The most interesting places you have seen in the United States

- Descriptions of your relatives appearing on your family tree

Each Part of this text is divided in the same way. There is an introduction to the paragraph type, a vocabulary acquisition section, a grammatical structures section, a writing skills section, a journal description and exercise(s), three skill-building units with specific activities and writing assignments, a Part summary page, a reflections page on which you will write your reactions to the Part, and Part and journal assignments checklists to record your progress.

A. Description Paragraphs

When we use adjectives to paint a picture of a person, place, or object, we are making a description. We perform this common activity many times a day. When someone asks about your new teacher, you describe him or her. When you tell your friends about your new apartment, you describe the space for them.

Description paragraphs are best understood when they are clearly organized. For example, when describing a room, you should describe it in a particular direction (left to right, top to bottom), as a video camera would move in capturing an image. In describing a person's appearance, you might begin with the hair and work downward. In describing a person's personality, you would probably begin with her most important characteristics.

The verb tense used in paragraphs of description is usually **simple present**. Common constructions also include *there is/there are* and **prepositional phrases** that indicate location (*beneath, on top of, next to, below, between,* etc.). Transitions used in paragraphs of description serve to add information and include *and, also, in addition, moreover,* and *furthermore.*

One aspect that usually separates good from excellent paragraphs of description is the quality of the **adjectives** used. This is a good time to expand your vocabulary to include as many rich and colorful adjectives as possible. In your reading this week, pay particular attention to adjectives. Underline them, and look them up in the dictionary. On pages 30 and 31, write the adjectives, their meanings, and their connotation (positive or negative); then use them in sentences.

Another good way to practice description is to look in magazines and newspapers for very expressive photographs. Cut out a few, write a description of what you see, and keep in mind that the audience hasn't read the accompanying article. This is a particularly interesting activity to do with photo advertisements for a particular product. You can also do this activity orally to improve your speaking skills.

Prewriting Assignment

Describe Photographs

Cut out or print three interesting photographs from a magazine, newspaper, or the Internet. Write brief descriptions of each photo; concentrate on using very expressive adjectives. Bring the photographs to class, and exchange them with your classmates. In this way, you will have an abundant supply of source material with which to practice description writing.

DESCRIPTION: AN INDUCTIVE APPROACH

Often in academic writing students do not get a chance to choose their own topics. Instead, they receive them from the teacher and are expected to produce articulate paragraphs and essays. One way to achieve this goal is to use an **inductive approach:** a five-step process that includes contemplation, paired work, listening, writing, and exchanging work. In this approach, you begin with a simple idea and slowly and meticulously develop it by working with a partner. You use oral skills (which might be more advanced than writing skills) to organize your work. In addition, you have the opportunity to analyze the writing of several different classmates.

Exercise 1   Do the following prewriting exercises in preparation for writing.

1. **Contemplation.** Not enough time is spent in quiet thought as preparation for writing. Before you begin writing, take a few minutes to think about your topic and possible approaches to writing about it. Use your imagination. Close your eyes, and open your mind. Ask yourself questions about the topic. Move from general to specific questions.

2. **Paired work.** Work with a partner and describe your thoughts and questions to him or her. Look in the person's eyes. If your partner seems to lose interest, change your pace or move on to another point. When he or she express perplexity and uncertainty, give more description.

3. **Listening.** Being a good listener implies maintaining interest, asking questions for clarification, and helping to move the conversation along. Short responses such as "Really?" "What do you mean?" "How?" "Why?" and "So what?" help the other person formulate ideas and organize thoughts.

4. **Writing.** After you have made an oral description for your partner, write it down.

5. **Exchanging work.** When you have finished writing, exchange papers. Read your partner's paragraph, and record your thoughts on the Peer Evaluation Form on page 23. Then discuss the work with your partner.

Exercise 2   Describe the worst (or the best) film that you have ever seen.

1. **Contemplation.** Think about the topic for five minutes. Organize your ideas, and think of reasons why you liked or disliked the film. Provide specific examples.

2. **Paired work.** Describe this film to your partner. Give full details. Then listen to your partner's description of his or her film.

3. **Listening.** Practice being a good listener. Pay close attention to what your partner says, and ask questions.

4. **Writing.** Write a paragraph in which you describe the worst or best film you have ever seen.

5. **Exchanging work.** When you have finished writing, exchange papers. Was everything your partner told you included in the paragraph, or was something left out? Is the description clear? Tell your partner three ways in which the paragraph is successful, and offer two ways in which it could be improved.

As a class, discuss **judgment** criteria about a good or bad film, working together to list the criteria on which a film should be judged. Judgment criteria might include an analysis of the quality of the plot and the acting performances, the cinematography and music. Were the costumes genuine, appropriate, or extravagant? A difference should be made between **objective** and **subjective** criteria. Objective criteria are agreed upon by the whole class, while subjective criteria are more personal. Then, work together as a class to compose a list of adjectives that best describe films in general and, more specifically, bad films.

B. Vocabulary Acquisition: Adjectives

Activity 1   *Adjectives*

In your reading this week, concentrate on *adjectives.* Find 15 new ones, and write them in the space below. (Hint: The Personal Ad [page 45] and Accommodations Activities [page 52] in this Part are filled with adjectives.) Write down the word. Indicate the part of speech, whether the word has a positive (+), negative (−), or neutral (=) connotation, and whether there are roots, prefixes, or suffixes that help you understand the meaning of the word. Then write a definition whether there are roots, prefixes, or suffixes that help you understand the meaning of the word. A prefix comes at the beginning of the word, while a suffix is found at the end of the word. *Pre* (before), *trans* (across), and *post* (after) are examples of prefixes. *-Ly* (adverb ending), *-ous* (full of), and *-gress* (step) are suffixes. A root may begin the word, appear in the middle, or at the end. For example, *mis* may be used at the beginning *(mission),* in the middle *(admission),* or at the end *(remiss).* After you have found the prefixes, suffixes, or roots, write a definition for the word. Finally, construct a sentence in your own words for each adjective. The first one on page 30 is a model.

Word	Part of Speech	Connotation (+, −, =)	Roots, Prefixes, or Suffixes	Definition
1. predictable	adj.	−	*pre* = before; *dict* = to say; *able* = able to be	that can be told beforehand, based on information or hints

SENTENCE: The film was so predictable that everyone in the theatre knew who the murderer was before it ended.

Word	Part of Speech	Connotation (+, −, =)	Roots, Prefixes, or Suffixes	Definition
2.				

SENTENCE:

Word	Part of Speech	Connotation (+, −, =)	Roots, Prefixes, or Suffixes	Definition
3.				

SENTENCE:

Word	Part of Speech	Connotation (+, −, =)	Roots, Prefixes, or Suffixes	Definition
4.				

SENTENCE:

Word	Part of Speech	Connotation (+, −, =)	Roots, Prefixes, or Suffixes	Definition
5.				

SENTENCE:

Word	Part of Speech	Connotation (+, −, =)	Roots, Prefixes, or Suffixes	Definition
6.				

SENTENCE:

Word	Part of Speech	Connotation (+, −, =)	Roots, Prefixes, or Suffixes	Definition
7.				

SENTENCE:

Word	Part of Speech	Connotation (+, −, =)	Roots, Prefixes, or Suffixes	Definition
8.				
SENTENCE:				
9.				
SENTENCE:				
10.				
SENTENCE:				
11.				
SENTENCE:				
12.				
SENTENCE:				
13.				
SENTENCE:				
14.				
SENTENCE:				
15.				
SENTENCE:				

CONNOTATION

Connotation means what is suggested in addition to the simple meaning. Most often, connotation denotes positive or negative meaning. Of course, not all words have positive or negative connotation; some are neutral. For example, *chair, book, student, pen, coffee, roast beef,* and *pilot* are neutral words. Many words, however, have a connotation in addition to the literal meaning. For example, analyze these four words, which basically have the same meaning:

slender   skinny   thin   slim

Which two words in the group are positive? Which word has a negative connotation? Which word is sometimes negative and sometimes positive? *Slender* and *slim* are compliments, while *skinny* is a put-down. *Thin* may be negative when grandma says it but positive when it describes a man who has been on a diet for eight months. The difference in these words is suggested in their connotation.

Exercise 3 Find the connotation for the following words.

Word	Connotation	Word	Connotation
1. punctual		**6.** compassion	
2. passionate		**7.** bellicose	
3. mugged		**8.** famous	
4. fanatic		**9.** moldy	
5. notorious		**10.** hasty	

LITERAL AND FIGURATIVE MEANING

There are two types of meaning: literal and figurative. **Literal** means using words in their exact meaning, without exaggeration or imagination. On the other hand, **figurative** means using words outside of their literal meaning to add beauty or force. In the Lloyd's Center description on page 59, for example, the mall is called a *circus*. There are no animals or lion tamers at the mall, no high-flying daredevils. *Circus* is used in its figurative sense, meaning a place where many activities are happening at the same.

Analyze the following two sentences:

Mr. Roberts is *dead*. He is buried in North Arlington Cemetery.

Mr. Roberts is *dead*. He worked 16 hours yesterday.

The first meaning of dead is *literal,* while the second is *figurative.* If Mr. Roberts is *literally* dead, his life is over. On the contrary, if Mr. Roberts is *figuratively* dead, he is exhausted. After a good night of sleep, he will be his old self again.

Exercise 4   Analyze the following sentences, trying to tell the literal or figurative meaning of the italicized words.

1. She was *buried* under a *ton* of homework. Mrs. Brown is *buried* in Valleau Cemetery.

2. I'm *sick* of doing the same old thing on my job. Last week I was *sick,* so I went to the doctor.

3. I am *hooked* on Mary. Last week on our first date we went fishing, and I *hooked* a big one.

4. Jack is so *thirsty* for knowledge that he stays up late every night reading.

5. France *whipped* Brazil in the finals of the 1998 World Cup, and the Brazilians felt *crushed.*

6. Enrico had a *crush* on Josephine, but she *had already fallen* for someone else.

C. Grammatical Structures: Subject–Verb Agreement

Quite often, the quality of writing is initially judged by the correctness of the grammar. Grammatically correct writing is one of the most visible signs of excellence. A common grammatical problem is *subject–verb agreement,* the use of a singular verb with a plural noun or a plural verb with a singular noun. For example, in the sentences *She like ice cream* or *My two brothers always arrives late,* there are mistakes in agreement. This is one aspect, though, that can be corrected rather easily in the proofreading phase of the writing process, when you go through your paragraph specifically looking for mistakes.

Editing Technique: Every time you finish writing a paragraph, <u>underline</u> all the verbs. Then check that the verb agrees with the subject.

The general rules for subject–verb agreement appear on page 35.

Exercise 5 Circle the correct verb in parentheses.

1. Geography *(is, are)* interesting. Physics *(is, are)* my favorite.

2. All of the doors in my house *(is, are)* made of glass.

3. How many people *(is, are)* there in Thailand?

4. The news on Channel 7 *(is, are)* always bad.

5. There *(has, have)* been times when I have felt very depressed.

6. Why *(does, do)* so many television programs show violence?

7. Four hours *(is, are)* too much to work without a break.

8. The United States of America *(is, are)* composed of 50 states.

9. The Japanese *(drinks, drink)* a great deal of tea.

10. Chinese *(consists, consist)* of many different characters.

11. Every man, woman, and child *(is, are)* protected by the law.

12. Some of the coffee *(is, are)* from Colombia.

13. Some of the students in the class *(comes, come)* from Asia.

14. Studying German *(is, are)* very time consuming.

15. Swimming across the ocean *(is, are)* impossible.

General Rules for Subject–Verb Agreement

Rule	Examples
1. Singular subjects take singular verbs. In the present tense, singular verbs end in -s. Two subjects take a plural verb.	Joe **works** in a factory. The Coordinator and the Dean **eat** tacos in the cafeteria every Friday.
2. Each and **every** take singular verbs.	Each student **has** to bring a book. Every woman in the class **is** studying medicine. Every man, woman, and child **is** protected by the law.
3. Several academic subjects such as physics, statistics, and economics are singular, even though they end in -s. They take a singular verb.	Physics **is** difficult while economics is easy. Statistics **is** very useful in analyzing elections.
4. Non-count nouns are singular. They have no plural and take a singular verb.	Your *advice* **is** excellent. *Coffee* **is** a very social drink. Her *hair* **is** long and curly.
5. A definite article (**the**) that precedes an adjective sometimes indicates people. In this case, the adjective acts as a noun and takes a plural verb.	The poor **are** struggling to survive. The English **drink** a lot of tea. The French **eat** cheese and baguettes for lunch. The poor **suffer** a great deal during cold weather.
6. An adjective for a country used without a definite article indicates a language. It takes a singular verb.	Chinese **is** very difficult to write. Italian **is** the language of opera.
7. Blocks of time, distance, and money are considered singular and take a singular verb.	Two hours **is** enough time to finish your homework. Four days **is** too long to go without food. Six miles **is** a long way to walk before breakfast.
8. With **some, all, a lot**—and with percentages and fractions—look at the noun that follows to decide between singular and plural.	Some of the *furniture* **is** used. Some of the *women* **are** from Taiwan. Forty percent of the *people* in the school **are** international students. A lot of the *tea* that I drink **comes** from Korea. All of the *students* in the class **keep** journals.

16. The police *(is, are)* coming to our school at nine o'clock.

17. *(Isn't, Aren't)* French spoken in Algeria?

18. A number of students *(has, have)* problems with pronunciation.

19. Nearly 60 percent of the people in Rome *(drinks, drink)* wine.

20. Most sugar *(is, are)* sold in five-pound bags.

Exercise 6 Circle the correct verb in parentheses.

1. A lot of the books in the library *(is, are)* about history.

2. A lot of the cheese sold in Walmart *(comes, come)* from Holland.

3. Where *(is, are)* Mozambique? Can you find it in the atlas?

4. Where *(is, are)* my brown pants?

5. Two-thirds of the book *(contains, contain)* recipes from Mexico.

6. All of the employees at the college *(is, are)* covered by insurance.

7. More men than women *(works, work)* in that company.

8. Seventy percent of the people in Ohio *(lives, live)* in detached houses.

9. Politics *(is, are)* a very interesting subject.

10. *(Was, Were)* there any reason to come late to the dinner?

11. Morroccans *(drinks, drink)* more tea than coffee.

12. Most of the food that I bought *(was, were)* eaten for dinner.

13. Every student in the class *(has, have)* a notebook.

14. Her hair *(is, are)* long and straight.

15. Waiter, come here quickly. There *(is, are)* a hair in my soup.

16. Sixteen days *(is, are)* a long time to go without eating lunch.

17. Most of the people I know *(comes, come)* from other countries.

18. The clothing in that store *(is, are)* very expensive.

19. The rich *(drive, drives)* beautiful cars.

20. The Philippines *(consists, consist)* of more than 7,000 islands.

Exercise 7 Circle the correct verb in parentheses.

1. The books on the Presidents of the U.S. *(is, are)* interesting.

2. A number of Jim's friends *(is, are)* coming to the party.

3. Three-fourths of the people I know *(is, are)* from Israel.

4. Only one of the children *(is, are)* able to read.

5. Statistics *(is, are)* very interesting to me.

6. The English *(drinks, drink)* ale rather than beer.

7. The advice she gave me *(was, were)* very useful.

8. A number of new books *(has, have)* appeared on that subject.

9. Some of the furniture in his home *(is, are)* used.

10. The government of the United States *(is, are)* elected by the people.

11. If you are going to run, three miles *(is, are)* enough.

12. Two hours *(is, are)* a long time to wait for a train.

13. Each child *(has, have)* two books and a crayon.

14. None of her friends *(works, work)*.

15. I *(has, have)* too much homework.

16. The army failed to advance. *(It was, They were)* defeated.

17. One of the books I read last night *(was, were)* about horse racing.

18. English *(comes, come)* from Latin, French, and German.

19. The poor *(lives, live)* in the southern part of town.

20. One of the places I want to visit *(is, are)* Turkey.

D. Writing Skills:
The Topic Sentence

The **topic sentence** is usually the first sentence in the paragraph, and it serves several functions. It describes what the paragraph will be about and thus introduces the main idea to the reader. It is usually a general statement that also indicates the type of paragraph that will follow. For this reason, the topic sentence for a description paragraph differs from that of a comparison and contrast or an opinion paragraph. The topic sentence:

- is the most important sentence in the paragraph because it makes a first impression on the reader

- indicates organization

- shows the direction the paragraph will take

The remainder of the paragraph will support, substantiate, illustrate, explain, or prove the topic sentence. Strong topic sentences contain an opinion that is supported by the paragraph or presents a statement of intentions, which is the plan for the paragraph.

TYPES OF TOPIC SENTENCES:
TESTING THE WATER OR JUMPING RIGHT IN

In addition to being a holiday commemorating those who died in wars, Memorial Day Weekend, at the end of May, in the United States marks the unofficial beginning of summer for many people. In Virginia, for example, this often means the first time they "go down the shore" to visit the miles of beach stretching along the Atlantic Ocean.

On Memorial Day the water is still very chilly, yet many people go into the ocean. In general, there are two types of beachgoers in late May. One type are the careful ones who approach the water slowly. They touch it with the very tips of their toes and then slowly proceed to get their ankles, knees, and legs under water. Eventually (perhaps), they are completely in the water and begin to swim. This process sometimes takes as much as 30 minutes, and some people never make it to the last step.

The other type are the fearless people. As soon as they park the car, they take off their outer clothes, run full-speed through the sand, and crash into the freezing water without stopping to let their body become accustomed to the shocking difference between body and water temperature. You can see them splashing and hear them screaming and urging you to keep them company in the frigid ocean.

TWO TYPES OF TOPIC SENTENCES

Topic sentences may be compared to the beachgoers in Virginia on Memorial Day. Just as there are timid, conservative, and complacent people, there are solid and well-structured topic sentences that clearly state the goal of the paragraph and the intention of the writer. Similar to those beachgoers who dive wildly into the frigid water, there are also topic sentences that catch the reader's attention or elicit surprise or curiosity.

Analyze the following topic sentences. How do they state the goal of the paragraph and the writer's intent?

1. In this paragraph, I will describe the most terrifying night of my life.

2. When I felt the cold steel of the operating instrument cutting through my skin, I knew that I might not make it through the night.

Now analyze three topic sentences.

1. There are many beautiful hotels in this area, and I would like to describe one of them.

2. The Dragon Motel is a lovely establishment located in downtown Philadelphia.

3. When I first walked through the paint-chipped doors of the Dragon Motel, I knew I would have an experience that would change my whole life.

Did you notice that the last sentence in each group is a little different from the others, that it tries to attract more attention and plunge the reader deeply into the paragraph?

Exercise 8   Analyze the following group of topic sentences relating to the topic "My Brother's Scar." Categorize each sentence by writing **T** (for toe, as in the careful approach to the water) or **B** (for body, as in the fearless approach to the water) next to the number.

_____T_____   **1.** There is a funny story about why my brother has a scar.

_____T_____   **2.** I would like to describe how my brother got his scar.

_____T_____   **3.** Scars are things that no one likes to have, including my brother.

_____T_____   **4.** I want to tell you about the accident that happened to my brother two years ago.

_____T_____ **5.** When my brother was young, he had an accident that caused him to receive lots of scars on his body.

_____B_____ **6.** Almost everyone of us has a scar, but my brother's is one of a kind.

_____B_____ **7.** Two years ago when my brother and I jumped from an airplane, his parachute didn't open.

_____B_____ **8.** Whenever I look at my brother's face, I think of the time two years ago when his parachute didn't open.

_____B_____ **9.** When my brother talks to people, he unconsciously keeps his hands near his face in an attempt to hide the large scar running across his cheek.

_____B_____ **10.** It is long and deep, white when the weather is cold and red when the weather is hot.

Writing Assignment

Write Topic Sentences

Write your own topic sentences for the following subjects. Try to write at least one "toe" type topic sentence and one "body" type topic sentence for each.

1. my best friend

2. the worst night in my life

3. breakfast in the U.S. and in my country

4. how to build a sandcastle

5. the mysterious death of a civil engineer

6. the arrest of the mass murderer

E. Journal Type 2: Creative Listings

The creative listings journal is linked with memory and personality. In this type of journal, you do not write paragraphs but short lists based on topics. The lists should be the result of deep thought and analysis. After you write a list, think closely about the significance of each entry. For example, you should analyze your answers to "Five things that you could not live without," and then ask these questions:

◆ Why are these things so important?

◆ How would your life be different without them?

◆ Can these things possibly be replaced?

Journal Activity

Write Creative Lists

For the next two weeks, write in your journal every day about two of the topics listed below. Write a list of five or more entries for each topic. After completing the lists, use the responses as sources of journal writing for next month. Follow the procedure used for Exercise 9 on page 42.

1. all the things you hide when people visit your home

2. the things you like to do when you are alone

3. your favorite animals

4. the aromas you really like

5. five foods you would not eat under any circumstances

6. five things you could not live without

7. the best gifts you have ever received

8. gadgets you bought but rarely (if ever) use

9. people who have had a strong influence on your life

10. five world leaders (living or dead) with whom you would love to speak

11. different eras in which you would like to live

12. smells from your grandparents' home

13. all the diseases and illnesses you have ever had

14. five excuses you use to say no to someone

15. reasons why people shouldn't get married

16. your five worst teachers

17. all the favorite items you have lost

18. your favorite snacks when you were a child

19. the people you really liked when you were growing up

20. your five favorite movies

21. your five favorite songs

22. your favorite toys when you were growing up

23. five actors or actresses with whom you would love to have a date

24. five classmates you really didn't like when you were in elementary or high school

25. your five best teachers

26. reasons why people should get married

27. your favorite meals your mother or grandmother used to cook

28. the neighbors you liked and disliked when you were growing up

Exercise 9 This exercise combines memory, critical thinking, vocabulary development, outlining, speaking and conversation, and writing skills. Follow the directions.

1. Make a list of the best gifts you have ever received. Include at least five. You may have received these gifts recently, or you may have received them as a child. From the list, choose what you consider to be the best gift. (5 minutes)

2. Write five adjectives to describe the gift. (3 minutes)

3. Write five adjectives to describe the way that you felt when you received the gift. (3 minutes)

4. Make a brief outline that includes answers to the following questions (5 minutes):

Why was the gift so significant to you?

Who gave you the gift?

On what occasion were you given the gift?

Do you still have the gift? (What happened to it?)

5. Have a conversation with a classmate. Tell your partner about your gift; use the adjectives you have just listed. Also include the information from point 4. After you finish telling your partner about your favorite gift, listen to his or her gift description. Remember to be a good listener and ask questions. (12–15 minutes)

6. Write a paragraph of description/narration on a separate piece of paper in which you describe the best gift you have ever received. Tell how and when you received it and why it is so important to you.

Building Your Skill in Describing People

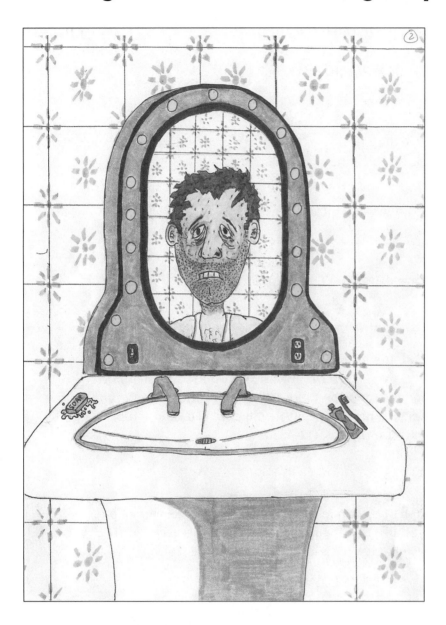

Activity 1 *The Face in the Mirror*

Analyze the drawing on page 44. Do you look like this when you first face the mirror each day?

Writing Assignment

Describe Yourself

In a short, descriptive paragraph, tell how you look when you first wake up in the morning. Try to be humorous. If you are too serious, it might ruin your mood.

Activity 2 *The Personal Ad*

Many Americans now try to meet their mates through personal ads placed in newspapers or magazines. The ads usually contain three parts:

♦ a title meant to attract readers

♦ a description of the person who has paid for the ad and is looking for a mate

♦ a description of the person being sought

Read the ads presented on page 46 from the *Strictly Personal* column to get a feel for the way in which they are constructed. Some are funny, while others are very serious. Whereas some seem to describe people who are almost perfect, other ads include a few shortcomings. Remember too that people often write what they think people want to read.

Because the people who submit ads usually pay by the word, they often use abbreviations to save space and money. **SWF** means single, white female. **DHM** means divorced, Hispanic male. **C** stands for Christian, **J** for Jewish, **A** for Asian, and **B** for Black. **NS** means non-smoking. **LTR** means long-term relationship.

Strictly Personal

SEEKING MEN

Country Girl, SWCF, 24, enjoys Broadway shows, sports, dancing, dinner, movies. Seeking SCM with similar interests. Call today?

Italian Beauty, a young 41, long hair, blue eyes, great cook; seeking tall, robust, romantic man to share the good times.

New Year, New Man. Are you a SWM, 40–55, NS, active, confident, and sincere? If so, contact this attractive DBF.

Outgoing, optimistic, and professional, 31, SHF, blond/blue, 130 lbs., seeks financially secure man for long-term relationship.

Petite, cute, shapely music lover, enjoys opera, ballet, dancing, and travel. Seeks professional, caring, sweet companion.

Hot-blooded Romance. Attractive SWF, aerobics instructor, great dancer, energetic. Seeking S/DM to share evenings cuddling by the fireplace and wild nights on the dance floor.

Circle this Ad! DJF, 44, Blue eyes, enjoys dining out, travel, romantic walks on the beach, seeks handsome, professional, sexy male with a sense of humor for LTR.

Plus-size SF seeking husky man, interesting, smart, fun-loving. Let's make magic together.

Beautiful, classy, SAF, seeking educated, professional SBM to create a happy family. Must be considerate, sensitive, passionate.

Looking for Tom Cruise. Meg Ryan look-alike seeks tall hunk for wild times, travel, partying.

Medical Professional, financially secure, intelligent, fun-loving, seeks emotionally stable, slim, and humorous SH/WM.

Caring and Outgoing mother of two, 27, seeks S/DM to go to the movies and have fun with, and to share quiet evenings at home.

Husky Male Wanted! Greek SF, 20, 5'1", chubby, enjoys country music, karoake bars, picnics in nature. Smokers OK.

SEEKING WOMEN

Secure JM, professional, 62, quite financially secure, seeks S/DF for candlelight dinners and intimate evenings.

Handsome Russian Gemini, 23, rugged construction worker, seeking my soulmate: slim, sweet, caring SWF.

Tired of the bar scene? SBM, 32, 6'0", athletic, likes to work out, seeks tall, intelligent woman to pamper and romance.

Call me! DWM, attractive, clean-cut Italian, seeks a traditional WF for a second chance. NS.

For sale: SWM, 32, runs/looks good, low mileage, body in good condition. Likes outdoors, shows, dining out. Seeks affectionate, down-to-earth woman.

Are you alone? Handsome Korean executive seeks attractive, artistic woman to set up a perfect house and family.

Wanted: Sincere Friend. SWM, attractive, clear-headed, just out of rehab, seeking SF to help me keep my life in order.

Commitment Wanted! SHM, 35, 5'8", 140 lbs., intelligent, caring, loves to dance the merengue, seeks smart, faithful, sincere SF.

African-American Male seeks SF, slender, passionate, warmhearted, for long walks in the country, treks in the mountains.

Let's Keep Warm This Winter! Muslim male. High-rise city resident. Seeks witty, energetic, cultured female.

Seeking Asian Girlfriend. I enjoy Asian cuisine/ culture, and can teach you English as well. Should be pretty and lively.

Any Good Women Left? Widowed white male, 53, seeks LTR with sincere, educated, shapely non-smoker to share outdoor and indoor activities.

Devout Muslim, seeks elegant, religious woman, 30–45, to share the good and difficult moments in life. Well-educated and secure.

The key to this activity is the quality of the adjectives used. Take a few minutes to underline some of the adjectives used in the ads and understand their meaning. Obviously, most of the adjectives have *positive connotations* because the writers are trying to offer and seek the best qualities. Your analysis of adjectives for this exercise will help you to complete Activity 1: Adjectives on page 29 in the Vocabulary Acquisition section of this Part.

Writing Assignments

Write Personal Ads

After you have read the ads on page 46, do the following on a separate piece of paper.

1. Above are caricatures of five people. Write five adjectives that best describe each person. The adjectives should explain physical characteristics and/or personality traits.

2. Write a humorous personal ad for each of the people. Keep the ads as short as the ones you just read. Because you pay by the word for ads, the writing must be very descriptive but economical and succinct.

3. Write a *serious* personal ad, perhaps with a romantic flavor, for each of the people.

4. Expand *one* of the brief personal ads into a paragraph in which you describe the person more fully. Include not only a physical description, but also an indication of his or her likes, dislikes, interests, hobbies, and dreams. Then describe the person that he or she would like to meet; give a more expanded description than you gave in the personal ad.

5. Write a personal ad about yourself; include five adjectives that best describe you and tell about some of your interests. Then describe the person you would find intriguing.

Activity 3　*A National Hero*

Every country has national heroes: people whom everyone admires and respects. These individuals have strong qualities, such as bravery, honesty, and dedication, that we wish to imitate. To be a national hero, a person likely has done something important on behalf of the country, such as liberation of the country or the initiation of social reform. U.S. heroes include George Washington, Abraham Lincoln, and Martin Luther King, Jr. Heroes often die for their cause.

Writing Assignment

Write about a National Hero

Research the biography of a national hero from the United States, the country of your birth, or another country of your choice. Go to the library and consult an encyclopedia and/or books on history, biography, or events, or use search engines on the Internet to find information. Take notes. **Do not copy directly from the book.** Write down the most important facts. Then compose a paragraph of description on this person's life. Read the paragraph a few times so you know it well. Practice oral communication skills by describing the person to a classmate. Then, when you are sure of yourself and your subject, be prepared to present what you have learned about the hero to your class.

Tomb of Kosciusko: West Point. Courtesy of The Library of Congress.

Writing Assignment

Paraphrase a Passage

The ability to paraphrase is an important writing skill when you use other materials (secondary sources) to help you gather ideas and provide facts for your composition work. When you paraphrase, avoid copying from the original. Instead, *use your own words.*

The following is an example of an encyclopedia article on the Polish hero Thaddeus Kosciusko.

> **Kosciusko, Thaddeus (1746–1817), was a Polish patriot who fought for freedom in America and Poland. Because of this, he is often called the Hero of Two Worlds. Kosciusko arrived in America in August 1776. He offered his services to the Continental Congress and was appointed colonel of engineers. He built fortifications near Saratoga and later was responsible for American defenses along the Hudson River. He constructed fortifications at West Point. After the war, Congress appointed him to the rank of brigadier general. Kosciusko returned to Poland in 1784. He led the uprising in 1794 that bears his name, in an effort to prevent the third and final partition of Poland by Russia, Prussia, and Austria. At first successful, he was later defeated and imprisoned. Kosciusko was born in Lithuania. His remains now rest in the historic Wawel Castle in Krakow, burial place of many of Poland's heroes.**

Source: *World Book Encyclopedia*

Paraphrase the article on Kosciusko into a paragraph of description by writing 10 to 12 sentences in your own words. Use a separate piece of paper. One way to begin the paragraph might be: *Thaddeus Kosciusko was a patriot who became a hero in two different countries, Poland and America. He was born in Lithuania in 1746. In 1776 . . .*

Activity 4   *Sherlock Holmes*

Read the excerpts from Sherlock Holmes stories written by Sir Arthur Conan Doyle and do the exercises and assignment that follow.

To Sherlock Holmes she is always *the* woman. I have seldom heard him mention her under any other name. In his eyes she eclipses and predominates the whole of her sex. It was not that he felt any emotion akin to love for Irene Adler. All emotions, and that one particularly, were abhorrent to his cold, precise, but admirably balanced mind. He was, I take it, the most perfect reasoning and observing machine that the world has seen; but, as a lover, he would have placed himself in a false position. He never spoke of the softer passions, save with a gibe and a sneer. They were admirable things for the observer—excellent for drawing the veil from men's motives and actions. But for the trained reasoner to admit such intrusions into his own delicate and finely adjusted temperament was to introduce a distracting factor which might throw a doubt upon all his mental results. Grit in a sensitive instrument, or a crack in one of his own high-power lenses, would not be more disturbing than a strong emotion in a nature such as his. And yet there was but one woman to him, and that woman was the late Irene Adler, of dubious and questionable memory.

Source: Introduction to *A Scandal in Bohemia* by Sir Arthur Conan Doyle

Sherlock Holmes was a man who seldom took exercise for exercise's sake. Few men were capable of greater muscular effort, and he was undoubtedly one of the finest boxers of his weight that I have ever seen; but he looked upon aimless bodily exertion as a waste of energy, and he seldom bestirred himself save where there was some professional object to be served. Then he was absolutely untiring and indefatigable. That he should have kept himself in training under such circumstances is remarkable, but his diet was usually of the sparest, and his habits were simple to the verge of austerity. Save for the occasional use of cocaine, he had no vices, and he only turned to the drug as a protest against the monotony of existence when cases were scanty and the papers uninteresting.

Source: Introduction to *The Yellow Face* by Sir Arthur Conan Doyle

Exercise 1   Answer the following questions about the passages.

    1. Why would a romantic attachment go against the nature of Sherlock Holmes?

    2. Why does Holmes take cocaine?

    3. Would you consider Holmes to be lazy?

    4. What is Holmes's reaction to others who fall in love?

    5. What is the attitude of Dr. Watson (who writes these passages) toward Holmes?

Exercise 2   Underline the adjectives used in the passages and then define them.

Writing Assignment

Describe Someone You Know

Using these two passages as models, describe one of your friends or someone you know. Concentrate both on physical appearance and on personality. Cite your friend's predominant traits.

Building Your Skill in Describing Places

Activity 1   *Accommodations*

Read the following passage, and then do the exercises that follow.

There are hundreds of hotels and inns scattered along the 12-mile strip of beach on Junao peninsula. If you arrive without reservations, go to the tourist information center near the train station for up-to-date listings on available places to stay. Most hotels are on the beach and require a three-day stay. During June and July it is generally difficult to find accommodations, so be certain to make reservations before you arrive. If you get here in May, early June, or September, you will have your choice of places.

The **Blue Lagoon Hotel** is in the center of town. It is a small, colorful place with moderate prices. Each room has a shower, television, radio, and air conditioning. The service is fair. There is a restaurant that serves standard quality food.

The **White Water Inn** is an immaculate and rustic hideaway a few blocks from the beach. It is very popular with locals because of its excellent restaurant. It is very relaxing, but the prices are high. You will have to share a bath, but the friendliness of the owners/hosts and the splendor of the service and food make staying here worth the inconvenience of sharing a bath.

The **Hotel Splendor** is a deluxe accommodation with all the amenities for a memorable stay. It has three swimming pools, four dining areas, a lounge, and nightly entertainment. All the rooms have a breathtaking view of the water, and the hotel has a private beach. The rooms are spacious and luxurious. Despite the exorbitant prices, the Hotel Splendor fills up quickly. The outdoor cafe is a wonderful place for people watching.

The **Proto Inn** has dormitory-style rooms that cater primarily to tour groups. The food will remind you of your school cafeteria, and the rooms are barely larger than prison cells. Heavy traffic can be heard all day, and the only attraction of this place is its extremely low price. If you are on a budget, or if you only use your hotel room for a nap, this may be the place for you. At least it's clean.

Exercise 1   Answer the following questions with complete sentences.

   1. How good is the food at the Proto Inn?

   2. Is the Hotel Splendor worth its high price?

   3. What does the phrase *people watching* mean?

   4. Describe the advantages and disadvantages of the White Water Inn.

   5. How does the evaluator rate the Blue Lagoon Hotel?

   6. Would you stay in the Proto Inn? Why or why not?

   7. What kind of people would you probably meet in the White Water Inn?

Exercise 2 The words in the first column appear in the text. Try to determine the definitions for them based on context clues. Do they have positive or negative connotations? Do they refer to money, prices, or rates? What nouns do they describe? Are they synonyms of "simple" or "fantastic"? After you have found a workable definition, match the word with its **opposite** in the second column.

_____ **1.** up-to-date	**a.** ultra-modern
_____ **2.** spacious	**b.** moderate
_____ **3.** rustic	**c.** very simple
_____ **4.** immaculate	**d.** concentrated
_____ **5.** deluxe	**e.** forgettable
_____ **6.** scattered	**f.** outdated
_____ **7.** luxurious	**g.** dirty
_____ **8.** breathtaking	**h.** cramped
_____ **9.** memorable	**i.** boring
_____ **10.** exorbitant	**j.** without extras

Writing Assignment

Describe a Hotel

Using some of the vocabulary words above, write a paragraph on a separate piece of paper in which you imagine the perfect place to stay for rest and relaxation. This may be a hotel in the mountains near a lake or a rustic cabin in the wilderness.

Activity 2 *Design a Living Space*

In the apartment or house into which you are moving, there is a large, sunny room that will probably serve as your living room/family room/ television room/den. The room is empty and has a beautiful, shiny, hardwood floor. There are several windows in the room and an entrance door. The shape and dimensions of the room are shown on page 56. You have some or all of the following pieces of furniture:

- ◆ a 32-inch plasma television
- ◆ a couch
- ◆ a loveseat
- ◆ 2 chairs
- ◆ bookshelves
- ◆ a stereo

- ◆ a 9- by 12-foot Oriental rug
- ◆ 2 end tables
- ◆ 2 table lamps
- ◆ a floor lamp
- ◆ a few framed posters, prints, or paintings

You may also add other furniture, as you see fit.

Using the living room plan on page 56, place the furniture in the room; make sure you consider comfort and style.

After you have arranged the furniture and decorated the walls, write a paragraph on a separate piece of paper that describes the room as you have designed it. You will probably have to use many prepositions of placement, such as *under, on top of, next to, between, over, on, beneath, in the corner of, in the middle of,* etc. To better organize your paragraph, describe the room using *spatial progression,* either left to right, right to left, or near to far. Follow a logical path around the room in your description.

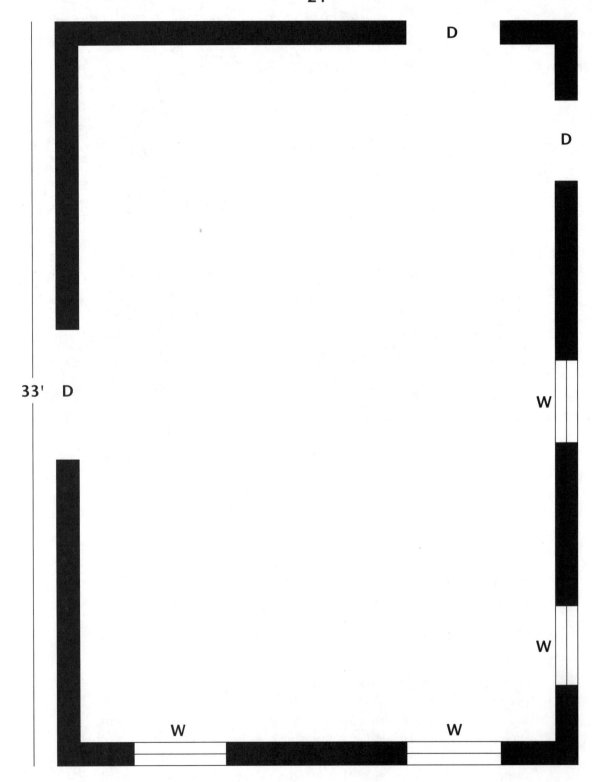

24'

33'

D

D

D

W

W

W

W

Activity 3   *Write a Travel Brochure*

Read the following passage, then do the activities that follow.

From the Palisade cliffs rising 500 feet above the Hudson River to the Passaic River in the west, from the Meadowlands in the south to the Ramapo Mountains in the north, Bergen County occupies the northeastern corner of the state of New Jersey. This suburban area is rather crowded, with a population of more than 830,000. However, the county has no big cities, which helps it keep a small town atmosphere. In terms of population, the largest towns are Teaneck (38,000), Hackensack (36,000), Fort Lee (32,000), Fair Lawn (31,000), Garfield (26,000), Paramus (26,000), and Ridgewood (25,000).

Bergen County has a long history. The Ramapo and Lenni Lenape Indians long inhabited the area. When we analyze the origins of several city names—Paramus ("where the wild turkeys run"), Ho-Ho-Kus ("maple trees by the brook"), and Mahwah ("mountain path")—we see evidence of the native Americans who first lived in the area. The first European settlers were the Dutch, who landed in Bergen County in 1630. The Dutch dominated Bergen County culture in important ways for 200 years, primarily in the habits of food and dress and methods of farming and housekeeping. Later settlers in the area included the English (in the "English neighborhood" of Ridgefield, Leonia, and Englewood), the French (led by Huguenot David Demarest who settled in River Edge), Germans, Poles, and Scots.

Bergen County stayed basically agricultural from the 17th to the end of the 19th century. One of the principal crops was strawberries. By 1859, 10 to 15 million baskets were produced each year. As Paterson, Newark, and New York City grew, so did the demand for Bergen County's agricultural products.

The transportation revolution of the last half of the nineteenth century brought profound changes to the county. By 1880, the Erie Lakawana Railroad was completed and thus eliminated slow journeys hauling merchandise down river. The trains reached inland to the farms, factories, foundries, and mills. The speed of the trains also made Bergen County a residential suburb. Now, businesspeople could travel back and forth to New York City with great speed. This caused many upper-class and middle-class families to leave the city and buy houses in the area. Real estate brokers stressed many positive aspects of life in Bergen County: spacious homes, impressive railroad stations, paved roads, and a real sense of community, with hospitals, libraries, fire and police protection, and quality education.

In the 20th century, Bergen County grew and prospered. The George Washington Bridge and Lincoln Tunnel (created from 1930 to 1935) made transportation even easier. Beginning in 1960 the construction of malls made the area a prime shopping center. Now, more than 50 percent of all the retail business in the county is done in one city: Paramus. The positive result is a vibrant, energetic atmosphere. The negative results are traffic jams and congestion. As the county begins a new millennium, several challenges lie ahead. The green areas must be preserved, growth must be controlled, and the quality of life must be maintained.

Writing Assignment

Write a Travel Brochure about Your County

Imagine you are asked to write a short travel brochure about the county where you currently live. Write a clearly organized paragraph in which you describe the places to see, the activities to do, the areas to visit, the stores, parks, historic sites, and towns to enjoy. Pretend that the reader knows very little about the county. Be as descriptive and as positive as possible.

Writing Assignment

Describe Your City/Town

Suppose that you have been asked by relatives to describe the city or town in which you live. Write a detailed description of your city or town. Make it sound as if you have made an excellent choice in terms of a place to live. Describe all the interesting places and people.

UNIT 2.3

Building Your Skills in Describing Scenes

Activity 1 *Description of Mall Activities at Lloyd's Center in Portland, Oregon*

Read the following passage, then do the activities that follow.

(1) Every Saturday afternoon, Lloyd's Center in Portland, Oregon, turns into a big circus. (2) People enjoy themselves and forget about their problems. (3) The main concourse fills up with shoppers. (4) Some of them race from store to store and try to complete their shopping in record time. (5) Other shoppers move leisurely. (6) They enjoy the art of window-shopping. (7) Parents lead small children by the hand. (8) The children tug in a different direction. (9) They want to visit the nearest toy store to see the new Harry Potter figures. (10) Teenagers come to the mall to hang out. (11) They really are not interested in shopping. (12) A four-piece hip-hop band plays a dance song in the square. (13) The band members wear baggy pants and baseball hats turned backward. (14) The shoppers gaze at them curiously. (15) The spinner at the twin turntables moves his hands at lightning speed. (16) There are three break-dancers in front of the band. (17) They really catch the attention of the crowd. (18) In the Food Court upstairs, people can choose from the cuisine of many countries. (19) There are Chinese, Italian, Greek, Japanese, and Mexican stands. (20) Many people stop at McDonald's to buy hamburgers and fries. (21) Others buy freshly baked cookies. (22) The aroma of the cookies is enticing. (23) The mall is very crowded. (24) No one complains. (25) Everyone seems to be having too much fun.

Exercise 1

Pretend that all the activities are occurring right now. On a separate piece of paper, change the entire paragraph to the present progressive tense beginning with the following words: *Right now Lloyd's Center in Portland, Oregon, is turning into a big circus.* Cross off the words, and write in the new tense. For a review of the present progressive tense, consult your grammar text.

Exercise 2

On a separate piece of paper, rewrite the entire paragraph combining sentences 1 and 2; 5 and 6; 7, 8, and 9; 10 and 11; 13 and 14; 15 and 16; 19 and 20; 21 and 22; and 24 and 25. One possibility for the first two sentences is the following: *Every Saturday afternoon, Lloyd's Center in Portland, Oregon, turns into a big circus where people enjoy themselves and forget about their problems.*

Writing Assignments

Describe Scenes

1. Go to the student center at your school and observe the students and their activities. When you get home, write a paragraph on a separate piece of paper that retells students' actions. For this assignment, you will use the **simple past** and **past progressive tenses.** For a review of these tenses, consult your grammar text.

2. Go to the library, and observe the students and their activities. Write a paragraph using the **simple present tense** to describe actions that occur there every day.

3. Do the same for the cafeteria, except pretend that the actions will take place tomorrow. Use the **simple future** and the **future progressive tenses.**

VOCABULARY FOR THE DESCRIPTION OF MALL ACTIVITIES

For the following vocabulary word or phrase found in the text, write a definition for each, indicate its part of speech, and use it in a sentence of your own.

Word/Phrase	Part of Speech	Definition
record time		
SENTENCE:		
leisurely		
SENTENCE:		
window-shopping		
SENTENCE:		

Word/Phrase	Part of Speech	Definition
tug		
SENTENCE:		
hang out		
SENTENCE:		
hip-hop band		
SENTENCE:		
baggy pants		
SENTENCE:		
lightning speed		
SENTENCE:		
cuisine		
SENTENCE:		
aroma		
SENTENCE:		

Describe an Indoor Entertainment Center

Indoor entertainment centers have become very popular. Protected from bad weather, filled with technological marvels, these places with the radio blasting and the bright lights shining provide fast-action fun one quarter at a time. Video games, action simulators, interactive play, miniature golf, bowling, and batting cages are just a few of the activities to be enjoyed in an indoor entertainment center.

Visit an indoor entertainment center or video arcade and observe the people and their activities. Take brief notes if you wish and use the Lloyd's Center in Portland, Oregon, paragraph on page 59 as a model. Then write a paragraph on a separate piece of paper in which you describe the scene at the indoor entertainment center or video arcade. Use as many descriptive words as you can.

F. Graded Writing Assignment: Describe a Painting or Work of Art

Describe a painting or a work of art by following this process.

1. Find the OVERSIZED BOOKS section in your school or community library. These are mostly books on art and architecture.

2. Look through the stacks and find a book on an artist who interests you. Look through the book and find a painting or work of art to describe.

3. Check the book out of the library (using your student identification card), or make a photocopy of the painting or work of art that you will describe.

4. Include a photocopy of the painting or work or art that you are describing when you hand in your assignment.

5. You may also research an artist on the Internet or at your local museum.

The paragraph ~~~~~~~~~ 12 to 14 sentences. It should have two parts:

~~de an analytical description of the painting. Tell
~~ scene, the positions of the subjects, the colors
~~cture for this part is *spatial progression* (that is,
~~ed manner from top to bottom, left to right, or
~~und).

~~he paragraph, comment on the painting or work
~~*ressions, reactions,* and *feelings* you get when you
~~l part of the paragraph should begin with the
~~*t the painting [or work of art], I feel. . . ."* If you use
~~u find the painting as source material for your
~~*paraphrase* the original and cite the source. Do
~~ the text. Use your own words.

~~ following list of words useful when you write
~~ painting or work of art. Write a definition, indi-
~~se it in a sentence of your own.

painter	sculptor
sculpture	work of art
background	subject
mood	

G. Part 2 Summary

Based on your work in Part 2, answer the questions below and discuss them as a class.

1. What is the importance of writing a journal entry every day?

2. Where do you find topics for journal writing?

3. What is a topic sentence?

4. Describe the two types of topic sentence.

5. What is the difference between *literal* meaning and *figurative* meaning? Give two examples of each.

6. What is the most important part of speech in a description paragraph and why?

7. What is the best way to check subject–verb agreement?

8. What verb tense is usually used in a paragraph of description? Are other tenses possible?

H. Reflections on Your Progress

Write your reflections or thoughts below on some of the writing you have done in Part 2.

1. Which two journal entries did you enjoy writing the most, and why?

2. Which lists were most effective in bringing back memories of your youth?

3. What was the most interesting writing assignment, and why?

4. What was the least interesting writing assignment, and why?

5. What is the most important thing about writing that you learned?

6. Were you satisfied with the progress you made in the assignments?

I. Part 2 Assignment Checklist

Assignment	Required or Optional	Grade	Revised	Returned and Filed
Describe Photographs (page 27)				
Write Topic Sentences (page 40)				
Write Creative Lists (Journal Activity) (page 41)				
Describe Yourself (page 45)				
Write Personal Ads (page 47)				
Write about a National Hero (page 48)				
Paraphrase a Passage (page 49)				
Describe Someone You Know (page 51)				
Describe a Hotel (page 54)				
Design a Living Space (page 54)				
Write a Travel Brochure about Your County (page 58)				
Describe Your City/Town (page 58)				
Describe Scenes (page 60)				
Describe an Indoor Entertainment Center (page 62)				
Describe a Painting or Work of Art (page 62)				

J. Part 2 Journal Summary

Date of First Journal	Date of Last Journal	Number of Journal Entries Written for Part 2

PART 3

Narration
Paragraphs

Suggested Journal Topics for Narration Paragraphs

- Tell a funny story or a joke

- Your most embarrassing experience

- A ghost story to be told late at night

- Review the plot of a movie or a book

- Tell how you met your best friend

- Narrate the proudest day of your life

- Your first day in the United States

- How you learned that not all people are nice

A. Narration Paragraphs

We live life in narration. When we retell the plot of a movie that we have seen, an exciting incident that happened on the way to class, or the way we spent our weekend, we are using the picture-creating facility in our brains. The ability to listen to narrative and understand fully involves the use of our *imagination*.

Narration, in the form of storytelling, is one of the oldest forms of communication and also one of the first forms to which we are introduced as small children. The bedtime story is a part of many wonderful childhood memories and an essential part of formation and development in many cultures.

Remember that *adjectives* were the predominant part of speech for description paragraphs. *Verbs,* rich and colorful, expressive and vivid, are the key elements of an interesting paragraph of narration. Structure is also quite important in narration: most times **chronological order**—that is, events in their natural sequence—is used. This is done to make the narration easier for the reader to follow.

Paragraphs of narration often use time clauses and phrases. Thus, it is common to see such words as **then, after, before, while, as soon as, until, when, as long as,** and **as** in narration. The sentences in narration paragraphs tend to be longer than in description paragraphs, so correct punctuation is important. The grammar exercises in this Part will work specifically on this point.

The word *narrate* comes from the Latin verb *narrare,* which means "to tell." An important part of telling a story is keeping the listener (or reader) in mind. The same narration, for example, would probably not be effective for both children and adults. It is advisable to practice paragraphs of narration aloud before writing them on paper. This simulates the natural processes of our everyday life in which we recount many episodes. It is also very important to become a good listener. When listening to other people's narrations, pay attention to their tone, their diction or choice of words, especially the verbs that they choose, and the length of their phrases. Listening well can help improve the writing process, because it keeps us aware of these essential elements.

B. Vocabulary Acquisition: Verbs

In your reading this week, concentrate on *verbs*. Find 15 new ones, and write them in the space below. Indicate the part of speech, whether the word has a positive or negative connotation, and whether you recognize parts of the word (prefixes or suffixes) that help you to find a definition. Then write a definition and construct a sentence for each verb. The first one serves as a model.

Word	Part of Speech	Connotation (+, −, =)	Roots, Prefixes, or Suffixes	Definition
1. propose	verb	+	*pro* = forward *pos* = put	To put forward for consideration or discussion
SENTENCE: The professor proposed a postponement of the test.				
2.				
SENTENCE:				
3.				
SENTENCE:				
4.				
SENTENCE:				
5.				
SENTENCE:				

Word	Part of Speech	Connotation (+, −, =)	Roots, Prefixes, or Suffixes	Definition
6.				
SENTENCE:				
7.				
SENTENCE:				
8.				
SENTENCE:				
9.				
SENTENCE:				
10.				
SENTENCE:				
11.				
SENTENCE:				
12.				
SENTENCE:				

Word	Part of Speech	Connotation (+, −, =)	Roots, Prefixes, or Suffixes	Definition
13.				
SENTENCE:				
14.				
SENTENCE:				
15.				
SENTENCE:				

C. Grammatical Structures: Independent Clauses

Independent clauses are complete sentences (and can stand alone), while dependent clauses are not complete (and cannot stand alone). In order to combine two independent clauses into a compound sentence, a comma and **conjunction** must be used. If there is no conjunction in the sentence, it is incorrect to combine two independent clauses with a comma alone. Even two seemingly simple independent clauses require a conjunction to combine them. For example: *He died. She cried.* These two clauses cannot be combined in this way: *He died, she cried.* Only if a conjunction is used can they be made into one sentence: *He died, and she cried.* Or: *He died, so she cried.*

Exercise 1 Punctuate the following sentences by adding periods or commas. Capitalize letters at the beginning of sentences. Do not add any other words.

1. I have read that article. It is very clear and concise.

2. Mary decided to stay home. She wanted to prepare for the test.

3. I opened the front door right away, but no one was there.

4. Marcus never comes to class on time. He sleeps late every day.

5. We arrived at the movie theatre early, but the movie had started.

6. The storm was raging outside. We were warm and dry in the cabin.

7. Last week we went camping. It rained every day and night.

8. A very common bird in Pennsylvania is the bluejay. It has bright colors, but it sometimes eats baby birds from nests.

9. I hurried to answer the telephone. I thought it was my mother.

10. I opened the window and the fresh air came right in.

11. I have not studied at all, I have to stay home tonight.

12. No one believed that he would pass, but he got a good grade.

13. English is difficult to read aloud, the words do not always sound like they look.

14. Jack works in a department store on Saturdays, and he works in an office during the week.

Exercise 2 Combine the two sentences using the word or words indicated in the parentheses. Punctuate carefully.

    1. He works nine hours every night. He is very tired when he gets to school in the morning. (because)

      He is very tired when he gets to school in the morning, because he works nine hours every night

    2. She studied French for three years in high school, and She is studying German now. (and)

3. John works 60 hours per week. ~~He~~ *, but he* never has money. (but)

4. ~~Although~~ *Although* He is 6 feet 11 inches tall~~,~~ *,* ~~He~~ *he* has never played basketball~~.~~ (although) *he is 6'11" tall.*

5. She always comes on time. ~~She~~ *because* believes that punctuality is important. (because)

6. He comes from a country where people speak Portuguese~~;~~ *; nevertheless* His Spanish is excellent. (nevertheless)

7. Max has never been to Egypt~~.~~ *; as a result,* He cannot discuss the pyramids from first-hand experience. (as a result)

8. Sicily is an island located between Italy and Africa~~.~~ *; consequently,* It produces many types of citrus fruits. (consequently)

9. The rain was very heavy last night. The grass was all wet this morning. (due to the fact that) *the rain was very heavy last night.*

10. In Vietnam the monsoon season lasts four months~~,~~ *,* There is sometimes flooding in the lowlands. (because of the fact that)

Exercise 3 Insert periods or commas in the following clauses. Do *not* add any extra words. Begin new sentences with capital letters.

1. She is very tall. He is short.

2. I have never seen Paris, but I am going later this year.

3. I love her so much because she is rich.

4. My brother lives in an apartment, my sister lives in an old house.

5. Brock never gives flowers to his wife. He gives flowers to his mistress.

6. Brock's mistress has another lover, his name is Ridge.

7. My uncle and aunt live in New York and work in New Jersey.

8. I have never eaten food from Thailand, but I have heard that it is spicy.

9. The woman talked to the man, and he whispered in her ear.

10. Because she is an excellent speaker, I always stay awake when she talks.

11. Professor Balongi speaks Chinese and French, Professor Jones speaks only English.

12. In the morning, I always look at the clouds. This way I can predict the weather.

13. Whenever I hear her voice, I start to cry.

14. In the late afternoon, it becomes difficult to play baseball. The sun is in your eyes.

15. After I saw his face I wanted to run away.

16. On Halloween my brother doesn't wear a mask he just walks around with a smile.

17. My mother cooks Thanksgiving turkeys for everyone in the neighborhood she is nice.

18. My father works in a restaurant he is a chef.

19. In the summer I go to the beach my sister stays home.

20. He died she cried.

21. The intelligent doctor married the wise nurse the nurse was very happy.

22. My car broke down so I had to take a taxi.

23. While I was driving to school I saw two cats and three dogs.

24. Last night a bird came into my house my cat ate it.

25. I will never go to Siberia It is too cold.

26. In the morning she makes coffee and drinks three cups.

27. Mrs. Jackson hates Mr. Jackson's dog but she loves his cat.

28. The professor gave a lot of homework no one could finish it.

29. You should take a shower you smell.

30. I take a shower in the morning and a bath in the evening.

31. She married her high school sweetheart He is a lawyer.

32. She married her first cousin this custom is against the law in 38 states.

33. When I came home I watched tv.

34. I watched tv when I came home.

35. While I was eating dinner I watched tv.

36. Tomorrow I will study all night after that I will take a shower.

37. When she cooks I eat out.

38. My mother is an excellent cook she knows how to make everything.

39. The teacher prepared the test her husband cooked pasta.

40. This exercise is too long I hate it.

D. Writing Skills: Outlining

Outlining is a writing skill that forces organization. By taking notes the writer can organize the work in chronological order. Here is an example of an outline from Aesop's fable "The Tortoise and the Hare."

1. **Introduction of Characters**

   a. Tortoise

   b. Hare

2. **The Bet**

   a. A race of speed

   b. Setting the distance

3. **The Beginning of the Race**

   a. The hare takes the lead

   b. The tortoise keeps on moving

4. **The Middle of the Race**

   a. The hare takes a nap

   b. The tortoise keeps on moving

5. **The End of the Race**

   a. The hare wakes up too late

   b. The tortoise keeps on moving

   c. The tortoise wins the race

6. **The Moral of the Story**

   a. Slow and steady wins the race

Exercise 4   After your teacher narrates the story (which can be found in the Answer Key, page 311), go around the class, with each person telling a bit of the story in chronological order. Then work in pairs and narrate the story to your partner. After you leave class, narrate the story again at least twice to two of your friends or relatives. Finally, write the story of the tortoise and the hare on a separate piece of paper.

WRITING CHRONOLOGICAL OUTLINES

Outlines are essential organizing tools. It is important to learn to write them quickly and effectively. Use bullets or lines in a vertical pattern. You do not have to write complete sentences. Just include a verb, noun, or key word to organize your thoughts. When you actually write the paragraph, the outline will serve as the basis for its arrangement. Follow each step and turn the brief note into a complete sentence. Add a topic sentence, a few details, and a conclusion, and the paragraph is finished.

Exercise 5 Write succinct outlines for the following topics:

1. a typical Sunday

2. an exciting date

3. the activities in a writing class

4. the plot of your favorite book

5. how to prepare your favorite meal

Exercise 6 **1.** Watch an episode of two of your favorite television programs.

2. Write an outline for each on a separate piece of paper that traces the plot of the shows.

Exercise 7 Go to a movie, rent a video, or watch a film on television. Then write an outline on a separate piece of paper that summarizes the plot.

Writing Assignment

Write a Paragraph of Narration

Using one of the outlines that you prepared in Exercise 6 or 7, write a complete paragraph of narration on a separate piece of paper in which you retell the plot of an episode of your favorite television program or a movie.

E. Journal Type 3: The Dream Journal

When Sigmund Freud published *The Interpretation of Dreams* in 1900, he introduced groundbreaking concepts and ushered in what some cultural historians call "the century of psychology." Freud said that dreams were wish fulfillments that disguise the wishes of the unconscious. In Freud's method of interpretation, dreams take on symbolic value. Dreamers may analyze and interpret their own dreams to understand the significance of the symbols, or they may turn to the trained psychoanalyst who might use the free association technique that was used in the Enhancing Creativity Activity in Part 5 on page 165.

Dreams are the "windows of our soul." In dreams—both happy fantasies and disturbing nightmares—our inner psyches are exposed. Many times when we have a particularly vivid dream, we turn to someone else for its interpretation. Perhaps your grandmother or a sibling is the master of interpretation. Many people remember their dreams and can retell them in great detail. Some of the most powerful memories in life are associated with dreams (especially with dreams that come true).

Journal Activities

Record Your Dreams

1. This activity will be performed for the next two to three weeks.

2. Keep your journal and a pen near your bed, so that you can record your dreams as soon as you wake up.

3. Go to sleep. Dream.

4. The next morning, try to recall your dream. Write a few notes in your journal as soon as you wake up so that later on in the day, when you have more time (and when you are fully awake), you can write about your dream.

5. Dreams are exercises in narration writing. You might retell your dream to several friends, family members, or classmates during the day in order to better organize your thoughts. Use distinct action verbs.

6. Write an entry each day about your dreams.

7. *If you do not dream on a particular night, or if you don't remember your dream,* then use your journal entry to recall powerful dreams that you have had in the past.

8. At the end of the two- or three-week period, write a final journal entry in which you analyze your experience with the dream journal.

UNIT 3.1

Building Your Skill in Writing Personal Narratives

Activity 1   *A Folktale from Your Culture*

One indication of the morals, standards, and goals of a culture is its story-telling tradition. This is because stories are often the most effective and subtle means of transmitting positive values from one generation to the next.

It should be an integral part of a culture to study its roots in folktale, because storytelling is the oldest art. Storytelling had its genesis with the birth of language itself. Storytelling is a mirror into the power and poetry of a language. A good story plants a seed in both children and adults, one that may germinate and flower through the power of the imagination not only of the storyteller, but also of the listener.

In order to reflect the intricate nuances of a culture, stories generally focus on the three unifying elements of a society: relationships, courtship, marriage and the family; the rituals of religion and the moral distinction between right and wrong; and the rites of burial. These elements demonstrate respect for family, for God, and for the dead, respectively.

Find a story that reflects your culture and its values. To do this, it is probably advisable to return to the source. If possible, find the oldest person in your family, perhaps a grandmother, grandfather, or a parent, and ask questions. Be prepared to *listen.* Your role is simply to encourage narration.

After you have listened to the story, write it down in your own words on a separate piece of paper. Remember that you cannot be wrong. Few others will know the story. It is your responsibility to reveal it to them. If you cannot get another person from your family to help you, think about a story you remember hearing when you were a child. You could also conduct research on the Internet; use the key word *folktale* and the name of a country to find an interesting piece. It is important to **paraphrase** the text as you did in Part 2 for the National Hero Activity on page 49. Copying text word-for-word is not only plagiarism, or academic theft, but it also does not improve writing and often produces stale and dated material.

Activity 2   *An Embarrassing Experience*

In this assignment you will narrate the most embarrassing experience you can remember and feel comfortable writing about. First, make an outline using chronological order. Keep the following aspects in mind:

1. Where were you?

2. Who was with you?

3. What happened?

4. What was your reaction?

5. What was the result of your action?

In order to further practice writing outlines and paragraphs of narration, you may substitute the word *embarrassing* with the terms *scary, saddest, proudest,* and *most memorable* experience. The topic, in general, involves key moments in your life—both positive and negative.

Activity 3   *My First Memory*

Some psychiatrists have stated that two of the determining causes in whether we are **optimists** or **pessimists** are the quality and the tone of our first memory in life. For example, if the first occurrence that we remember is listening to a folktale told by our grandmother in front of a fireplace in the winter, we have this positive foundation on which to base our existence. On the other hand, if our first memory involves the death of a family pet and the *trauma* that this caused, we might tend to be more pessimistic. People whose experiences are more neutral, neither too positive nor too negative, tend to become **realists.**

Writing Assignment

Narrate Your First Memory

In a clearly written, well-organized paragraph, narrate the first memory you have on a separate piece of paper. Or interview several of your friends, relatives, or coworkers about their first memories. Write about the most interesting one(s).

Building Your Skill in Retelling Stories

Activity 1   *"The Hyena of Zimbabwe"*

Read the following story and answer the questions that follow.

The Hyena of Zimbabwe

In the land of Zimbabwe, there once lived a hyena, who spent his nights preying on other animals. One day after eating a big meal of young animals, he was very thirsty. He went to the well to drink, but the bucket broke, and he got stuck in the deep well. He called out for many hours and had no response from the animals that passed by. Then he heard the heavy steps of Ox. Hyena shouted, "Ox, help me! I'm stuck in the well. Hang your tail down the well so I can climb out."

Ox shook his head and said, "You're a bad one. You ate those two young heifers on the farm last night."

Hyena answered, "No, Ox, that wasn't me. It was somebody else in the dark."

Ox continued, "No, you're a bad one. If I help you up, you'll bite me and attack me and eat me."

Hyena called out, "No, Ox, if you get me out, I'll be your best friend."

Well, Ox, who was a friendly creature, hung down his tail, and hyena scampered up. As soon as he got close, though, Hyena started to bite Ox, getting ready to eat him. Just then, Elephant passed by, and said, "What's all this? Fighting like little children? Let us reason things out calmly as they do in my part of the forest. Explain the situation to me." Ox couldn't talk. He was in too much pain. Hyena lied and lied and lied. Finally, Elephant answered, "This seems like a complicated situation. Perhaps if you could show me how it happened, I could understand better."

Hyena was much meaner than he was intelligent, and he went back down to the bottom of the well. Elephant turned to Ox and said, "Come on, Ox. Let's take a walk and talk about this some more." So Elephant walked away. And Ox walked away. And Hyena was left in the well. And he is still there today.

Source: Traditional African folktale

1. In four or five sentences, describe how Hyena is the bad character of the story.

2. Describe the fundamental characteristics of Hyena, Ox, and Elephant.

3. Sometimes in beast fables, animals are meant to represent humans. Are you ever like Ox? Explain. Are you ever like Hyena? Explain.

4. Do you know of any jobs in which the workers need the characteristics of Ox, Hyena, and/or Elephant?

5. Sometimes fables can be very political. If Hyena, Ox, and Elephant represented countries, which might they be?

6. Discuss the impact of changing the gender of the animals. For example, how would the situation change if Ox were female and Hyena male, or if Hyena were female and Ox male?

7. Try to look at the story in a different way. Prove that Elephant is wrong in its actions.

Activity 2   *"The Diamond Necklace"*

Read "The Diamond Necklace" on pages 86–90. Then do the activities on pages 90–92.

The Diamond Necklace

by Guy de Maupassant

She was one of those pretty, charming young ladies, born, as if through an error of destiny, into a family of clerks. She had no dowry, no hopes, no means of becoming known, appreciated, loved, and married by a man either rich or distinguished; and she allowed herself to marry an entry-level clerk at the Board of Education.

She was simple, not being able to adorn herself; but she was unhappy, as one out of her class; for women belong to no caste, no race; their grace, their beauty, and their charm serving them in the place of birth and family. Their inborn finesse, their instinctive elegance, their suppleness of wit are their only aristocracy, making some daughters of the people the equal of great ladies.

She suffered incessantly, feeling herself born for all delicacies and luxuries. She suffered from the poverty of her apartment, the shabby walls, the worn chairs, and the faded material. All these things, which another woman of her station would not have noticed, tortured and angered her.

When she seated herself for dinner, before the round table where the tablecloth had been used three days, opposite her husband who uncovered the tureen with a delighted air, saying, "Oh! the good potpie! I know nothing better than that!" she would think of the elegant dinners, of the shining silver, of the tapestries peopling the walls with ancient personages and rare birds in the midst of fairy forests; she thought of the exquisite food served on marvelous dishes, of the whispered gallantries, listened to with the smile of the sphinx, while eating the rose-colored flesh of the trout or a chicken's wing.

She had neither fancy dresses nor jewels, nothing. And she loved only those things. She felt that she was made for them. She had such a desire to please, to be sought after, to be clever, and courted.

She had a rich friend, a schoolmate at the convent, whom she did not like to visit, she suffered so much when she returned. And she wept for whole days from chagrin, from regret, from despair, and disappointment.

****

One evening her husband returned elated bearing in his hand a large envelope. "Here," he said, "here is something for you."

She quickly tore open the wrapper and drew out a printed card on which were inscribed these words:

> *"The Minister of Public Instruction and Madame George Ramponneau ask the honor of Mr. and Mrs. Loisel's company Monday evening, January 18, at the Minister's residence."*

Instead of being delighted, as her husband had hoped, she threw the invitation spitefully upon the table, murmuring, "What do you suppose I want with that?"

"But, my dearest, I thought it would make you happy. You never go out, and this is an occasion, and a fine one! I had a great deal of trouble to get it. Everybody wishes one, and it is very select; not many are given to employees. You will see the whole official world there."

She looked at him with an irritated eye and declared impatiently, "What do you suppose I have to wear to such a thing as that?"

He had not thought of that, he stammered, "Why, the dress you wear when we go to the theatre. It seems very pretty to me—"

He was silent, stupefied, in dismay, at the sight of his wife weeping. Two great tears fell slowly from the corners of his eyes toward the corners of his mouth; he stammered, "What is the matter? What is the matter?"

By a violent effort, she had controlled her anger and responded in a calm voice, wiping her moist cheeks, "Nothing. Only I have no dress and consequently I cannot go to the affair. Give your card to some colleague whose wife is better fitted out than I."

He was grieved, but answered, "Let's see, Matilda. How much would a suitable outfit cost, something that would serve for other occasions, something very simple?"

She reflected for some seconds, making estimates and thinking of a sum that she could ask for without bringing with it an immediate refusal and a frightened exclamation from the economical clerk.

Finally she said, in a hesitating voice, "I cannot tell exactly, but it seems to me that 400 francs ought to cover it."

He turned a little pale, because he had saved just this sum to buy a gun that he might be able to join some hunting parties the next summer, on the plains at Nanterre, with some friends who went to shoot larks up there on Sunday. Nevertheless, he answered, "Very well. I will give you 400 francs. But try to have a pretty dress."

****

The day of the ball approached and Mme. Loisel seemed sad, disturbed, anxious. Her dress was almost ready. Her husband asked, "What is the matter with you? You have acted strangely for two or three days."

And she responded, "I am vexed not to have a jewel, not one stone, nothing to adorn myself with. I shall have such a poverty-laded look. I would prefer not to go."

He replied, "You can wear some natural flowers. This season they look very *chic*. For ten francs you can have two or three magnificent roses."

She was not convinced. "No," she replied, "there is nothing more humiliating than to have a shabby air in the midst of rich women."

Then her husband cried out, "How stupid we are! Go and find your friend Mme. Forestier and ask her to lend you her jewels. You are close enough to her to do this."

She uttered a cry of joy, "It is true! I had not thought of that."

The next day she took herself to her friend's house and related her story of distress. Mme. Forestier went to her closet, took out a large jewel case, opened it, and said, "Choose, my dear."

She saw at first some bracelets, then a collar of pearls, then a Venetian cross of gold and jewels. She tried the jewels before the mirror, hesitated, but could not decide to take them or leave them. Then she asked, "Do you have anything else?"

"Why yes. Look for yourself. I do not know what will please you."

Suddenly she discovered, in a black satin box, a superb necklace of diamonds, and her heart beat fast with immoderate desire. She placed them about her throat against her dress, and remained in ecstasy before them. Then she asked, in a hesitating voice, full of anxiety, "Could you lend me this? Only this?"

"Why, yes, certainly."

She fell upon the neck of her friend, embraced her with passion, then went away with her treasure.

****

The day of the ball arrived. Mme. Loisel was a great success. She was the prettiest of all, elegant, gracious, smiling, and full of joy. All the men noticed her, asked her name, and wanted to be presented. All the members of the Cabinet wished to waltz with her. The Minister of Education paid her some attention.

She danced with enthusiasm, with passion, intoxicated with pleasure, in the triumph of her beauty, in the glory of her success, in a cloud of happiness that came of all this homage, and all this admiration, of all these awakened desires, and this victory so complete and sweet to the heart of woman.

She went home around four o'clock in the morning. Her husband had been half asleep in one of the little salons since midnight, with three other gentlemen whose wives were enjoying themselves very much.

He threw around her shoulders the wraps they had carried for the return trip, modest garments of everyday use, whose poverty clashed with the elegance of the ball costume. She felt this and wished to hurry away in order not to be noticed by the other women with rich furs.

When they were in the street, they found no carriage, and they began to look for one. They walked along toward the Seine, hopeless and shivering. Finally they found a cab, which took them to their door on Martyr Street, and they went wearily up to their apartment. It was all over for her. And on his part, he remembered that he would have to be at the office by ten o'clock.

She removed the wraps from her shoulders before the glass, for a final view of herself in her glory. Suddenly she uttered a cry. Her necklace was not around her neck.

Her husband, already half undressed asked, "What is the matter?"

She turned toward him excitedly, "I have—I have—I no longer have Mme. Forestier's necklace."

He arose in dismay, "How is that? It is not possible!"

And they looked in the folds of the dress, in the pockets, everywhere. They could not find it.

He asked, "You are sure you still had it when we left the house?"

"Yes. I felt it in the doorway as we came out."

"But if you had lost it in the street, we should have heard it fall. It must be in the cab."

"Yes. It is probable. Did you take the number?"

"No."

They looked at each other, utterly downcast. Finally, Loisel got dressed again.

"I am going," he said, "over the road we walked, to see if I can find it."

And he went. She remained in her evening gown, not having the strength to go to bed. Toward seven o'clock her husband returned. He had found nothing.

He went to the police and the cab offices, and put an ad in the newspapers, offering a reward.

She waited all day in a state of bewilderment before this frightful disaster. Loisel returned home at evening with his face pale; he had discovered nothing.

"It will be necessary," he said, "to write to your friend that you have broken the clasp of the necklace and that you will have it repaired. That will give us time."

She wrote as he dictated.

At the end of a week, they had lost all hope. And Loisel, older by five years, declared: "We must take measures to replace the necklace."

The next day they took the box which had enclosed it to the jeweler whose name was on the inside. He consulted his books. "It is not I, Madame, who sold this necklace. I only furnished the box."

Then they went from jeweler to jeweler seeking a necklace like the other one. In a shop of the Palais Royal, they found a necklace of diamonds which seemed to them exactly like the one they had lost. It was valued at 40,000 francs. They could get it for 36,000.

They begged the jeweler not to sell it for three days. Loisel possessed 18,000 francs that his father had left him. He borrowed the rest, asking for 1,000 francs from one, 500 from another. He gave notes, made ruinous promises, took money from usurers and the whole race of moneylenders. He compromised his whole existence, in fact, risked his signature, without even knowing whether he could make good or not, and harassed by anxiety for the future, and the prospect of all physical privations and moral torture, he went to get the new necklace, depositing on the merchant's counter 36,000 francs.

When Mme. Loisel took back the jewels to Mme. Forestier, she said to her in a frigid tone, "You should have returned them sooner. I might have needed them."

She did not open the jewel box as her friend feared she would. If she perceived the substitution, what would she think or say? Would she take her for a robber?

****

Mme. Loisel now knew the horrible life of necessity. She did her part, however, completely, heroically. It was necessary to pay this frightful debt. She would pay it. They sent away the maid; they changed their lodgings; they rented some rooms under a mansard roof.

She learned the heavy cares of a household, the odious work of a kitchen. She washed the dishes, using her rosy nails on the greasy pots and bottoms of stewpans. She washed the dirty clothes, which she hung on the line to dry; she took down the garbage to the street each morning and brought up the water, stopping at each landing to breathe. And, clothed like a woman of the people, she went to the grocer, the butcher, the fruit store, with her bag on her arm, shopping, haggling to the last sou of her miserable money.

Her husband worked evenings, putting the books of some merchants in order, and nights he often did copying at five sous a page.

And this life lasted for ten years.

At the end of ten years, they had restored all, with interest, usurer's interest, and accumulated interest.

Mme. Loisel seemed old now. She had become a strong, hard woman, the crude woman of the poor household. Her hands were red, she spoke in a loud tone, and washed the floors in large pails of water. But sometimes when her husband was at the office, she would sit at the window and think of that evening party, of that ball where she was so beautiful and so flattered.

How would it have been if she had not lost the necklace? Who knows? Who knows? How strange is life, and how full of changes!

****

One Sunday, she took a walk on the Champs-Elysees to rid herself of the cares of the week, she suddenly perceived a woman with a child. It was Mme. Forestier, still young, still pretty, still attractive. Mme. Loisel was affected. Should she speak to her? Yes, certainly. And now that she had paid, she would tell her all. Why not?

She approached her, "Good morning, Jeanne."

Her friend did not recognize her and was astonished to be so familiarly addressed by this common person. She stammered, "But, Madame— I do not know— You must be mistaken."

"No, I am Matilda Loisel."

Her friend uttered a cry of astonishment, "Oh! my poor Matilda! How you have changed!"

"Yes, I have had some hard days since I saw you, and some miserable ones—and all because of you."

"Because of me? How is that?"

"You recall the diamond necklace that you loaned me to wear to the Commissioner's ball?"

"Yes, very well."

"Well, I lost it."

"How is that, since you returned it to me?"

"I returned another to you exactly like it. And it has taken us ten years to pay for it. You can understand it was not easy for us who have nothing. But it is finished and I am decently content."

Mme. Forestier stopped short. She said, "You say that you bought a necklace to replace mine?"

"Yes. You did not perceive it then? They were just alike."

And she smiled with a proud and simple joy. Mme. Forestier was touched and took both her hands as she replied:

"Oh! my poor Matilda! Mine were false. They were not worth over 500 francs!"

Source: *Short Stories of the Tragedy and Comedy of Life*

Complete the following chronological outline for "The Diamond Necklace." Include the most important events in the short story. Add adjectives whenever possible.

1. Matilda—sad—she is poor

2. Invitation to a ball

3.

4.

5.

6.

7.

8.

9.

10.

11.

12.

Answer the following reading comprehension questions.

1. Why is Matilda so unhappy at the beginning of the story?

2. What is her reaction when she learns of the invitation to the ball?

3. After Matilda loses the necklace, how does her life change? (Reread the paragraph beginning "Matilda now knew the horrible life of necessity" and the next paragraph.)

4. Using the answer to question 3 as your basis, reassess Matilda's financial status and duties at the beginning of the story. How did she pass her day before she lost the necklace? Did she have to cook? Wash the dishes? Clean the house? After reading the two paragraphs describing her life after she loses the diamond necklace, why do you think Matilda was so unhappy at the beginning of the story?

Writing Assignment

Write a Conclusion to "The Diamond Necklace"

At the end of de Maupassant's piece, the story is not really over. In fact, the writer chose to finish "The Diamond Necklace" at the precise moment of truth, when Matilda finds out that she had worked for many years for nothing. However, we are not given her reaction to this new and startling information.

On a separate piece of paper, write a conclusion to "The Diamond Necklace" in which you present Matilda's reaction to her friend's news that the necklace was made of imitation diamonds. Write the results of this news in your paragraph. There are many possibilities, from quite happy to tragic. Describe one.

Building Your Skill in Creative Narratives

Activity 1   *The Telephone Call*

Read the following passage and complete the story in the space below.

> **I was sitting at home, all alone, feeling very sorry for myself. I was sad and lonely. It had been months since anything interesting had happened to me. I hadn't seen any old friends in a while. My job was the same—boring and repetitive. Just as the daylight outside was dwindling and I was about to turn on the lights in the house, the telephone rang. That was the phone call that probably changed my life. . . .**

GRAMMAR REVIEW: THE USE OF QUOTATION MARKS IN DIRECT SPEECH

In writing the conclusion to the "The Telephone Call," you will probably have to use quoted speech (direct speech). Pay close attention to the rules of punctuation. Analyze the following sentences.

He said, "My name is Taddeus Testa."

I asked, "Is it really you?"

He answered, "Yes, it is!"

"I can't believe it," I shouted.

As you can see, you must place a comma after the words that are like *said*.

Activity 2   *A Movie Review*

We are quickly becoming a review-oriented society. Turn on the television almost every evening, and you will see critics offering reactions to movies, plays, books, CDs, television programs, baseball games, and the latest fashions. Many have a very simple formula. A movie reviewer recounts the plot, analyzes the acting performances, and gives a thumbs up (approval) or thumbs down (disapproval) rating.

The movie reviews given on television or radio serve several purposes. First, they are meant to inform. Since so many movies are produced and available to consumers, it is believed that they want guidance to avoid bad films and select good ones. Because it can be expensive to go to the movies, more consumers do their homework on a film instead of just appearing at a movie theatre and choosing a movie based on the title or the names of the stars. Second, movie reviews are also forms of entertainment. Several movie reviewers have become famous in their own right and might even exercise some power over the success of a movie by influencing whether viewers see it.

Although reviews are usually brief (no more than three minutes), they are quite lively and often include clips from the movie. A good review should be interesting and fun and should reveal the joy of watching a good movie and the justified anger at having wasted time and money on a bad movie.

Writing Assignment

Write and Present a Movie Review

1. Watch a movie review program on television or listen to one on the radio. Notice the structure of the review as well as the tone and the pacing. Pay attention to the reviewers' facial gestures and voice quality when they like a movie and when they don't like one.

2. Read the review of the movie *Titanic* on pages 95–97. Notice how the reviewer analyzes the various aspects of the film. Find new vocabulary words that might help you write your review.

3. Attend any movie that you like. Keep in mind while you are watching it that you are going to write and then perform a review.

4. On a separate piece of paper, write a paragraph in three parts:

   a. Recount the action of the movie; tell whether it is a good story or if it has weaknesses.

   b. Analyze the performances of the actors and actresses, the setting, special effects, and cinematography.

   c. Offer a final recommendation to your audience (whether they should see it or not).

5. Correct and revise the review, and read it over a few times. Then present the review in front of the class.

Titanic: A Spectacle as Sweeping as the Sea

by Janet Maslin

The long-awaited advent of the most expensive movie ever made, the reportedly $200 million "Titanic," brings history to mind, and not just the legendary seafaring disaster of April 15, 1912. Think back also, exactly 58 years ago, to the Dec. 19 New York premiere of another grand, transporting love story set against a backdrop of prideful excess, cataclysmic upheaval and character-defining trial by fire.

Recall how that cultural landmark wowed audiences with its bravado, mad extravagance and state-of-the-art Hollywood showmanship, all fueled by one unstoppable filmmaker and his obsessive imagination. Just as David O. Selznick had Atlanta to burn, now James Cameron has a ship to sink, but he also has much more than calamity to explore in this gloriously retrograde new epic. Cameron's magnificent "Titanic" is the first spectacle in decades that honestly invites comparison to "Gone with the Wind."

What a rarity that makes it in today's world of meaningless gimmicks and short attention spans: a huge, thrilling three-and-a-quarter-hour experience that unerringly lures viewers into the beauty and heartbreak of its lost world. Astonishing technological advances are at work here, but only in the service of one spectacular illusion: that the ship is afloat again, and that the audience is intimately involved in its voyage.

What's more, Cameron succeeds magically in linking his film's young lovers, played enchantingly by Leonardo DiCaprio and Kate Winslet, with established details of the "Titanic" story. And let's not forget the offscreen drama: delayed release and outrageous costs made "Titanic" the joke of the summer. Now it's the movie of the year.

Though the tender moments in Cameron's earlier films have mostly involved Arnold Schwarzenegger, graceful storytelling from this one-man army of a filmmaker (a director, a producer, a writer and an editor) is the biggest of many surprises here. Swept away by the romance of his subject matter, Cameron rises to the occasion with a simple, captivating narrative style, one that cares little for subtlety but overflows with wonderful, well-chosen Hollywood hokum. In its own sobering way, the film is forward-looking, too, as its early brashness gives way to near-religious humility when the moments of reckoning arrive. Ultimately a haunting tale of human nature, with endless displays of callousness, gallantry or cowardice, it offers an unforgettable vision of millennium-ready unease in the sight of passengers adrift in icy seas on that last, moonless night.

That Cameron allowed flashlights into what should have been a pitch-black sequence is one of the rare times when "Titanic" willingly departs from established fact. Otherwise, with an attention to detail that goes well beyond fanatical, the film flawlessly recreates its monument to Gilded Age excess. Behind-the-scenes details here, which prove no less fascinating than Selznick's "Gone with the Wind" memos, include Cameron's having persuaded the original carpet manufacturer to make an 18,000-square-foot reproduction of its "Titanic" weave and his having insisted that every sign, uniform and logo for the

Southampton sailing sequence also be created in mirror image, so that the camera could reverse the apparent direction of the nearly life-size model ship.

Sets match old photographs right down to the sculpture and woodwork; costumes incorporate fragments of vintage clothing; even the silver White Star Line ashtrays had to be right. A core group of 150 extras worked with an Edwardian etiquette coach throughout the filming, furthering the illusion that the privileged past had returned to life.

"Titanic" is no museum piece, however. It's a film with tremendous momentum right from its deceptive, crass-looking start. The story opens in the present day, with a team of scientist-cowboys (led by Bill Paxton) hunting for lost treasure amid the Titanic wreckage. Though Cameron made his own journey to the ocean floor to film amazing glimpses of the ship, he treats these explorers as glib '90s hotshots, the kind of macho daredevils who could just as easily be found tracking twisters or dinosaurs in a summer action film.

"Oops, somebody left the water running," one of them wisecracks about the sunken ship. Then the film begins, ever so teasingly, to open its window to the past. A 101-year-old woman (played spiritedly by Gloria Stuart, an 87-year-old beauty who appeared in "Gold Diggers of 1935") hears of the expedition and says it has links to her own history. It seems that she, Rose, was the model for a nude sketch found by the present-day fortune hunters in a Titanic safe. It is the only thing of value to be retrieved there. The money in the safe has turned to mud.

But where is the Heart of the Ocean, the egg-size blue diamond Rose wears in the drawing? Rose begins telling her story, and at long last 1912 is at hand. In an introductory sequence mounted on a colossal scale, Cameron shows the ship being boarded by its full economic range of passengers, from the haughty rich to the third-class passengers being checked for head lice.

Young Rose (Ms. Winslet) arrives at the dock in the show-stopping plumage of Deborah L. Scott's costume designs, and in the unfortunate company of Cal Hockley (Billy Zane), the tiresome snob whom she has agreed to marry, largely at the urging of her impecunious mother (Frances Fisher). The Rose—Cal story line, which is the weakest part of the film thanks to Cal's unwavering odiousness, plays like Edith Wharton Lite.

Meanwhile, in a nearby tavern, adorable Jack Dawson (DiCaprio) is winning a third-class Titanic ticket in a poker game. It won't be long before Jack is bounding happily into steerage, showing off the boyish adventurousness that makes him such a cure for what's ailing Rose. Aboard the ship of dreams, as the Titanic is often called here, Jack is one serious dreamboat.

A bohemian artist (whose drawings were done by Cameron) who has spent the requisite time in Paris, he offers all the fun and flirtatiousness that Rose has been missing. This 20-year-old has also shown his share of worldly wisdom by the end of the story. It goes without saying that it's Jack, not Cal, who is the film's true gentleman. And that DiCaprio has made an inspired career move in so successfully meeting the biggest challenge for an actor of his generation: a traditional role.

Among the many miracles of "Titanic" is its way of creating a sweet, life-changing courtship between Jack and Rose in the course of only a few days. At the risk of turning into a women's picture, "Titanic" brings these two together through a dramatic meeting, an invitation for Jack at a formal first-class dinner, a dancing romp among steerage passengers and even enough intimate moments to give the love story heat. Splendid chemistry between the stars, along with much color from the supporting cast and careful foreshadowing from Cameron, keeps the romance buoyant even after the dread iceberg gets in its way.

Comfortable even in suggesting that the ship's lookouts missed the danger because they were busy watching lovestruck Jack and Rose, Cameron lets tragedy strike midway through the film. That way, the disaster can unfold in almost real time, with terrifying precision on a par with all the other details here.

Not for "Titanic" the shrill hysteria of ordinary disaster stories; this film is especially delicate in its slow way of letting the gravity of the situation become clear. Much scarier than any explosion-filled caper film is the simple assessment from the ship's master builder, played with great dignity by Victor Garber: "In an hour or so, all this will be at the bottom of the Atlantic."

As Cameron joked during production, about a film that pitilessly observes the different plights of the rich and the poor, "We're holding just short of Marxist dogma." (A lavish "Titanic" coffee table book from Harper-Collins is filled with fascinating data about the film, from the director's casual asides to accounts of the technological wizardry, like computerized hydraulics, that were devised for repeatedly sinking the ship.) By this point, the audience knows the ship so fully, from Cal and Rose's elaborate suite to the depths of the boiler room, that the film is on shockingly familiar territory as Rose searches every newly waterlogged area for Jack.

Very much to Cameron's credit is the lack of logistical confusion. Indeed, the film's modern-day characters even watch a computerized version of how the ship split and then rose vertically just before it plunged straight down, events that are later re-enacted with awesome power. Despite all this advance information and the revelation that Rose lives to be 101, "Titanic" still sustains an extraordinary degree of suspense.

Tiny, devastating touches—how the same doll whose face rests on the ocean floor in 1996 is clutched in the arms of a pretty little girl who idolizes Jack, or a four-hanky coda seen in Rose's dream—work as well as the film's big spectacle in giving the tragedy of "Titanic" its full dramatic impact. Though many of the story's minor characters are one-note (hardly the case with Kathy Bates's hearty Molly Brown or Bernard Hill's brave captain), the cumulative effect of their presence is anything but shallow.

Beyond its romance, "Titanic" offers an indelibly wrenching story of blind arrogance and its terrible consequences. It's the rare Hollywood adventure film that brings mythic images of tragedy—the fall of Icarus, the ruin of Ozymandias—so easily to mind.

The irony is that Cameron's "Titanic" is such a Titanic in its own right, a presumptuous reach for greatness against all reasonable odds. The film itself gambles everything on visual splendor and technological accomplishment, which is one reason its extravagance is fully justified on screen. But if Cameron's own brazenness echoes that seen in his story, remember the essential difference. This "Titanic" is too good to sink.

Source: *The New York Times*, December 19, 1997

F. Graded Writing Assignment: A Night in Chicago

Read the following passage and complete the story in the space below.

A Night in Chicago

Everything had been going along too well. I just knew that something had to go wrong. After all, we had won the plane tickets and the free five-night stay in the luxury hotel in a raffle at my cousin's school. Now, here we were. Chicago. We were in the restaurant of the Four Seasons Hotel on Michigan Avenue, having a candlelight dinner for two, with soft dance music playing in the background. Suddenly, a man walked over to our table and stood above us. He had a strange smile, the kind of smile that was not from happiness. He asked, "Don't you remember me?" I felt a sudden pain in my heart. Could it really be him? After all these years? He still had that crazy look in his eyes, and a few scars on his face to remind me of that fateful night.

You see, we were only 13 years old back then, in the seventh grade. On Friday nights we used to travel from suburban Oak Park to Chicago to walk around and see the street life. On one of those Friday nights we went to Chicago and. . . .

G. Part 3 Summary

Based on your work in Part 3, answer the questions below and discuss them as a class.

1. What is the importance of chronological order in organizing a paragraph of narration?

2. What is an outline, and what purpose does it serve?

3. What is the most common type of topic sentence that may be used in paragraphs of narration?

4. What does the author mean when he says, "We live life in narration?" Do you agree or disagree?

5. Summarize the sequence of tenses in time clauses and provide an example. What tenses are used with the following words when you are writing about the past? The first one is done for you.

   While SV, SV.

   > **While + subject + past progressive, subject + simple past**
   > **While I was studying last night, my brother called me.**

   By the time SV, SV

   After SV, SV

SV since SV

At precisely 9:00 A.M., SV

6. What tense is usually used in a paragraph of narration? Are other tenses possible?

H. Reflections on Your Progress

Write your reflections or thoughts below on some of the writing you have done in Part 3.

1. Which were your two favorite journal entries, and why?

2. What was the most interesting writing assignment, and why?

3. What was the least interesting writing assignment, and why?

4. What is the most important thing about writing that you learned?

5. Were you satisfied with the progress you made in the assignments?

I. Part 3 Assignment Checklist

Assignment	Required or Optional	Grade	Revised	Returned and Filed
Write a Paragraph of Narration (page 79)				
Record Your Dreams (Journal Activity) (page 80)				
A Foltale from Your Culture (page 81)				
An Embarrassing Experience (page 82)				
My First Memory (page 82)				
The Hyena of Zimbabwe (page 83)				
The Diamond Necklace (outline) (page 90)				
The Diamond Necklace (conclusion) (page 92)				
The Telephone Call (page 93)				
Write and Present a Movie Review (page 94)				
A Night in Chicago (page 98)				

J. Part 3 Journal Summary

Date of First Journal	Date of Last Journal	Number of Journal Entries Written for Part 3

PART 4

Process Paragraphs

Suggested Journal Topics for Process Paragraphs

- Give advice to someone who wishes to get high grades in English courses

- Present the process by which a person learns how to dance

- How can you meet "the dream date"?

- Give techniques on saving money

- Tell how to get along with people from many different cultures

- Give simple directions to get from school to your house

- How to clean up your house in ten minutes when you receive a phone call from a friend who is arriving shortly to see you

A. Process Paragraphs

If you enter a bookstore, you will see that one of the largest sections is the "How to" section. Here you'll find books on how to learn a language in 30 days (they must be dreaming), how to catch big fish in the ocean, how to cook Thai food, how to build a bookshelf, and just about anything else you wish to learn.

One aspect that all of these books have in common is that they use a **process structure.** They demonstrate the correct step-by-step method, accompanied by illustrations, photographs, personal examples, hints for success, or tips for clearer understanding. Many of the books claim that a particular process is easy (such as *Gardening Made Easy*)—but, of course, it is easy only to the person writing the book and not to the person who has purchased it. However, if the book is well organized and the steps are clear, it should be possible to follow.

The writing you will do in this Part includes giving instructions on the preparation of a meal and imparting advice. Many times every day we give advice to our friends and family members. In fact, it is probably true that we are much more willing to give advice to others than take our own advice.

In giving advice, we often use **modals** (words like *should, would,* and *might*) to convey our message. Most times this is done in the present tense. Yet, there are times when we give foolproof advice (that is, when the situation has already occurred), and then we use the past tense. For example, if a friend saw *Scooby Doo* instead of *My Big Fat Greek Wedding* and did not enjoy it, you could say, "You should have seen *My Big Fat Greek Wedding.*" This type of advice is easy to give: you know the correct answer. However, this advice cannot be followed and can be of no assistance.

It is essential for the process paragraph to be well organized. Have you ever seen assembly instructions that are so complicated and so poorly written that you cannot follow them? The result is a product that remains in the box until you pay an expert to assemble it.

STRUCTURE OF THE PROCESS PARAGRAPH

Verb Tense: Present (with modals), imperative
                         (or command) voice

Order: Steps or phases

Discourse markers: *first, next, after, before, while* (time words)

Below is a typical structure for a process paragraph.

   1. Topic Sentence

> **If you want to learn to swim, follow these instructions.**

   2. Step 1

> **First, you should buy a book about swimming.**

   a. Support 1 (Answers the question "Why?"):

> **Buying a book will acquaint you with the techniques necessary to learn how to swim.**

   b. Support 2 (Answers the question "So what?"):

> **In this way, you will be familiar with what to do before you jump in the water.**

3. Step 2

Next, you should go to a pool with shallow water.

a. Support 1 (Answers the question "Why?")

You will not be afraid to try if you know that you cannot drown.

b. Support 2 (Answers the question "So what?")

You can practice as much as you want.

c. Support 3 (Specific example)

In fact, this is the way that I learned. I had been really afraid of deep water, so I never tried to swim.

4. Step 3

You should bring an experienced swimmer with you.

a. Support 1 (Answers the question "Why?"):

This person can really help you, and you will feel more comfortable.

5. Conclusion (encouragement)

If you follow these instructions, you will learn how to swim quickly and easily. After that, a new world will open to you.

Below is a sample process paragraph.

If you want to learn to swim, follow these directions. First, you should buy a book about swimming. Buying a book will acquaint you with the techniques necessary to learn. In this way, you will be familiar with what to do before you jump in the water. Next, you should go to a pool with shallow water. You will not be afraid to try, if you know that you cannot drown. You can practice as much as you want. In fact, this is the way that I learned how to swim. I had been really afraid of deep water, so I never tried to swim. You should bring an experienced swimmer with you. This person will help you, and you will feel more comfortable. If you follow these instructions, you will learn to swim quickly and easily. After that, a new world will open to you.

B. Vocabulary Acquisition: Adverbs

Exercise 1 In your reading this week, concentrate on *adverbs*. Find 15 new ones, and write them in the space below. Indicate the part of speech, whether the word has a positive (+), negative (−), or neutral (=) connotation, and whether there are prefixes, suffixes, or roots that help you understand the meaning of the word. Write a definition for the word. Then construct a sentence for each adverb. The first one below is a model.

Word	Part of Speech	Connotation (+, −, =)	Roots, Prefixes, or Suffixes	Definition
1. gracefully	adverb	+	*ly* = adjective suffix	done with great poise, smoothness of movement, and seemingly without effort
SENTENCE: The tall woman danced gracefully as the musicians played a waltz.				
2.				
SENTENCE:				
3.				
SENTENCE:				
4.				
SENTENCE:				
5.				
SENTENCE:				

Word	Part of Speech	Connotation (+, −, =)	Roots, Prefixes, or Suffixes	Definition
6.				
SENTENCE:				
7.				
SENTENCE:				
8.				
SENTENCE:				
9.				
SENTENCE:				
10.				
SENTENCE:				

Word	Part of Speech	Connotation (+, −, =)	Roots, Prefixes, or Suffixes	Definition
11.				
SENTENCE:				
12.				
SENTENCE:				
13.				
SENTENCE:				
14.				
SENTENCE:				
15.				
SENTENCE:				

C. Grammatical Structures: Modals

The modals that will be used in this chapter indicate *ability, advisability, possibility, probability,* and *necessity.* In general, modals are followed by the **base form** of the verb. Modals are also used in the past tense, but their meaning is slightly different. The distinction in meaning between **must, have to,** and **have got to** (*must* is stronger) is lost in the past tense. All three modals use *had to* in the past. When *had to* is used, the action was certainly performed. For example, when you hear, "I had to clean my house," you know that the speaker surely cleaned the house. On the other hand, if the speakers says, "I should have cleaned my house," you can be sure that he or she didn't do it.

Use of the past tense is common but does not serve a purpose when offering advice. The action is finished, so giving advice on something that has already happened does not help the situation. However, people love to be right, so they use *should have* (plus the past participle) all the time.

The chart below shows the modals that we will use in this chapter and their functions.

Modal Chart		
Function	Present Tense	Past Tense
Necessity	*must* *have to* *have got to* *don't have to* (lack of necessity)	*had to* *had to* *had to* *didn't have to*
Advisability	*should* *ought to* (rare) *had better* (strong)	*should have* + past participle *ought to have* (rare) —
Possibility/Probability	*may* *might* *could* *must* (he must be sick)	*may have* + past participle *might have* + past participle *could have* + past participle *must have* + past participle (I don't see her anywhere. She must have left.)
Ability	*can* *be able to* (am able to, is able to, are able to)	*could* *was able to* (were able to)

Exericse 2   Complete the following sentences.

1. Students must never _____

2. Teachers don't have to _____

3. When you go to Dallas, you should _____

4. Grandma used to say, "You ought to _____

5. When you want someone to check the oil, you say, " _____

6. When I was six years old, I _____

7. The doctor told the heavy smoker, you had better _____

8. I get nervous every time I'm stuck in traffic. I should _____

9. Married people are never supposed to _____

10. To make a delicious meal, you _____

Exercise 3   Read the following passage. Write a paragraph on a separate piece of paper in which you give Ali advice. He loves his parents and his aunt and uncle, and he does not want to hurt them or disobey them. What *can* he do? What *should* he do? What *must* he do?

Ali comes from a conservative Moslem family. He wants to be an engineer, and his parents allowed him to come to the United States to study at an excellent engineering school. However, they insisted that he live with his aunt and uncle, who are also conservative Moslems. His aunt and uncle do not let him go out on weekends or attend parties at the college. If he goes out at night, he must go to the university library to study. Because the apartment is small and because his aunt and uncle are so strict, Ali does not want to invite his friends to visit him. He is becoming lonely and unhappy, and his studies are beginning to suffer.

Exercise 4 Read the following passage. Then write a paragraph on a separate piece of paper in which you give Mr. And Mrs. Iwabata some advice. What *should* Mrs. Iwabata *have said* in her note? What *could* (and *should*) Mr. Iwabata *have done* instead of doing nothing?

> Mrs. Iwabata was called to the hospital suddenly one afternoon to see a friend who had been in an automobile accident. Mr. Iwabata, who prided himself on the fact that he never lifted a finger in the kitchen, came home late from work and found a note from his wife that said, "I have gone to see Yukiko at the hospital. I will be home at 10 o'clock." On this particular night, Mr. Iwabata was very hungry, but he just sat in the living room feeling sorry for himself and waiting impatiently for his wife to come home to fix dinner.

Exercise 5 Read the following passage. Write two paragraphs on a separate piece of paper. In the first paragraph, use the following topic sentence: "Generally speaking, Inez's problem is difficult but not impossible." In the rest of the paragraph, use modals to explain what Inez *can* do, what she *should* do, and what she *must* do. For the second paragraph, use this topic sentence: "On the whole, Inez and her parents made several mistakes that caused Inez to have this problem." In the rest of the paragraph, use past tense modals to explain what Inez and her parents *should have* done, *should not have* done, and *could have* done before she left her country for the United States.

> Inez has just arrived in the United States. Her cousin was supposed to meet her at the airport and take her to her uncle's house, but she cannot find him. Her parents forgot to give her the address of her uncle, and she has no other friends or relatives in the United States. She comes from a very small town, and she is confused by the noise and the crowd at the airport. In addition, she does not speak English well, and she has only ten dollars with her. The rest of her money is in checks, which are somewhere in her luggage.

D. Writing Skills: Proofreading

Proofreading is the implementation of several procedures, in a methodical manner, to correct mistakes in grammar, punctuation, and spelling. Very often, the difference between a good paragraph and an excellent paragraph is the quality of the proofreading done before the work is handed in. Every writing assignment should be checked and proofread before it is submitted. At first, each step should be done separately.

1. Underline all the verbs in your paragraph.

   a. Check verb tense—is it correct?

   b. Check agreement with subject

2. Is the punctuation correct?

   a. Circle all the commas—are they correct, or should they be periods?

   b. Have semicolons been used before conjunctions, and does a comma follow the conjunction? (For example: ; however,   ; in addition,   ; as a result,   )

3. Check spelling of the following:

   a. words used more than once

   b. words in the introduction and conclusion

   c. For paragraphs written at home, you must check *every word*. **Spelling mistakes in paragraphs written at home are unacceptable.**

4. Check short sentences. Is it possible to combine two of them?

5. Are there elements of advanced grammar in your writing? Check for:

   a. adjective and noun clauses

   b. correct use of articles

   c. correct use of modals

6. Check that the correct parts of speech have been used. Put a box around all the adjectives. Do they have the correct ending? Have they been placed in the correct position? What about the adverbs? Put a triangle around all the adverbs. Is the form correct? Have they been placed in the correct position?

7. Make sure that the topic sentence and the conclusion are excellent. That is, they must make a strong first and last impression.

8. Analyze the structure of the paragraph.

   a. Is there a sufficient number of examples?

   b. Ask questions such as why? so what? as a result? really?

9. Have you used discourse markers (transition words)?

Exercise 6   Find and correct the mistakes in the following paragraph. Make the changes in the space provided or rewrite the corrected paragraph on a separate piece of paper.

I would like to give some advices to those who ~~are~~ taking the exit examination next week. The first, students should take ~~his~~ their time during the test. The test lasts 70 minutes, So there is no need to rush. Second, I believe that students should ~~to~~ be creative, Because this impresses those who reads the test. Third, be on time. In addition, students should bring an English-English dictionary ~~for~~ to chekc the spelling of words, it is important to do this because most readers stress correct spelling, and students should care about this, to. There is another advise that I want to give. Do not worry. Those students who have done well all semester will certainly pass the exit examination. If they will not get nervousness, they will surely do well. ~~I should use some sort of~~ In conclusion, ~~conclusion here.~~ Come on time, In short, Bring a pencil and a dictionary, and do'nt worry. Be creative. The exit test is just like any other writing assignment.

E. Journal Type 4:
The Double-Entry Journal

The double-entry journal gives you the opportunity to practice two types of writing: description and opinion. Concentrate on filling up the two columns with clear, organized summaries and strong, persuasive thoughts on the subject. The following is the process for writing the double-entry journal.

1. From a magazine, newspaper, book of short stories, book of poetry, or the Internet, choose an article, story, or poem that interests you.

2. Read the piece. Underline important points, key words, and new vocabulary.

3. Use a two-entry journal format. Divide your paper in half by drawing a vertical line down the middle of the page.

4. In the left-hand column, write a summary of what you have read. Include key points, specific examples, and anything else that you consider important. You may also quote what you consider to be the most important line in the text.

5. In the right-hand column, give your opinion on the topic covered. React to the subject of the piece. Personalize your reaction as much as possible. You might also try to write **process paragraphs** in the right-hand column in which you give advice on the problem presented in the article.

6. On the back of the page, list five new vocabulary words that you have found in the piece. The more information you write about a word, the greater your chances of remembering it and making it part of your *active* vocabulary. Thus, for each word, provide the following:

   a. part of speech

   b. connotation (positive [+], negative [−], or neutral [=])

   c. any prefixes, suffixes, or roots that help determine the meaning

   d. a definition of the word

   e. a sentence using the new vocabulary word

   > **terrorist:** (noun); negative; ist = someone involved in, someone who acts on; a person who revolts against authority, usually by using violence, especially bombing. Terrorists often act alone or in small groups.
   >
   > **The military officers captured the *terrorist* who had planted the bomb in the subway station.**

7. All work will be done in the journal. The work should not be done on loose papers.

UNIT 4.1

Building Your Skill in Giving Instructions

Activity 1   *Write a Recipe*

Read the following two recipes and do the Writing Assignment that follows.

Tortellini all'Altano

Traditional Italian New Year's Pasta Dish

Italians believe that the first dinner of the year is very important: the way they begin the year is the way it will continue. Therefore, New Year's Day is a traditional feast in most Italian homes. The meal usually has five courses: the antipasto (appetizer), the pasta course, the meat or fish course, the fruit and cheese course, and the dessert.

Grandma used to make fresh tortellini, small hat-shaped dough filled with meat by hand, while she told stories at the table. It was a New Year's morning ritual to hear her talk about the times during the Second World War when meat was rationed, and she made "meatballs" from eggs and flour, and she stuffed the tortellini with cheese. When better times returned, the tortellini were filled with prosciutto and parsley just as they have been made for many generations. Today, few people make pasta by hand; tortellini are now available at most supermarkets.

Ingredients (makes eight servings)

2 pounds of meat tortellini	freshly ground pepper
2 cups of heavy cream	fresh nutmeg
1 stick of butter	10 tablespoons of fresh basil
1 medium onion, chopped	
6 ounces of parmesan cheese	

Preparation

1. Bring 8 quarts of water to a boil in a large pasta pot.
2. Add the tortellini and cook for 8–10 minutes until they are *al dente* (firm to the bite).
3. Drain the tortellini in a colander.
4. While the pasta is cooking, melt the butter in a large saucepan.
5. Add the onion and fresh basil, and cook at low heat for 5 minutes.
6. Add the heavy cream. Turn up the heat until the mixture boils, and cook until it is reduced by one-half.
7. Turn down the heat. Add the parmesan cheese, and stir until the sauce is creamy.

8. Add the tortellini to the sauce, and turn down the heat.
9. Grind the fresh pepper, and grate the fresh nutmeg over the tortellini.
10. Cook for 2 minutes.

Serve as the pasta course during a New Year's dinner, or with a salad for a mid-week supper.

Yakitori Grilled Chicken

Japanese Fast Food

After a long day at the office, many Japanese businesspeople stop at a *yakitori* shop, where they cook chicken morsels on skewers over a charcoal grill. Yakitori is one of the most traditional meals in Japan, and it is eaten all around the country. Bamboo skewers are used in Japan, but it is possible to use the stainless steel or wood skewers found in America. Although Japan is quite far from the Middle East, this dish is very similar to shish kabob, one of the most important dishes in Arabic cuisine.

Ingredients (makes 6 servings)

½ cup chicken broth
1½ cups dark soy sauce
1 cup sugar
1 cup *sake,* or dry white wine

2 pounds chicken cutlet (breast or thigh) cut into 1-inch chunks
4 leeks, white part only

Preparation

1. Combine the chicken broth, soy sauce, sugar, and sake in a saucepan, and bring to a boil.
2. Reduce heat, and simmer for 10 minutes.
3. Remove from the stove, and cool for 1 hour.
4. Cut the chicken and the leeks into 1-inch chunks.
5. Insert the chicken and leeks onto the skewers; alternate chicken cubes with pieces of leek.
6. Marinate the chicken and leek skewers in the yakitori sauce for 1 hour.
7. Barbecue over a very hot grill; turn the skewers to avoid burning one side of the meat.
8. Be careful not to overcook the chicken.
9. Serve the yakitori with a little extra sauce for dipping.

Of course, yakitori is eaten with the hands. No forks or knives, fancy napkins, or tablecloths are necessary. This is fast food meant to satisfy hunger quickly and cheaply.

Writing Assignment

Write Your Own Recipe

You are going to write a recipe that is typical of your culinary heritage, or that is a favorite dish of yours. It is probably advisable to avoid dishes that are too complicated in their preparation.

The assignment has three parts: a presentation of the **background** of the dish (when the dish is served, on what occasion, the importance of the particular ingredients, what usually accompanies the dish), a listing of the **ingredients** with quantities, and a description of the **process**, divided into steps. The process writing should be done using the **imperative** (command) **voice** (e.g., slice the onion, boil the broth, etc.).

Your recipe should follow the outline below. Use the recipes presented on the previous pages as models.

Outline

1. **Introduction to the dish**

    a. Background

    b. When eaten

    c. Parts of the country where it is served most

    d. Other interesting information about the dish or the ingredients

2. **Ingredients**

    a. Quantity (e.g., 4 ounces, two pieces)

    b. Method of preparation (e.g., chopped finely, in chunks, etc.)

    c. Other information (e.g., at room temperature, frozen, etc.)

3. **The Preparation Process**

    a. Steps involved in the cooking process

    b. How served

Activity 2   *Weddings*

Read the following article and do the Exercises and Writing Assignment that follow.

Here Comes the Bride, and Here Comes the Bill
Large Weddings: Love! Fantasy! Bankruptcy?

During the month of June, thousands of couples will take their wedding vows and join their lives together "for richer or for poorer, in sickness and in health, until death do us part." Most of them will celebrate this momentous occasion with a wedding reception that may surpass $25,000, or the equivalent of a down payment on a house. The traditional wedding involves so many expenses that the entire ordeal may be frightening to the unprepared.

Because weddings are dominated by fantasy, they are usually not very practical. It is a good idea to analyze a list of the various expenses incurred in order to make recommendations on how to cut costs without making a bad impression by seeming cheap. The total cost of a wedding may be high, but it is the basis of many happy memories.

Who pays? In traditional American society, the father of the bride pays for the wedding reception and most of the other expenses. However, the ethnic heritage of the bride and groom often dictates who foots the bill.

In addition, since the average age of couples marrying for the first time has risen, it is not uncommon for the bride and groom to share expenses and pay for their own wedding. As a result, the number of guests invited has decreased.

The reception. This is the most expensive part of the wedding. Most wedding receptions take place in a catering hall, where the price may exceed $100 per guest for a Saturday evening wedding in June. For this sum, the couple can expect a five-hour reception: a one-hour cocktail hour where guests enjoy an open bar and unlimited hors d'oeuvres, followed by a four-hour full-course dinner with appetizer, salad, pasta, prime rib, and perhaps a dessert buffet (sometimes called a Venetian Table). Usually the drinks are included in the price.
How to save. The best way to save money is to make small adjustments in the menu. Serve chicken instead of prime rib (a $5–10 savings), serve the wedding cake as the dessert (save $4), and limit the drinks to wine and beer ($3 off). In addition, the timing of the wedding can save a great deal of money. A February reception will bring a 20 percent discount. Afternoon weddings are cheaper than evening ones, and a Sunday brunch reception can save an additional 10 percent.

The rings. An engagement becomes official when the man gives his betrothed (fiancée) a diamond ring, which may cost more than $3,500. Recent advertisements in newspapers and on television have indicated that a man should pay approximately two months' salary for the ring. The woman also may give the man a diamond ring, but this is not a requirement.
How to save. Buy direct from the wholesaler instead of buying from a retail jewelry store. Sacrifice on the clarity and purity of the diamond. Few people, except the bride's mother, will be able to tell the difference.

The photographer and videographer. Photographs and videos are permanent memories of the festive occasion. In addition to the couple's wedding photo album, the parents of both the bride and groom receive a smaller wedding album. We must also add the cost of creating videotapes for the couple and their parents. The photographer charges more than $1,000, the videographer somewhat less.
How to save. Trusting a brother-in-law who says that he almost became a professional photographer is risky business, but it can save a great deal of money. According to an advertisement, even a child can use a videocamera. Is it worth a try to hire relatives or friends to perform some of the functions that would normally be done by professionals?

The limousines. Part of the fantasy of weddings is that the bride and groom pretend they are rich. This includes riding to the ceremony and the reception in a limousine or a Rolls Royce at a cost of $100 per hour.
How to save. Find a friend with a luxury car and have him or her play the role of chauffeur.

The wedding gown and tuxedo. Many women analyze magazines such as *Brides* to choose designer wedding dresses. Because more than 100 photographs will be taken, the gown must be beautiful. The men rent their tuxedos, including shirt, tie, and even shoes.
How to save. Women can be traditional and wear their mother's or grandmother's gown. A rented or used dress may be available, but it may also bring bad luck, depending on who wore it previously. Most brides keep their wedding dresses to show their children and grandchildren. Of course, if the marriage ends in divorce, they probably do not hold onto it.

The band. Guests probably remember the band at the reception even more than they remember the food. An excellent band sets a party mood and keeps everyone dancing. Bands are expensive; also, the band members eat the dinner served to the guests.

How to save. The house band (the regular band of the wedding hall) might be an inexpensive choice, but this could also ruin the party because most times it is inferior to freelance bands. Do you remember how bad the band in the Adam Sandler movie *The Wedding Singer* was? A disk jockey (DJ) with a good collection of CDs can be fine, but for some people, nothing replaces live music. If a DJ is chosen, make sure to find one with a lively personality.

The honeymoon. Flush with the gift money received from the guests, the honeymooners often spend a great deal of money on their first vacation together. Because this is one of the most important memories of their lives, perhaps it is worth it to stay in a luxury hotel on a lush island in the Caribbean or on a sandy beach in Mexico. Hawaii is a tropical paradise that attracts many honeymooners. Those flying from the East or Midwest might want to stop over in San Francisco for a few days.

How to save. Instead of flying to an exotic place, the couple could drive to their destination, thus extending their honeymoon. Grandma went to Niagara Falls for her honeymoon; perhaps a drive to Orlando, Florida, or to California will make a memorable trip.

Wedding Expenses: Traditional Breakdown			
Item	Cost	Who Pays?	How to Save
Engagement ring	$3,500	Groom	The rule of thumb is that the ring costs two months' salary made by the groom. Buy direct from the wholesaler. Sacrifice on the clarity and purity of the diamond.
Bride's dress	$2,500–$3,000	Bride	Use Mom or Grandma's dress; buy a used dress; rent a dress.
Groom's tuxedo	$75–$100	Groom	Rent a tuxedo.
Tuxedos for the men in the wedding party	$75–$100 each	The men pay for their own	
Dresses for the women in the wedding party	$200 each	The women pay for their own	
The wedding shower	$35 × 50 guests = $1,750	Bride	This is a simpler dinner than the wedding reception and more than pays for itself because of the gifts received.

Wedding Expenses: Traditional Breakdown *(continued)*

Item	Cost	Who Pays?	How to Save
Invitations	$400	Bride	Print them on the computer; choose lower-quality paper.
Gifts for the wedding party (a better gift for the Best Man and the Maid of Honor)	($250 × 2) + ($100 × 8) = $1,300	Bride and Groom	The gift is usually a watch for men and jewelry for women; buy less expensive products.
Photographer/ Videographer	$1,000 each = $2,000	Bride	A relative who is a "semi-professional" could take the photos or the video—but this is a great risk.
Minister/Priest/Rabbi/ Judge	$100–$200	Groom	This is a fixed cost.
The wedding reception (a cocktail hour followed by a four-hour full-course dinner, including dessert and liquor)	($75–$100 each) × 150 guests = $11,250–$15,000	Bride	*The main course:* choose chicken instead of beef. *Timing:* Friday or Sunday weddings cost less, as do receptions held in January, February, March, and November. Or you can have a garden reception in your own backyard (save $7,000).
The band (for the reception)	$1,500	Bride	Book the house band, but remember: if the band is terrible, no one will dance, and the party will be dead. A DJ is a good alternative.
Flowers	$500	Bride	The Bride and Groom may arrange the centerpieces for the tables themselves.
Limousines	$300 each × 3 = $900	Bride	A friend with a luxury car could serve as driver.

Wedding Expenses: Traditional Breakdown (continued)			
Item	Cost	Who Pays?	How to Save
Favors (gifts from the Bride and Groom to the guests)	$20 each × 90 gifts = $1,800	Bride	One per couple or per single guest. Buy a less expensive gift.
The honeymoon	$5,000	Bride and Groom (usually from the wedding gifts)	Paid with the wedding gift money. Drive instead of fly. Stay in a less expensive hotel. Take a shorter trip.
TOTAL	$27,500 without the honeymoon		

Exercises 1–4

The article about marriage introduces many aspects of the wedding reception in America and its rising cost. After you read the article, do the following Exercises.

1. List the various parts of the wedding reception and the methods for saving money with each.

2. Make a list of new vocabulary words presented in the article. These will probably be necessary for the Writing Assignment below.

3. Working in pairs with a classmate with different wedding customs, explain a typical wedding from your culture. Tell how people decide to marry (by arranged marriage or by meeting and dating), and describe the wedding ceremony and the wedding reception. This oral practice will make writing your paragraph on the subject easier. When your partner describes weddings in his or her family or culture, be a good listener, ask questions, and make comments.

4. How do you feel about the extravagance of a large wedding as presented in the article? Write a paragraph on a separate piece of paper in which you give your opinion on this subject.

Writing Assignment

Describe a Wedding Reception

Using the article on pages 119–21 as your basis, write a paragraph on a separate piece of paper in which you describe a typical wedding reception in your family or culture. Use a process approach by telling your audience (people who are not from your culture) about the best way to have a wonderful and memorable reception. You might include costs if you think that it would be interesting and if you are familiar enough with them to list them.

Activity 3 *Making a Good Impression*

For this assignment you will have to interview someone who is from a different culture. Assume that you have been invited to dinner at your classmate's house. You are not familiar with the customs of your classmate, and you need advice on how to behave because you want to make a very good impression. You wish to know what time to arrive (the invitation is for 6:00 P.M.) because you do not know if it is customary to arrive early, on time, or a few minutes late. You also wish to know whether you should bring a gift, and what that gift should be (flowers, wine, dessert, candy, etc.). How should you dress for the dinner? Will you have to take off your shoes? Can you smoke during the meal? What will you probably be served to drink during the meal? What will you be served for dinner? Is the dinner served individually or family style? Should you ask for second helpings? Should you help bring the plates into the kitchen after the meal? How late should you stay after the meal is over? Are there topics you should not talk about during the meal?

Your teacher will explain the rules of etiquette for behavior at a typical American meal. After that, working in pairs, ask your partner questions about customary dining behavior in his or her culture. Take notes. Then your partner will ask you the same questions about your culture.

Writing Assignment

How to Make a Good Impression

After you finish the interview, use your notes to write a paragraph on a separate piece of paper that begins: "If you wish to make a good impression when you are invited to dinner in a _____ (your partner's culture) house, follow these directions." Be specific and include things that your reader should *certainly avoid* doing.

VOCABULARY

The following words might be useful in your paragraph.

impression	seconds
individually	family style
host	guest
customary	compliment
invitation	etiquette

OUTLINE OF POINTS TO LEARN

1. Time to arrive
2. Gift? What?
3. How to dress
4. Shoes off?
5. Seconds?
6. Dishes to kitchen?

7. Smoke?
8. Drinks
9. Food
10. Individual or family style?
11. How late to stay
12. Topics for conversation

Activity 4 *Finding an Apartment*

Suppose that you receive a letter from a good friend of yours from another country in which she tells you that she is moving to America. She would like to know how to find a nice apartment in your neighborhood.

Writing Assignment

Write a Letter

Write a letter back in the space below. Give her advice based on your personal experience and the experiences of other people you know.

Dear _____,

Sincerely yours,

VOCABULARY FOR FINDING AN APARTMENT

The following words might be useful for your paragraph.

real estate agent	newspaper advertisement (newspaper ad)
apartment	house
condominium	townhouse
first floor (second floor)	neighborhood (good, safe, dangerous)
owner	landlord
renter	tenant
rent (verb) (*to rent an apartment*)	rent (noun) (*to pay rent; to pay $800 rent*)
lease (a long-term agreement to rent)	a one-year lease
utilities (electricity, heat, water)	the utilities are included
the utilities are extra	gas and electric
convenient (convenient location)	rooms (a four-room apartment)
bathroom (bathrooms don't count as rooms)	My apartment has two bedrooms and one bathroom
location (where the apartment is)	a good location (near the train station, near the bus)

Building Your Skill in Problem Solving and Analytical Writing

Activity 1 *Brainteaser*

This old fable is actually a brainteaser. See if you can figure out a way for the boatman to transport three things across a river. After you read the fable below, do the Writing Assignment on page 129.

The Basket of Cabbages, the Goat, and the Wolf

Once upon a time there was a boatman who made a humble living by transporting people, animals, and items across a deep river. His boat was so small that he could only take one person or thing at a time. Despite the fact that he lived in a simple cottage near the river, and his clothes had been mended more than a few times, he was widely known throughout the kingdom for his intelligence. One day, word of the man's keen wit reached the King, who immediately wanted to test his subject. The King approached the shore, bringing with him a basket of cabbages, a goat, and a wolf. He asked the boatman to transport the three across the river, where a nobleman was waiting to bring them to his castle. The King said, "If you serve me well and deliver the cabbages, the goat, and the wolf to my nobleman, I will reward you richly. However, if you fail me, you will be punished."

The boatman thanked the King for his trust, and the King returned to his castle. Now the boatman had a problem. Because his boat was so small, he could only take one thing at a time. That meant that he would have to leave two of them behind and come back for them. That was the problem!

If the boatman took the wolf and left the goat with the cabbages, the goat would eat them all up. If he transported the basket of cabbages and left the goat and wolf, the wolf would eat the goat. What a fine mess!

Actually, he could bring the goat across first, leaving the wolf with the cabbages. In this way, they would be safe. However, what would he do after that? On his second trip, he would have to carry either the wolf or the cabbages; something would be gobbled up while he returned for the last thing.

The boatman searched his brain for an answer to his problem. He had to carry the three things across the river, one at a time, and he couldn't leave behind the goat and the cabbages or the goat and the wolf.

Because he was wise, he finally found the correct way out of his bad situation. He didn't protect the goat by tying the wolf to a tree. Nor did he hang the big basket from a high branch so that the goat couldn't eat the cabbages. He managed to get the three things across the river and earn the King's reward. He did this without leaving the goat with the cabbages or the wolf with the goat.

Writing Assignment

Write a Process Paragraph on a Brainteaser

1. Working in pairs or groups, discuss the boatman's problem, and try to find the solution.

2. Discuss the problem as a class, and write the solution on the board. Use a chart to show the solution.

3. Write a process paragraph in which you trace the steps that the boatman must take to carry the basket of cabbages, the goat, and the wolf across the river.

Note: The solution to the problem is in the Answer Key (page 312), but do not look there until you have fully analyzed the situation.

Activity 2 *Mystery Math Magic*

The following are some interesting mysteries involving mathematics and using process paragraphs.

1. Multiply the number of your brothers by 2, add 3, multiply by 5, add the number of your sisters, and multiply by 10. Then, add the number of your living grandparents and subtract 150 to get your final answer. The first digit of your answer will be the number of your brothers. The second digit represents the number of sisters that you have. The third digit is the number of grandparents still living. (Note: The first digit may be zero.)

2. Which would make you richer: If you accepted a million dollars in cash today, or if you received a penny today and twice its value every day for 31 days?

3. Take a number from 1 to 10. Double it. Add 10. Divide by 2. Subtract the number you first started with. Your answer is always the same (5).

See if you can add any curious math problems to the list.

Activity 3 *A Letter of Advice*

Assume that you write a column for a newspaper in which you advise readers who write to you asking for help with their problems. One reader has written you the following letter.

> **Dear Advisor:**
>
> I am a 21-year-old male who started this school one month ago from a different area. My parents sent me here to study engineering because of the excellent facilities and professors at this school. I began classes two weeks ago. My teachers and the facilities are as good as I thought they would be. I can understand the lectures well, and I am able to understand the difficult textbooks and assignments.
>
> However, I do have one problem. I have not met any friends yet. Although the people I have met are nice, I am already becoming lonely. I miss my friends and family and would like to eat some of the food that I am used to. I want to feel part of the group, but it seems as if everyone knows each other, and that I am an outsider.
>
> Will you please give me some advice on how to make friends and feel more comfortable? Thank you.
>
> Sincerely yours,
>
> Lonely

Writing Assignment

Write a Letter Giving Advice

Write a letter beginning "Dear Lonely." In the letter, explain how the reader can make friends and feel more comfortable in the new environment.

Activity 4 *Anonymous Problems*

This activity is a three-part process. Complete Part One at home on a separate piece of paper and bring your letter to class. The success of this activity is based on every student having a letter to exchange.

Part One. Using the Dear Advisor letter above written by "Lonely" as a model, write a letter in which you describe a problem (real or imaginary) that you are having this semester. Do not sign your name, but use another term to identify yourself. Provide as many details as possible. State your problem clearly, and request advice.

Part Two. Bring your problem letter to class. The teacher will collect all of the letters and distribute them to the class. Each student will receive a different problem. Students should answer the letter and provide advice to remedy the situation. On an attached piece of paper, respond directly to the problem, and address the issues raised.

Part Three. Read the letters and responses aloud to the class, but maintain the anonymity of the writers. The material may be read by either the person who has answered the letter or by the teacher in front of the class. This will also serve as the point of departure for a short classroom discussion on each problem, with students presenting their own ideas on possible advice.

UNIT 4.3

Building Your Skill in Political Analysis

Activity 1   *John F. Kennedy's Inaugural Address*

The election of 1960 was the first in which television played a pivotal role. Richard Nixon, the vice-president under Dwight D. Eisenhower and the Republican candidate for president, was leading in the polls. However, in a series of four debates broadcast on television, America got a closer look at the Democratic candidate, John Fitzgerald Kennedy. A World War II hero and senator from Massachusetts, Kennedy was handsome and well-spoken. He was also young, only 43 years old. While Nixon stressed his record of service during the prosperous 1950s, the Eisenhower years, Kennedy looked to the future and promised to lead Americans to a "New Frontier." The election results were very close. Kennedy received 34,221,344 votes to Nixon's 34,106,671, but Kennedy received 303 electoral votes to Nixon's 219.

Kennedy became president at the height of the Cold War between America and Russia. The Kennedy years would also bring public awareness to the civil rights movement and bring Martin Luther King, Jr., to national prominence. It was a time of great change and great excitement. However, the youngest man ever elected president was also the youngest to die in office. Kennedy was assassinated in Dallas, Texas, on November 22, 1963, after only two years and ten months as chief executive. The entire world mourned his passing.

The speech that he delivered on the day that he took the oath of office is one of the most famous American addresses. Kennedy challenges Americans to become active in making America a better country and the world a better place. "Ask not what your country can do for you. Ask what you can do for your country," he told the nation, and this call to volunteerism and activism set the tone for a new generation.

John F. Kennedy's Inaugural Address, January 20, 1961

Vice President Johnson, Mr. Speaker, Mr. Chief Justice, President Eisenhower, Vice President Nixon, President Truman, reverend clergy, fellow citizens. We observe today not a victory of party, but a celebration of freedom—symbolizing an end, as well as a beginning—signifying renewal, as well as change. For I have sworn before you and Almighty God the same solemn oath our forebears prescribed nearly a century and three quarters ago.

The world is very different now. For man holds in his mortal hands the power to abolish all forms of human poverty and all forms of human life. And yet the same revolutionary beliefs for which our forebears fought are still at issue around the globe—the belief that the rights of man come not from the generosity of the state, but from the hand of God.

We dare not forget today that we are the heirs of that first revolution. Let the word go forth from this time and place, to friend and foe alike, that the torch has been passed to a new generation of Americans—born in this century, tempered by war, disciplined by a hard and bitter peace, proud of our ancient heritage—and unwilling to witness or permit the slow undoing of those human rights to which this Nation has always been committed, and to which we are committed today at home and around the world.

President John F. Kennedy delivering his inaugural speech in 1961. Courtesy of United States Army Signal Corps/John Fitzgerald Kennedy Library, Boston.

Let every nation know, whether it wishes us well or ill, that we shall pay any price, bear any burden, meet any hardship, support any friend, oppose any foe, in order to assure the survival and the success of liberty.

This much we pledge—and more.

To those old allies whose cultural and spiritual origins we share, we pledge the loyalty of faithful friends. United, there is little we cannot do in a host of cooperative ventures. Divided, there is little we can do—for we dare not meet a powerful challenge at odds and split asunder.

To those new States whom we welcome to the ranks of the free, we pledge our word that one form of colonial control shall not have passed away merely to be replaced by a far more iron tyranny. We shall not always expect to find them supporting our view. But we shall always hope to find them strongly supporting their own freedom—and to remember that, in the past, those who foolishly sought power by riding the back of the tiger ended up inside.

To those peoples in the huts and villages across the globe struggling to break the bonds of mass misery, we pledge our best efforts to help them help themselves, for whatever period is required—not because the Communists may be doing it, not because we seek their votes, but because it is right. If a free society cannot help the many who are poor, it cannot save the few who are rich.

To our sister republics south of our border, we offer a special pledge—to convert our good words into good deeds—in a new alliance for progress—to assist free men and free governments in casting off the chains of poverty. But this peaceful revolution of hope cannot become the prey of hostile powers. Let all our neighbors know that we shall join with them to oppose aggression or subversion anywhere in the Americas. And let every other power know that this Hemisphere intends to remain the master of its own house.

To that world assembly of sovereign states, the United Nations, our last best hope in an age where the instruments of war have far outpaced the instruments of peace, we renew our pledge of support—to prevent it from becoming merely a forum for invective—to strengthen its shield of the new and the weak—and to enlarge the area in which its writ may run.

Finally, to those nations who would make themselves our adversary, we offer not a pledge but a request: that both sides begin anew the quest for peace, before the dark powers of destruction unleashed by science engulf all humanity in planned or accidental self-destruction.

We dare not tempt them with weakness. For only when our arms are sufficient beyond doubt can we be certain beyond doubt that they will never be employed.

But neither can two great and powerful groups of nations take comfort from our present course—both sides overburdened by the cost of modern weapons, both rightly alarmed by the steady spread of the deadly atom, yet both racing to alter that uncertain balance of terror that stays the hand of mankind's final war.

So let us begin anew—remembering on both sides that civility is not a sign of weakness, and sincerity is always subject to proof. Let us never negotiate out of fear. But let us never fear to negotiate.

Let both sides explore what problems unite us instead of belaboring those problems which divide us.

Let both sides, for the first time, formulate serious and precise proposals for the inspection and control of arms—and bring the absolute power to destroy other nations under the absolute control of all nations.

Let both sides seek to invoke the wonders of science instead of its terrors. Together let us explore the stars, conquer the deserts, eradicate disease, tap the ocean depths, and encourage the arts and commerce.

Let both sides unite to heed in all corners of the earth the command of Isaiah—to "undo the heavy burdens . . . and to let the oppressed go free."

And if a beachhead of cooperation may push back the jungle of suspicion, let both sides join in creating a new endeavor, not a new balance of power, but a new world of law, where the strong are just and the weak secure and the peace preserved.

All this will not be finished in the first 100 days. Nor will it be finished in the first 1,000 days, nor in the life of this Administration, nor even perhaps in our lifetime on this planet. But let us begin.

In your hands, my fellow citizens, more than in mine, will rest the final success or failure of our course. Since this country was founded, each generation of Americans has been summoned to give testimony to its national loyalty. The graves of young Americans who answered the call to service surround the globe.

Now the trumpet summons us again—not as a call to bear arms, though arms we need; not as a call to battle, though embattled we are—but a call to bear the burden of a long twilight struggle, year in and year out, "rejoicing in hope, patient in tribulation"—a struggle against the common enemies of man: tyranny, poverty, disease, and war itself.

Can we forge against these enemies a grand and global alliance, North and South, East and West, that can assure a more fruitful life for all mankind? Will you join in that historic effort?

In the long history of the world, only a few generations have been granted the role of defending freedom in its hour of maximum danger. I do not shrink from this responsibility—I welcome it. I do not believe that any of us would exchange places with any other people or any other generation. The energy, the faith, the devotion which we bring to this endeavor will light our country and all who serve it— and the glow from that fire can truly light the world.

And so, my fellow Americans: ask not what your country can do for you—ask what you can do for your country.

My fellow citizens of the world: ask not what America will do for you, but what together we can do for the freedom of man.

Finally, whether you are citizens of America or citizens of the world, ask of us the same high standards of strength and sacrifice which we ask of you. With a good conscience our only sure reward, with history the final judge of our deeds, let us go forth to lead the land we love, asking His blessing and His help, but knowing that here on earth God's work must truly be our own.

Writing Assignment

How a Person Becomes a Good Citizen

The responsibilities inherent in Kennedy's famous charge—"My fellow Americans: ask not what your country can do for you—ask what you can do for your country"—have been affirmed, questioned, and redefined many times since 1961. The idea that citizenship involves more giving than taking and a greater acceptance of responsibility than reliance on government assistance has been a major topic of debate. Attitudes toward mandatory enlistment in the armed forces, especially during the Vietnam War, brought the concept of service of country into question. On the other hand, many believe that a benign public assistance program run by the government to help the underprivileged is the best sign of a country that takes care of its citizens.

Do you agree with Kennedy's concept that citizenship implies many responsibilities, or do you feel that paying taxes is enough to satisfy your duty? What responsibilities does citizenship imply? Using a process approach, write a paragraph on a separate piece of paper that tells how a person becomes a good citizen.

Activity 2   *Franklin Delano Roosevelt's First Inaugural Address*

Franklin Delano Roosevelt was born in 1882 in Hyde Park, New York. He became the 32nd president of the United States and the only president elected four times. He served as president for more than 12 years, from 1933 until his death in 1945 near the end of World War II. He was president during two major crises: the Great Depression of the 1930s and World War II in the 1940s. His impassioned and resonant voice calmed the fears of many Americans during his "fireside chat" broadcasts on the radio throughout his presidency. Despite suffering from polio he had contracted in 1921, Roosevelt was a vigorous leader who directed the economic recovery in America and the American participation in the war in Europe and Asia.

Roosevelt took office in March 1933 during the depth of the Great Depression. Almost 25 percent of all Americans were unemployed. Many families had no money for food, and some had even lost their homes. With most people overcome by fear of what would happen next, Roosevelt stated: "The only thing we have to fear is fear itself." He began a new era in American history called the New Deal in which the federal government, under his direction, started programs to ease unemployment and help the average worker and the farmer. Roosevelt tried to spread a feeling of optimism across the country, a message that Americans had the power and the might to survive the Depression. His inaugural address outlined a program of assistance and a reassessment of the true nature of prosperity.

Franklin Delano Roosevelt's First Inaugural Address March 4, 1933

I am certain that my fellow Americans expect that on my induction into the Presidency I will address them with a candor and a decision which the present situation of our Nation impels. This is preeminently the time to speak the truth, the whole truth, frankly and boldly. Nor need we shrink from honestly facing conditions in our country today. This great Nation will endure as it has endured, will revive and will prosper. So, first of all, let me assert my firm belief that the only thing we have to fear is fear itself—nameless, unreasoning, unjustified terror which paralyzes needed efforts to convert retreat into advance. In every dark hour of our national life a leadership of frankness and vigor has met with that understanding and support of the people themselves which is essential to victory. I am convinced that you will again give that support to leadership in these critical days.

In such a spirit on my part and on yours we face our common difficulties. They concern, thank God, only material things. Values have shrunken to fantastic levels; taxes have risen; our ability to pay has fallen; government of all kinds is faced by serious curtailment of income; the means of exchange are frozen in the currents of trade; the withered leaves of industrial enterprise lie on every side; farmers find no markets for their produce; the savings of many years in thousands of families are gone.

More important, a host of unemployed citizens face the grim problem of existence, and an equally great number toil with little return. Only a foolish optimist can deny the dark realities of the moment.

Yet our distress comes from no failure of substance. We are stricken by no plague of locusts. Compared with the perils which our

President Franklin Delano Roosevelt delivering his inaugural speech in 1933, courtesy of the Franklin Delano Roosevelt Presidential Library.

forefathers conquered because they believed and were not afraid, we have still much to be thankful for. Nature still offers her bounty and human efforts have multiplied it. Plenty is at our doorstep, but a generous use of it languishes in the very sight of the supply. Primarily this is because the rulers of the exchange of mankind's goods have failed, through their own stubbornness and their own incompetence, have admitted their failure, and abdicated. Practices of the unscrupulous money changers stand indicted in the court of public opinion, rejected by the hearts and minds of men.

True they have tried, but their efforts have been cast in the pattern of an outworn tradition. Faced by failure of credit they have proposed only the lending of more money. Stripped of the lure of profit by which to induce our people to follow their false leadership, they have resorted to exhortations, pleading tearfully for restored confidence. They know only the rules of a generation of self-seekers. They have no vision, and when there is no vision the people perish.

The money changers have fled from their high seats in the temple of our civilization. We may now restore that temple to the ancient truths. The measure of the restoration lies in the extent to which we apply social values more noble than mere monetary profit.

Happiness lies not in the mere possession of money; it lies in the joy of achievement, in the thrill of creative effort. The joy and moral stimulation of work no longer must be forgotten in the mad chase of evanescent profits. These dark days will be worth all they cost us if they teach us that our true destiny is not to be ministered unto but to minister to ourselves and to our fellow men.

Recognition of the falsity of material wealth as the standard of success goes hand in hand with the abandonment of the false belief that public office and high political position are to be valued only by the standards of pride of place and personal profit; and there must be an end to a conduct in banking and in business which too often has given to a sacred trust the likeness of callous and selfish wrongdoing. Small wonder that confidence languishes, for it thrives only on honesty, on honor, on the sacredness of obligations, on faithful protection, on unselfish performance; without them it cannot live.

Restoration calls, however, not for changes in ethics alone. This Nation asks for action, and action now.

Our greatest primary task is to put people to work. This is no unsolvable problem if we face it wisely and courageously. It can be accomplished in part by direct recruiting by the Government itself, treating the task as we would treat the emergency of a war, but at the same time, through this employment, accomplishing greatly needed projects to stimulate and reorganize the use of our natural resources.

Hand in hand with this we must frankly recognize the overbalance of population in our industrial centers and, by engaging on a national scale in a redistribution, endeavor to provide a better use of the land for those best fitted for the land. The task can be helped by definite efforts to raise the values of agricultural products and with this the power to purchase the output of our cities. It can be helped by preventing realistically the tragedy of the growing loss through foreclosure of our small homes and our farms. It can be helped by insistence that the Federal, State, and local governments act forthwith on the demand that their cost be drastically reduced. It can be helped by the unifying of relief activities which today are often scattered, uneconomical, and unequal. It can be helped by national planning for and supervision of all forms of transportation and of communications and other utilities which have a definitely public character. There are many ways in which it can be helped, but it can never be helped merely by talking about it. We must act and act quickly.

Finally, in our progress toward a resumption of work we require two safeguards against a return of the evils of the old order; there must be a strict supervision of all banking and credits and investments; there must be an end to speculation with other people's money, and there must be provision for an adequate but sound currency.

There are the lines of attack. I shall presently urge upon a new Congress in special session detailed measures for their fulfillment, and I shall seek the immediate assistance of the several States.

Through this program of action we address ourselves to putting our own national house in order and making income balance outgo. Our international trade relations, though vastly important, are in point of time and necessity secondary to the establishment of a sound national economy. I favor as a practical policy the putting of first things first. I shall spare no effort to restore world trade by international economic readjustment, but the emergency at home cannot wait on that accomplishment.

The basic thought that guides these specific means of national recovery is not narrowly nationalistic. It is the insistence, as a first consideration, upon the interdependence of the various elements in all parts of the United States— a recognition of the old and permanently important manifestation of the American spirit of the pioneer. It is the way to recovery. It is the immediate way. It is the strongest assurance that the recovery will endure.

In the field of world policy I would dedicate this Nation to the policy of the good neighbor—the neighbor who resolutely respects himself and, because he does so, respects the rights of others—the neighbor who respects his obligations and respects the sanctity of his agreements in and with a world of neighbors.

If I read the temper of our people correctly, we now realize as we have never realized before our interdependence on each other; that we can not merely take but we must give as well; that if we are to go forward, we must move as a trained and loyal army willing to sacrifice for the good of a common discipline, because without such discipline no progress is made, no leadership becomes effective. We are, I know, ready and willing to submit our lives and property to such discipline, because it makes possible a leadership which aims at a larger good. This I propose to offer, pledging

that the larger purposes will bind upon us all as a sacred obligation with a unity of duty hitherto evoked only in time of armed strife.

With this pledge taken, I assume unhesitatingly the leadership of this great army of our people dedicated to a disciplined attack upon our common problems.

Action in this image and to this end is feasible under the form of government which we have inherited from our ancestors. Our Constitution is so simple and practical that it is possible always to meet extraordinary needs by changes in emphasis and arrangement without loss of essential form. That is why our constitutional system has proved itself the most superbly enduring political mechanism the modem world has produced. It has met every stress of vast expansion of territory, of foreign wars, of bitter internal strife, of world relations.

It is to be hoped that the normal balance of executive and legislative authority may be wholly adequate to meet the unprecedented task before us. But it may be that an unprecedented demand and need for undelayed action may call for temporary departure from that normal balance of public procedure.

I am prepared under my constitutional duty to recommend the measures that a stricken nation in the midst of a stricken world may require. These measures, or such other measures as the Congress may build out of its experience and wisdom, I shall seek, within my constitutional authority, to bring to speedy adoption.

But in the event that the Congress shall fail to take one of these two courses, and in the event that the national emergency is still critical, I shall not evade the clear course of duty that will then confront me. I shall ask the Congress for the one remaining instrument to meet the crisis—broad Executive power to wage a war against the emergency, as great as the power that would be given to me if we were in fact invaded by a foreign foe.

For the trust reposed in me I will return the courage and the devotion that befit the time. I can do no less.

We face the arduous days that lie before us in the warm courage of the national unity; with the clear consciousness of seeking old and precious moral values; with the clean satisfaction that comes from the stern performance of duty by old and young alike. We aim at the assurance of a rounded and permanent national life.

We do not distrust the future of essential democracy. The people of the United States have not failed. In their need they have registered a mandate that they want direct, vigorous action. They have asked for discipline and direction under leadership. They have made me the present instrument of their wishes. In the spirit of the gift I take it.

In this dedication of a Nation we humbly ask the blessing of God. May He protect each and every one of us. May He guide me in the days to come.

Writing Assignment

How to Achieve Happiness

The words of Franklin Delano Roosevelt in his inaugural address—"Happiness lies not in the mere possession of money; it lies in the joy of achievement, in the thrill of creative effort. The joy and moral stimulation of work no longer must be forgotten in the mad chase of evanescent profits"—are perhaps as applicable today as they were in 1933.

Do you agree with Roosevelt's definition of happiness? How do you measure happiness and success? Write a clearly organized paragraph on a separate piece of paper that presents your definition of happiness and success, and, using a process approach, presents the steps necessary to attain this goal.

A good topic sentence might be: "If you want to be truly happy, follow my advice."

Activity 3   *Abraham Lincoln's Gettysburg Address*

Abraham Lincoln was born in a log cabin in Kentucky in 1809. Despite the poverty of his youth and the fact that he received little formal education, he became the 16th President of the United States. He ran for the presidency in a turbulent era in American history. The country was divided over the issue of slavery. Immediately after Lincoln was elected in 1860, South Carolina seceded from the Union. Before he took office a few months later, six other states had followed. The Civil War began on April 12, 1861, and did not end until April 9, 1865. Just five days later, Lincoln attended a play at Ford's Theatre in Washington and was assassinated by John Wilkes Booth, a well-known actor of the day. Most Americans deeply mourned Lincoln's passing, and today he is considered one of our greatest Presidents.

During the Civil War, the Battle of Gettysburg, which took place from July 1 through July 3, 1863, was crucial. The Northern army was led by General George Meade, and the Southern forces were led by General Robert E. Lee. Lee's attack directly at the center of the Northern forces was at first successful, but the Southern troops were unable to hold the position. Lee then withdrew his battered forces to Virginia, and the balance of the war tipped to the Northern army. Meade's and Lee's armies both suffered approximately 23,000 casualties in one of the worst debacles in the history of the United States. In November 1863, Lincoln traveled to Pennsylvania to deliver an address at ceremonies for the dedication of a portion of the battlefield as a military cemetery.

Lincoln wrote five different versions of this brief speech, which many consider his best. The speech is inscribed on a large plaque on the left wall of the Lincoln Memorial in Washington, D.C., and it evokes deep emotions in most Americans. The first draft was probably written on a train from Washington to Pennsylvania. Lincoln held the second revised version in his hand as he delivered the speech, but he made several additions and changes as he spoke. The most important modification was the addition of the phrase "under God" after the word *nation* in the last paragraph. The last copy of the address, the fifth version, was made in 1864; it was the only copy that Lincoln signed.

Abraham Lincoln's Gettysburg Address
November 19, 1863

Four score and seven years ago our fathers brought forth on this continent a new nation, conceived in Liberty, and dedicated to the proposition that all men are created equal.

Now we are engaged in a great civil war, testing whether that nation, or any nation, so conceived, and so dedicated, can long endure. We are met here on a great battlefield of that war. We have come to dedicate a portion of it as a final resting place for those who here gave their lives that that nation might live. It is altogether fitting and proper that we should do this.

But in a larger sense we can not dedicate—we can not consecrate—we can not hallow—this ground. The brave men, living and dead, who struggled here, have consecrated it far above our poor power to add or detract. The world will little note, nor long remember, what we say here, but it can never forget what they did here. It is for us the living, rather to be dedicated here to the unfinished work which they who fought here have thus far so nobly advanced. It is rather for us to be here

Abraham Lincoln, courtesy of the Defense Visual Information Center.

dedicated to the great task remaining before us—that from these honored dead we take increased devotion to that cause for which they gave the last full measure of devotion—that we here highly resolve that these dead shall not have died in vain—that this nation, under God, shall have a new birth of freedom—and that this government of the people, by the people, for the people, shall not perish from the earth.

Writing Assignment

Are Causes Worth Defending with Your Life?

Lincoln reserves the highest praise and the greatest respect for those soldiers who sacrificed their lives for a cause. Are there any causes to which you are so dedicated that you would risk your life to defend them? Or do you feel that no cause is strong enough for you to sacrifice your life in defending it? Write a clearly organized paragraph on a separate piece of paper that presents your position.

F. Graded Writing Assignment: Write a Process Paragraph on Observation and Deduction

Read the excerpt on pages 142–43 from the Sir Arthur Conan Doyle story "The Blue Carbuncle." Then write a paragraph of 10 to 12 sentences that summarizes the steps used by Sherlock Holmes to deduce information about the owner of the hat.

The Powers of Observation

"I continue to retain the hat of the unknown gentleman who lost his Christmas dinner."

"Did he not advertise?"

"No."

"Then, what clue could you have as to his identity?"

"Only as much as we can deduce."

"From his hat?"

"Precisely."

"But you are joking. What can you gather from this old battered felt?"

"Here is my lens. You know my methods. What can you gather yourself as to the individuality of the man who has worn this article?"

I took that tattered object in my hands and turned it over rather ruefully. It was a very ordinary black hat of the usual round shape, hard, and much the worse for wear. The lining had been of red silk, but was a good deal discolored. There was no maker's name; but, as Holmes had remarked, the initials "H.B." were scrawled upon one side. It was pierced in the brim for a hat-securer, but the elastic was missing. For the rest, it was cracked, exceedingly dusty, and spotted in several places, although there seemed to have been some attempt to hide the discolored patches by smearing them with ink.

"I can see nothing," said I, handing it back to my friend.

"On the contrary, Watson, you can see everything. You fail, however, to reason from what you see. You are too timid in drawing your inferences."

"Then, pray tell me what it is that you can infer from this hat?"

He picked it up and gazed at it in the peculiar introspective fashion which was characteristic of him. "It is perhaps less suggestive than it might have been," he remarked, "and yet there are a few inferences which are very distinct, and a few others which represent at least a strong balance of probability. That the man was highly intellectual is of course obvious on the face of it, and also that he was fairly well-to-do within the last three years, although he has now fallen upon evil days. He had foresight, but has less now than formerly, pointing to a moral retrogression, which, when taken with the decline of his fortunes, seems to indicate some evil influence, probably drink, at work upon him. This may account also for the obvious fact that his wife has ceased to love him."

"My dear Holmes."

"He has, however, retained some degree of self-respect," he continued, disregarding my remonstrance. "He is a man who lives a sedentary life, goes out little, is out of training entirely, is middle-aged, has grizzled hair which he has had cut within the last few days, and which he anoints with limecream. These are the more patent facts which are to be deduced from his hat. Also, by-the-way, that it is extremely improbable that he has gas laid on in his house."

"Your are certainly joking, Holmes."

"Not in the least. Is it possible that even now, when I give you these results, you are unable to see how they are attained?"

"I have no doubt that I am very stupid; but I must confess that I am unable to follow you. For example, how did you deduce that this man was intellectual?"

For answer Holmes clapped the hat upon his head. It came right over the forehead and settled upon the bridge of his nose. "It is a question of cubic capacity," said he; "a man with so large a brain must have something in it."

"The decline of his fortunes, then?"

"This hat is three years old. These flat brims curled at the edge came in then. It is a hat of the very best quality. Look at the band of ribbed silk and the excellent lining. If this man could afford to buy so expensive a hat three years ago, and has had no hat since, then he has assuredly gone down in the world."

"Well, that is clear enough. But how about the foresight and the moral retrogression?"

Sherlock Holmes laughed. "Here is the foresight," said he, putting his finger upon the little disk and loop of the hatsecurer. "They are never sold upon hats. If this man ordered one, it is a sign of a certain amount of foresight, since he went out of his way to take this precaution against the wind. But since we see that he has broken the elastic, and has not troubled to replace it, it is obvious that he has less foresight now than formerly, which is a distinct proof of a weakening nature. On the other hand, he has endeavored to conceal some of these stains upon the felt by daubing them with ink, which is a sign that he has not entirely lost his self-respect."

"Your reasoning is certainly plausible."

"The further points, that he is middle-aged, that his hair is grizzled, that it has been recently cut, and that he uses limecream, are all to be gathered from a close examination of the lower part of the lining. The lens discloses a large number of hair-ends, clean cut by the scissors of the barber. They all appear to be adhesive, and there is a distinct odor of limecream. This dust, you will observe, is not the gritty, gray dust of the street, but the fluffy brown dust of the house, showing that it has been hung up indoors most of the time, while the marks of moisture upon the inside are proof positive that the wearer perspired very freely, and could, therefore, hardly be in the best of training.

"But his wife—you said that she had ceased to love him."

"This hat has not been brushed for weeks. When I see you, my dear Watson, with a week's accumulation of dust upon your hat, and when your wife allows you to go out in such a state, I shall fear that you also have been unfortunate enough to lose your wife's affection."

"But he might be a bachelor."

"Nay, he was bringing home the goose as a peace-offering to his wife. Remember the card upon the bird's leg."

"You have an answer to everything. But how on earth do you deduce that the gas is not laid on in his house?"

"One tallow stain, or even two, might come by chance; but when I see no less than five, I think that there can be little doubt that the individual must be brought into frequent contact with burning tallow—walks upstairs at night probably with his hat in one hand and a sputtering candle in the other. Anyhow, he never got tallow stains from a gasjet. Are you satisfied."

"Well, it is very ingenious," said I, laughing.

Source: "The Blue Carbuncle" by Sir Arthur Conan Doyle

G. Part 4 Summary

Based on your work in Part 4, answer the questions below and discuss them as a class.

1. What is the importance of using steps in organizing a process paragraph?

2. What verb forms and tenses are most common in process paragraphs?

3. What is the intent of a self-improvement program? How is it organized?

4. Explain the most important aspects in the proofreading process.

5. Why is "past tense advice" useless? Can you recall situations in which you have given or received this type of advice?

H. Reflections on Your Progress

Write your reflections or thoughts below on some of the writing you have done in Part 4.

1. Which were your two favorite journal entries, and why?

2. What was the most interesting writing assignment, and why?

3. What was the least interesting writing assignment, and why?

4. What is the most important thing about writing you learned?

5. Were you satisfied with the progress you made in the assignments?

I. Part 4 Assignment Checklist

Assignment	Required or Optional	Grade	Revised	Returned and Filed
Write Your Own Recipe (page 118)				
Describe a Wedding Reception (page 124)				
How to Make a Good Impression (page 125)				
Write a Letter (page 126)				
Write a Process Paragraph on a Brainteaser (page 129)				
Write A Letter Giving Advice (page 130)				
How a Person Becomes a Good Citizen (page 134)				
How to Achieve Happiness (page 139)				
Are Causes Worth Defending with Your Life? (page 141)				
Write a Process Paragraph on Observation and Deduction (page 142)				

J. Part 4 Journal Summary

Date of First Journal	Date of Last Journal	Number of Journal Entries Written for Part 4

PART 5

Comparison and Contrast Paragraphs

Suggested Journal Topics for Comparison and Contrast Paragraphs

- Compare the educational system in the U.S. with the system in another country

- Contrast your brothers and/or sisters

- Are you more like your mother or father?

- Compare two television programs

- Compare two of your classmates (ones with very dissimilar characteristics)

- Where you live now and a place you lived earlier

- The best and worst teachers that you have ever had

A. Comparison and Contrast Paragraphs

Many people tend to see life in comparative terms. Because the fixed point of reference is usually something familiar and customary, anything new is seen in relative terms. Try to recall your first month living in a new place and the impressions that you experienced. Most of these impressions were the result of comparisons with the area where you previously lived. Here are some examples:

1. The people in your new neighborhood were friendlier than the people where you used to live.

2. There were more people on the streets in your old neighborhood at 9:00 PM.

3. People drove more safely in your new area.

4. The stores were open later where you lived previously.

In fact, almost every new object you saw and every new characteristic that you learned about American people likely prompted a comparison with a similar object in your culture. This is a natural phase of development. In general, when people move to a new place, the *comparison phase* lasts from a few months to a year, although for some it has a longer duration.

Making intelligent comparisons is an important skill and is required in many of the college courses that you will take. History professors might request a comparison between the French and American revolutions on the final examination, while psychology professors could ask for a comparison of the way that Freud and Jung analyzed women. Many essay examinations in art history demand a comparison of two slides of paintings or sculptures.

Comparison paragraphs concentrate on the *similarities* between two things; **contrast paragraphs** focus on *differences*. **Comparison** and **contrast paragraphs** focus on both similarities and differences. Organization in these types of paragraphs is essential. The structure of the paragraph is based on **points of comparison,** the basis for the analysis.

Points of comparisons are usually **nouns.** A comparison of restaurants might center on price, food quality, and service, while a comparison of hotels could be based on comfort, location, facilities, and rates. People may be compared in terms of personality traits and physical characteristics, and a comparison of movies would revolve around the quality of the performances, the plot, and the visual effects. It is important to choose solid points of comparison that are rich in possibilities.

Comparison and contrast paragraphs usually use the **simple present tense.** The order is either *descending*—from the most important to the least important point of comparison—or *ascending*—designed to build interest in the paragraph. Discourse markers include *however, nevertheless, on the other hand, while, although, but, on the contrary,* and the *comparative form* of adjectives and adverbs (*bigger, faster*). There are two possible structures for the comparison paragraph: **direct comparison** and **separated structure.** Outlines for each method are presented on pages 153 and 156, respectively.

THE COMPARISON PARAGRAPH

Paragraph type:	Comparison and contrast
Verb tense used:	Simple present
Organization:	Based on three or four differences
	Direct comparison structure or separated structure
Discourse markers:	Comparison words; *the first difference is; another difference is;*
Grammar points:	Comparison sentences may be formed in the following way:

Typical Structure of Comparison Paragraphs	
Structure	**Examples**
1. Independent Clause comma conjunction independent clause (with **but** and **yet**)	I am tall, **but** my brother is short. She studies hard, **but** her sister is somewhat lazy. He works many hours, **yet** he never has any money.
2. Independent Clause semicolon conjunction comma independent clause (with **however, nevertheless, nonetheless, on the other hand,** and **on the contrary**)	Min is 7 feet 3 inches tall; **however,** he doesn't play basketball. I left early from my house this morning; **nevertheless,** I was late for class. I bought six bags of candy to give to the trick-or-treaters on Halloween; **nonetheless,** I didn't have enough for all of them. My brother has never been to South America; **on the other hand,** my sister has visited six countries there. Senator Johnson did not approve the education bill; **on the contrary,** she has voted against it six times in a row.
3. Dependent clause comma independent clause (with **although, while,** and **whereas**)	**Although** my brother lives 100 miles away from me, we still see each other every weekend. **While** my sister loves gardening, I don't have the patience for it. **Whereas** Koreans eat soup for breakfast, Americans usually eat cereal.
4. Independent clause (no punctuation) dependent clause (with **although, while,** and **whereas**)	I never get an A **although** I study a great deal. Dorothy loves jogging **while** her sister hates it. Yoonhee takes the highway to school **whereas** Angelica takes the back roads.

BRAINSTORMING AND THE PROCESS FOR ORGANIZING AND WRITING CONTRAST PARAGRAPHS

1. When you are given a topic for comparison, the first step is to *brainstorm differences.* Think about the topic for a few minutes. Then write as many differences as you can in two minutes. Do not stop to analyze or reject any differences. Simply write them down.

2. Choose the *four differences* that are richest in possibilities for discussion. You will probably need only three for your paragraph, but keep the fourth in reserve in case you find that you have not written enough.

3. Fill out a comparison chart like the one on page 152, entering the *points of comparison* in the first vertical column on the left and the *objects of comparison* in the next two columns.

4. Write as many details as you can in the chart.

5. Select a structure for the comparison paragraph; choose between direct comparison and separated structure.

6. Write the paragraph; follow the comparison chart closely.

An excellent way to organize ideas in a comparison paragraph is to chart the points of comparison using the chart like the one on page 152. Use the appropriate boxes to provide supporting information, details, or specific examples. The chart on page 152 has been filled in; it compares breakfast in the U.S. to breakfast in Korea.

Writing Assignment

Write Comparison Charts

Write comparison charts for the topics below. Use the sample Comparison Chart format on page 152.

1. two people in your family who are very different

2. two very different places that you have visited

3. the major differences between typical American food and the food eaten in your house

4. two musical groups (or soloists) with very different styles

5. the place where you live now and a place where you used to live

Comparison Chart		
Points of Comparison	Object of Comparison 1:	Object of Comparison 2:
Point of Comparison 1		
Point of Comparison 2		
Point of Comparison 3		
Point of Comparison 4		

Comparison Chart		
Points of Comparison	Object of Comparison 1: *Breakfast in the U.S.*	Object of Comparison 2: *Breakfast in Korea*
Usual foods	Based on carbohydrates (bagels, toast, rolls, donuts, cereal, buns, pancakes), sometimes bacon and eggs	A variety of hot foods (vegetables, rice, soup)
Time of preparation	Usually a quick meal if eaten at home; little prep time. Sunday breakfast is usually more elaborate and may even become *brunch.*	Requires time to prepare, so someone must wake up early.
Drinks	Coffee is an important part of the American breakfast. Orange juice. Some drink tea. Kids have milk or hot chocolate.	Tea

STRUCTURE 1: DIRECT COMPARISON

In direct comparison, you start with the first point of comparison. Then you should discuss the two objects. For example, in the paragraph on breakfast in the U.S. and Korea, you should introduce the subject of usual foods. Then present an analysis of typical breakfast foods in the U.S. and in Korea. For example, you could write the following:

> **The first important difference in breakfast in the two countries is that the American breakfast is usually based on carbohydrates and starches. Most Americans eat a quick bagel, donut, muffin, or a bowl of cereal. Sometimes, if they have more time, they will eat bacon and eggs, the customary meal of their parents and grandparents. On the other hand, Koreans usually eat a hot breakfast composed of soup, meat, vegetables, and rice. They believe that it is important to eat a rich breakfast in order to have more energy for morning activities.**

These sentences would be followed by the introduction of the second point of comparison, followed by an analysis of the two objects (i.e., preparation time for a U.S. breakfast and a Korean breakfast), the third point of comparison (drinks), and a conclusion. Below is the general structure for a comparison paragraph using the direct comparison structure.

1. Topic sentence (establishes the comparison)

2. Point of comparison 1 (the most important point)

   a. Analyze A (object of comparison 1)

      1. Support

      2. Explanation

   b. Analyze B (object of comparison 2)

      1. Support

      2. Explanation

3. Point of comparison 2

   a. Analyze A

      1. Support

      2. Explanation

   b. Analyze B

      1. Support

      2. Explanation

4. Point of comparison 3

   a. Analyze A

      1. Support

      2. Explanation

   b. Analyze B

      1. Support

      2. Explanation

5. Conclusion

(You may make a decision to reiterate the qualities of each. Do not feel obliged to choose one over the other.)

Exercise 1 Read the sample paragraph below and do the analysis exercises that follow.

There are many differences between living in Miami and living in Hallendale, a suburb 20 miles away. Each has several advantages and disadvantages. The first important difference is convenience. I work in Miami, so if I live there I can walk to work or take a short bus ride. As a result, I can go out more in the evening because I am able to go to bed and sleep later. On the other hand, if I live in Hallendale, I have to leave my house at 6:30 A.M. to make it to work by 8:30. It costs $12.00 every day to drive and park my car, or $11.00 to take the bus. Another important difference is safety. Miami is a large city, so there is some crime. On the contrary, Hallendale is a safe place to live. I like to jog in the evening, and I feel very secure running in the park near my house in Hallendale. However, when I lived in Miami, I was sometimes too afraid to run downtown in the early morning or late evening, especially after watching the news. The third point of comparison between living in the city and the suburbs is variety. Miami is a vibrant, multicultural city with people from all around the world. I can go to different restaurants from many countries and try all kinds of new food. In Hallendale, though, it sometimes seems as if there are very few interna-

Key Biscayne and the Miami Skyline. Courtesy of the Miami Downtown Development Authority.

tional people. There is one Chinese restaurant, two pizza places, and six hamburger restaurants. It may get boring in such a small and closed place. I really cannot make up my mind where to live because I recognize that there are several good and bad aspects to living in both places.

Exercise 1

1. Underline the discourse markers used to structure the comparison paragraph.

2. Analyze the points of comparison. Are they the best ones? Could you find several others on which to base a paragraph?

3. Does the writer support the points through example and explanation? Analyze the quality of the support.

4. Does the writer make a choice regarding the best place to live? If you were writing this paragraph, what choice would you make, and how would you support it?

5. Pretend that you prefer to live in the suburbs rather than in the city. Which points of comparison would you choose to present a more favorable image of the suburbs?

STRUCTURE II: SEPARATED STRUCTURE

The separated structure is similar to two description paragraphs joined together by a major transition word (such as *on the other hand* or *however*). The writer begins by analyzing the first object of comparison and going through the points of difference. Thus, with the breakfast in the U.S. and Korea topic, the first part of the paragraph using separated structure concentrates entirely on the U.S. and discusses food, preparation time, and drinks. Then, after a transition, breakfast in Korea is discussed; the points of comparison are covered in the same order (food, preparation time, and drinks).

The separated structure is probably easier to write but slightly more difficult to read as a comparison than the direct comparison method. The separated structure (shown below) is particularly suitable for writing long pieces such as essays.

   1. Topic sentence

   2. Object of comparison 1

   　a. Point of comparison 1

   　　1. Support

   　　2. Example

   　b. Point of comparison 2

   　　1. Support

   　　2. Example

   　c. Point of comparison 3

   　　1. Support

   　　2. Example

Transition (on the other hand)

   3. Object of comparison 2

   　a. Point of comparison 1

   　　1. Support

   　　2. Example

b. Point of comparison 2

    1. Support

    2. Example

c. Point of comparison 3

    1. Support

    2. Example

B. Vocabulary Acquisition: Nouns

In writing points of comparison to organize your paragraphs in this chapter, you will use nouns. So in your reading this week, concentrate on *nouns*. Find 15 new ones, and write them in the space below. Indicate whether the word has a positive (+), negative (−), or neutral (=) connotation and whether there are prefixes, suffixes, or roots that help you understand the meaning. Write a definition for the word. Then construct a sentence for each noun. The first one below is a model.

Word	Part of Speech	Connotation (+, −, =)	Roots, Prefixes, or Suffixes	Definition
1. materialism	noun	−	*ism* = noun ending	the tendency to care too much for the things of this world and neglect spiritual needs
SENTENCE: My uncle's house resembles a shrine to materialism because he has too many showy things.				
2.				
SENTENCE:				
3.				
SENTENCE:				

Word	Part of Speech	Connotation (+, –, =)	Roots, Prefixes, or Suffixes	Definition
4.				
SENTENCE:				
5.				
SENTENCE:				
6.				
SENTENCE:				
7.				
SENTENCE:				
8.				
SENTENCE:				
9.				
SENTENCE:				

Word	Part of Speech	Connotation (+, −, =)	Roots, Prefixes, or Suffixes	Definition
10.				
SENTENCE:				
11.				
SENTENCE:				
12.				
SENTENCE:				
13.				
SENTENCE:				
14.				
SENTENCE:				
15.				
SENTENCE:				

C. Grammatical Structures: Connectors

Exercise 2   As a class, form into groups of four, and do the following Exercises.

1. Each group should choose a scribe and a leader. The scribe will record the group's work. The leader will make sure that everyone in the group participates. The groups will discuss the following connectors:

yet	on the other hand	thus
in addition	moreover	inasmuch as
also	since	while
as a result	furthermore	so
but	nevertheless	whereas
consequently	on the contrary	because
therefore	although	hence
however	in conclusion	nonetheless
for this reason	and	

2. Divide the above connectors into three groups. One group is called Adding Information, with the key word *and;* another is Result, with the key word *so;* the last is Contrast, with the key word *but.* The scribe will write the words.

3. Place all the words into the three categories. The scribe from each group will write a complete list on the board. As a class, review the lists and decide whether the connectors have been placed in the correct columns.

4. Finally, compose one sentence for each connector. It is essential that everyone in each group participates. Write samples of these sentences on the board for analysis by the whole class.

5. Punctuation of connectors is important. Review when to use periods, commas, and semicolons.

Sample sentences with semicolons:

He works hard all week; however, he doesn't earn much money.

Sue is 6 feet 2 inches tall; nevertheless, she cannot play basketball well.

Maria has a job at Sears; in addition, she works nights at a restaurant.

Gianna studies hard every night; as a result, she gets good grades.

Her brother is quite lazy; on the other hand, Mary is energetic.

Sample sentences with commas:

> **Because she stayed up all night, Elizabeth looks exhausted today.**
>
> **Although they have a great deal of money, they have no taste.**
>
> **While the Yankees have a young team, the Angels are all veterans.**
>
> **It has rained all week, but it should be nice tomorrow.**
>
> **The weather is wonderful in San Diego, so many tourists go there.**

Writing Assignment

Write Sentences with Connectors

Write two sentences for each of the words listed in #1 on page 160. Pay particular attention to punctuation. You will write 52 sentences in all. During the next class, you will write some of the sentences on the board so the whole class can analyze them.

Exercise 3   Complete the sentences below. Punctuate carefully.

1. While some people enjoy jogging _____

2. My sister is an extrovert on the other hand _____

3. Mario was well qualified for that job however _____

4. Although we live very close to Los Angeles _____

5. That Indian restaurant has fair prices in addition _____

6. We have never been to Singapore but _____

7. The Chileans are proud of their wine and _____

8. She is the vice-president of that company nevertheless _____

   _____

9. Keiko lives far away from her friend Nabuko as a result _____

   _____

10. Joseph cannot keep a secret however _____

Exercise 4 Write sentences on "two professors who are very different" using the constructions below.

1. S V ; *however,* S V.

2. *Since* S V, S V.

3. S V , *although* S V.

4. S V ; *as a result,* S V.

5. S V , *so* S V.

6. S V . *Nevertheless,* S V.

7. *While* S V, S V.

8. S V ; *thus,* S V.

Exercise 5 Insert the following transition words in the paragraph below. Write the corresponding number from the paragraph in the blank next to each word below.

_____ thus	_____ both	_____ or example
_____ on the other hand	_____ but	_____ though
_____ however	_____ despite	_____ in fact
_____ in order to	_____ while	_____ therefore
	_____ and	_____ so

Baseball and Football

Two of the most popular sports in America—baseball and football—are (1) _____ the two that probably differ most. Baseball is a spring and summer sport played on a grassy field in a place called a ballpark. The goal of the game is to reach home safely. (2) _____, football is played in the fall and winter, when the field becomes muddy, frozen, slippery, or hard. Weather is a very important factor. (3) _____ baseball games are cancelled when it rains, football is played in all weather. Football is a game of constant and violent physical contact. The goal of the defense is to smash the ball carrier to the ground, tackling him before he can reach a first down.

Football is a game of violence, (4) _____ baseball is a game of peace. Football players must lift weights constantly (5) _____ to keep themselves in peak physical condition. Baseball players, (6) _____, are not always in perfect shape. (7) _____, when a reporter saw former Philadelphia Phillies first-baseman John Kruk drinking a large beer and eating two hot dogs, he asked, "How can an athlete eat and drink like that?" Kruk replied, "Buddy, I'm not an athlete. I'm a baseball player."

To love baseball, which is known as the national pastime, is to love spring, soft grass, blue skies, and sunshine. Its colors are green, blue, and

Courtesy of University of Michigan Photo Services.   Courtesy of University of Michigan Photo Services.

white. Baseball, like life, is a game of hope, a game of multiple chances. There are 162 games in a season, (8) _____ every day is a new game, a new chance to win. (9) _____, even the best team loses 60 times a season. The worst team will beat the best team 40 percent of the time. (10) _____, baseball teaches how to win gracefully and humbly and how to lose without becoming hopeless.

(11) _____, to love football is to love the fall, with its infinite variety of colors and tones. The season begins with the last rush of summer still in the air, continues to the resplendence of the oranges, reds, and yellows of the autumn leaves, (12) _____ concludes when late fall turns into dreary winter with all hope gone, death reflected in the bare trees, the grass and flowers dormant, and the days short.

(13) _____ their differences, (14) _____ baseball and football are important parts of American culture. The two sports represent two sides of the American spirit—violent and peaceful, energetic and thoughtful, in-your-face and laid-back.

Note: The answers to this exercise are in the Answer Key (page 314). But do not look there until you have completed the Exercise.

D. Writing Skills: Enhancing Creativity

These exercises are intended to return you to a time when your imagination ran free. Do not limit yourself. Express the first thing that comes into your mind.

Exercise 6 Do the following Exercises on a separate piece of paper.

1. Picture a perfect place in your mind. Where are you? Describe the scenery. Are you alone or with someone else? Describe the weather. What are you doing? Picture yourself in paradise, and write notes.

2. Imagine yourself in a terrifying situation, one from which it would be very difficult to escape. Picture the action and the fear, and write notes.

Exercise 7 Write down the first word that pops into your mind when you read the following words. Then compare your answers with your classmates' answers.

1. Cold _____
2. Expensive _____
3. Mountain _____
4. Warm _____
5. Woman _____
6. Book _____
7. Summer _____
8. Home _____
9. Food _____
10. Chocolate _____
11. Morning _____
12. Saturday _____
13. Family _____
14. School _____
15. Bitter _____
16. Cheap _____
17. Lonely _____
18. Death _____
19. Jealous _____
20. Children _____

Exercise 8 Give five examples for each of the following.

1. things that you love

2. things that get better with age

3. things that really get you angry

4. characteristics of a good friend

5. things that you love to touch

Exercise 9 Give five examples for the situations below.

1. a romantic place

2. a remote place

3. an exciting afternoon

4. a beautiful outfit of clothes

5. wild behavior

6. a terrible day

7. a great place to hide

8. summer sounds

E. Journal Type 5: The Four-Entry Journal

The four-entry journal is an important step in understanding writing as a group dynamic. It is an expansion of the double-entry journal in which you summarized ideas and presented themes in the first column and introduced your own ideas and analysis in the second column. The four-entry journal gives you a chance to see how your classmates think and how they express themselves in writing. Columns 1 and 2 are your work. In column 3, one classmate will comment on your ideas and react directly to what you have written. In column 4, another classmate will respond to the ideas introduced in the first three columns and react both to your writing and to that of the classmate who has filled in column 3. The Four-Entry Journal Chart on page 168 shows the structure of this type of journal.

Journal Activity

Four-Entry Journal Practice

This journal works best on controversial pieces that offer a variety of possible interpretations. Follow the procedure on page 167.

The Four-Entry Journal			
Column 1	Column 2	Column 3	Column 4
Summarizes the main idea in a passage; describes the characters, their traits, and the setting in a passage of fiction; and summarizes the opinions expressed in a persuasive piece, and any other points that you consider important in the reading.	Presents your own ideas and reactions to the reading. How do you feel about it? Do you agree or disagree with the ideas presented? Do your personal experiences affect the way that you have read the passage?	This column is filled in by one of your classmates, who reacts to your ideas and introduces his or her own thoughts on the subject. This column may include questions on how you arrived at your conclusion. Disagreement is welcome here.	This column is done by another classmate, who reacts either to the ideas presented in column 3 or to the thoughts expressed in column 2. This classmate should present reasons of his or her own in analyzing the situation presented in the reading.

1. Take a piece of blank unlined paper (8½- by 11-inch) and make four equal columns. Or open your journal book so that two blank pages are side to side and make four equal columns.

2. Read the article discussing Dr. Kevorkian and euthanasia.

3. In column 1, write a summary of the facts presented in the article. Include the key points set forth by the writer. Do not exceed one column in your writing.

4. In column 2, write your reactions to the themes introduced. State your own opinion on the topic. You might also include personal experiences if the topic directly affects you or someone you know well. Describe how you feel about Dr. Kevorkian specifically and euthanasia in general. Be strong in your decision, and set forth your ideas clearly.

5. Exchange journals with a classmate. In column 3 write your reactions to what is written in the second column, and comment on the ideas and opinions expressed. Someone else will do the same with your journal.

6. Pass the journal on to another classmate, and receive someone else's journal. Fill in column 4 by commenting on the ideas expressed in the columns 2 and 3.

Dr. Kevorkian Sentenced to 10–25 Years in Jail

PONTIAC, MICH. JUNE 14—A Michigan judge sentenced Dr. Jack Kevorkian today to 10 to 25 years in jail, in spite of an emotional courtroom plea from the widow and brother of the terminally ill man he was convicted of killing.

The judge, Jessica Cooper of Oakland County Circuit Court, denied bail to Dr. Kevorkian, who is 70 years old. Kevorkian said that he had planned to appeal. The judge declared that the fact that Dr. Kevorkian had blatantly disregarded the law gave the court no choice but to remove him from society.

"The trial was not about the morality of euthanasia," the judge said. "It was about you, sir. It was about lawlessness."

The judge was referring to a "60 Minutes" program that showed a videotape of Dr. Kevorkian administering the lethal injection that resulted in the charges. Judge Cooper said to Dr. Kevorkian, "You had the audacity to go on national television, show the world what you did, and dare the legal system to stop you.

"Well, sir, consider yourself stopped."

Dr. Kevorkian, a retired pathologist who says that he has assisted more than 130 people to commit suicide in a decade-long campaign of death that has made him a courageous pioneer to some and an arrogant predator to others, did not answer the judge.

The corridor outside the courtroom was filled with foes of Dr. Kevorkian, many in wheelchairs, who burst into applause after the sentencing. Dr. Kevorkian, who had talked on a cellular telephone in court before the sentencing, smiled as he was led out by bailiffs. He had declined to speak in his defense.

A jury convicted Dr. Kevorkian in March of second-degree murder in the death of Thomas Youk, a 52-year-old man who lived in suburban Detroit and suffered from amyotrophic lateral sclerosis, or Lou Gehrig's disease. His widow, Melody Youk, gave a statement to the court that bitterly criticized prosecutors and cast Dr. Kevorkian as someone who was merely carrying out the wishes of her husband.

VOCABULARY

Highlight the following words in the passage, and try to find the meaning from the context.

sentenced	terminally	bail
euthanasia	lethal	courageous
widow	prosecutor	second-degree murder

UNIT 5.1

Building Your Skill in Cultural Comparisons

Activity 1   *Cats and Dogs*

 Read the passage below and answer the questions that follow.

Domestic cats and dogs differ greatly, and so do their owners. In fact, many believe that human pet owners share similar characteristics with their animals. Aspects such as desire for freedom and independence, the relationship that develops between the animals and their owners, and their particular forms of development are some of the fundamental differences between cats and dogs and their owners.

The domestic cat is a contradiction. No other animal has developed such an intimate relationship with humanity, while at the same time demanding and getting such independent movement and action.

The cat manages to remain a tame animal because of the sequence of its upbringing. By living both with other cats (its mother and litter-mates) and with humans (the family that has adopted it) during its infancy and kittenhood, it becomes attached to and considers that it belongs to both species. It is like a child who grows up in a foreign country and as a result becomes bilingual. The young cat becomes bimental. It may be a cat physically, but mentally it is both feline and human. Once it is fully adult, though, most of its responses are feline, and it has only one major reaction to its human owners. It treats them as pseudoparents. The reason is that they took over from the real mother at a sensitive stage in the kitten's development and went on giving it milk, solid food, and comfort as it grew up.

This is rather different from the kind of bond that develops between human and dog. The dog sees its human owners as pseudoparents, as does the cat. But the dog has an additional link. Canine society is group-organized; feline society is not. Wild dogs live in packs with strong status relationships: there are top dogs, middle dogs, and bottom dogs. So the adult pet dog sees its human family both as pseudoparents and as the dominant members of the pack. For this reason, the dog has a well-known reputation for obedience and a celebrated capacity for loyalty. In the wild, most cats spend most of their day in solitary hunting. Going for a walk with a human, therefore, has no appeal for cats. And as for learning to "sit" and "stay," cats are simply not interested.

As a result, the moment a cat manages to persuade a human to open a door, it is off and away without a backward glance, and it transforms into a wildcat. In this situation, a dog may look back to see that the human is following. The dog wants companionship; the cat's mind has floated off into another, totally feline world, where humans have no place at all.

Because of the difference between domestic cats and domestic dogs, cat-lovers tend to be rather different from dog-lovers. As a rule, cat-lovers tend to have a stronger personality bias toward working alone, independent of the larger group. Artists tend to like cats; soldiers tend to like dogs. The "group loyalty" phenomenon is alien to both cats and cat-lovers. If you are a member of a team, the chances are that you love dogs. It is difficult to picture football players with cats in their laps; it is much easier to imagine them taking their dogs for a walk.

Those who have studied cat owners and dog owners also have reported a gender difference. The majority of cat-lovers are female. This may be due to differences in personality between men and women. Or it may be due to development in personalities from prehistoric times, when men were more commonly engaged in group hunting and fishing activities and thus developed a "pack mentality" that is far less marked in women.

The argument will always go on—feline self-sufficiency and individualism versus canine camaraderie and good fellowship. Perhaps, though, many of us have both feline and canine elements in our personalities. We have moods when we want to be alone and thoughtful, and other times when we wish to be in the center of a crowded, noisy room.

1. If you own cats or dogs or if you know people who own them, do their characteristics mirror those of their pet, or are they somewhat different?

2. Summarize the characteristics of dog owners and cat owners as presented in the article.

3. How do dogs and cats differ in their relationship with their owners?

Writing Assignment

Summarize an Article

Write a paragraph on a separate piece of paper in which you summarize the piece "Cats and Dogs." Include the points of comparison and the support used. Do not copy directly from the text. Use your own words.

Activity 2   *Enhancing Creativity through Creating a Cartoon*

Watch cartoons at home for at least an hour. The best time to find them on television is Saturday morning, although the Nickelodeon cable channel and Cartoon Network show cartoons throughout the day. After watching and analyzing the cartoons, create two of your own animal cartoon characters. For the sake of argument, you will make up two characters with opposite, or antagonistic, qualities.

1. Work in groups of four, and select an animal to be represented.

2. Select four characteristics for your animal.

3. Check to see that the attributes within one character are complementary, not contradictory.

4. Select another animal to serve as the rival of the first animal.

5. Select a geographical place and time to set the cartoon.

6. Finally, plan an episode with action.

Consider the following when developing your characters.

1. What would happen to the character if it were changed from a man to a woman? Does gender affect personality and behavior?

2. What would happen if the character were African-American instead of Caucasian? Or Asian? South American? From the Middle East? From California or the American South? From Amish country? Do people behave a certain way according to their background, culture, or environment?

3. What if we changed the character from middle class to rich? To poor? To homeless? Do people behave in a certain way according to their social class?

4. What would happen if we changed the character from 15 to 30 years old? To 90? To 6? Do people behave in a certain way according to their age?

Activity 3 *Cultural Characteristics*

1. Discuss the meaning of the 14 vocabulary words appearing in the chart on page 175 as defining characteristics. Evaluate whether they have positive or negative connotations, and whether they are absolute (the same standard for each country) or relative (different standards for each culture). For example, the term *punctual* varies from culture to culture. If you are invited to dinner at 6:00 P.M. in America, you should probably come at 6:15. On the other hand, in Middle Eastern countries you should arrive at 5:45. In Japan you should come at precisely 6:00 P.M. So, the concept of punctuality is relative rather than absolute.

2. Evaluate Americans according to your sensibilities and experiences; mark 1 (very), 2 (somewhat), or 3 (not very) in the boxes of the chart. Realize that any characteristic that you score a 2 is not a determining one for Americans.

3. Next, evaluate the people from your culture according to your sensibilities and experiences; mark 1 (very), 2 (somewhat), or 3 (not very) in the boxes. Realize that any characteristic that you score a 2 is not a determining one for the people from your country.

4. Finally, evaluate yourself; mark 1 (very), 2 (somewhat), or 3 (not very) in the boxes.

5. After you have filled in the chart, discuss it in small groups to find similarities and differences in your responses.

Cultural Characteristics			
Characteristic	Americans	People from Your Cultural Heritage	You
hurried			
efficient			
hospitable			
outgoing			
showy			
devious			
traditional			
polite			
punctual			
tolerant			
pushy			
friendly			
frank			
cosmopolitan			

Writing Assignments

 Write about Cultural Characteristics

1. On a separate piece of paper, write two short paragraphs: one that concentrates on Americans, and the other that concentrates on the people from your country. Discuss only the four or five most important characteristics (those you have scored 1 or 3), and give examples for each.

2. Write a comparison paragraph about the four characteristics that differ the most between Americans and people from your country. Again, use specific examples and explanations.

3. Find the points that describe *you* best, and write a paragraph in which *you* are the focus.

Building Your Skill in Understanding Poetry and Varying Perspectives

Activity 1 *"Lament"*

Read the poem below and answer the questions that follow.

Lament

by Edna St. Vincent Millay (1892–1950)

Listen, children:
Your father is dead.
From his old coats
I'll make you little jackets;
I'll make you little trousers
From his old pants.
There'll be in his pockets
Things he used to put there,
Keys and pennies
Covered with tobacco;
Dan shall have the pennies
To save in his bank;
Anne shall have the keys
To make a pretty noise with.
Life must go on,
And the dead be forgotten;
Life must go on,
Though good men die;
Anne, eat your breakfast;
Dan, take your medicine;
Life must go on;
I forget just why.

Source: *Collected Poems*, © 1921, 1948

1. Describe the *mood* of the poem. Does the mood change from the beginning to the end of the poem?

2. What is the significance of the last two verses: *"Life must go on;/ I forget just why."*?

3. How is the poet trying to cope with the death of her loved one?

Writing Assignment

How to Cope with the Loss of a Loved One

Write a paragraph (or a poem) in which you give advice on how to cope with the loss of a loved one.

Activity 2   *"To a Poor Old Woman"*

Read the following poem and answer the questions that follow.

To a Poor Old Woman

by William Carlos Williams (1883–1963)

munching a plum on
the street a paper bag
of them in her hand

They taste good to her
They taste good
to her. They taste
good to her

You can see it by
the way she gives herself
to the one half
sucked out in her hand

Comforted
a solace of ripe plums
seeming to fill the air
They taste good to her

Source: *Collected Poems: 1939-1962, Vol. II* © 1962

1. Is this poem happy or sad? Why?

2. What is the effect of the repetition of the line, "They taste good to her."?

3. Do plums have a symbolic value? What do they represent?

Writing Assignment

Write about a Common Object

Write a paragraph or poem in which you take a common object (as Williams does with plums) and make it the focus of your writing.

Activity 3   *"Good-Bye My Fancy!"*

Read the following poem and answer the questions that follow.

Good-Bye My Fancy!

by Walt Whitman (1819–1892)

Good-bye my Fancy!
Farewell dear mate, dear love!
I'm going away, I know not where,
Or to what fortune, or whether I may ever see you again,
So Good-bye my Fancy.

Now for my last-let me look back a moment;
The slower fainter ticking of the clock is in me,
Exit, nightfall, and soon the heart-thud stopping.
Long have we lived, joyed, caressed together;
Delightful-now separation-Good-bye my Fancy.

Yet let me not be too hasty,
Long indeed have we lived, slept, filtered, become really
    blended into one;
Then if we die together (yes, we'll remain one),
If we go anywhere we'll go together to meet what happens,
Maybe we'll be better off and blither, and learn something,
Maybe it is yourself now really ushering me to the true songs,
    (who knows?)
Maybe it is you the mortal knob really undoing, turning-so
    now finally,
Good-bye-and hail! my Fancy.

(1891)

Source: *Leaves of Grass*

1. Why is the poet leaving his beloved?

2. Do you think that he will actually leave?

Writing Assignments

Literary Format and Point of View

1. Change the poem into a letter written by the lover and sent to his (or her) beloved that explains the reasons why he (or she) is leaving.

2. Write a response to this poem from the point of view of the beloved. The poem should express that the beloved either cares a great deal about the departure, or that she (he) doesn't care at all.

UNIT 5.3

Building Your Skill in Understanding Points of View

Activity 1   *A Comparison of Two Restaurants*

The homework for this writing assignment may seem more pleasant than usual. It includes visiting and eating at two restaurants of your choice. Choose two that are similar in price so that the comparison is fair. To say that a restaurant whose prices are $25 for a main course is better than one that charges $9 for a main course is not fair to the restaurant with the lower prices.

Writing Assignment

Write a Restaurant Review

Write a restaurant review that compares the two restaurants you visit. Before you go to the restaurants, decide on your criteria for analysis and comparison. Make a list of possible points of comparison, and be perceptive during your visit. You might interview other diners to get their opinions on the quality of the place. If possible, go to the restaurant with a few people (perhaps other classmates, or else family or friends) so that you can try a variety of food and drinks. Have the others help you with your work. After all, this assignment is a combination of work and pleasure!

Imagine also that there are people who do this for a living. If you wish to read further on the subject before you write, a good place to turn is the restaurant review section of your local newspaper. Notice the points of analysis and the tone of the article. The review of Chap's Chophouse on pages 181–83, a restaurant in the vacation village of Vail, Colorado, is a good model.

Fine Dining Meets Rocky Mountain Eclectic

Grill & Chophouse Transforms the Cascade Resort

by Stephen Lloyd Wood

Daily Staff Writer

It's not often one finds a perfect balance between refined, world-class cuisine and bountiful, hungry-man fare. But amid Colorado High Country splendor and a rustic Western style dubbed Rocky Mountain Eclectic, that delicious, satisfying combination is réalité tous les jours at Grill & Chophouse, located deep within Vail Cascade Resort. Open since June, Chap's has quickly become perhaps the Vail Valley's hottest dining establishment, following a complete remodel of its predecessor, Alfredo's Restaurant.

Through the Cascade's grand entrance and tucked quietly behind the Resort's lively Lobby Lounge, guests are welcomed into a glowing, candle-lit dining room furnished with wrought iron fixtures, ample distressed-wood tables and cozy, horsehair-upholstered chairs and booths. Once the diners are seated, copper-backed menus present extensive fare, served on sturdy, blue-steeled flatware accompanied by Chap's distinctive steam-engine-sturdy pepper grinders, stemware and steak knives. Blue steel water pitchers and Mexican pottery serving dishes complete the eclectic mix. In spring, summer and fall, diners can enjoy it all amid views of Vail Mountain, fresh air and the roar of Gore Creek from an adjoining patio.

"It goes with casual elegance," says restaurant manager Russ Craney, acknowledging Alfredo's more formal atmosphere was a bit stuffy. "And the food speaks for itself."

Indeed. For starters, imagine Chap's succulent Seafood Sampler of oysters, jumbo shrimp, a chilled crab claw, clams, scallops and Maryland-style crabcakes so fresh they scream for lemon juice and a touch of fresh horseradish, cocktail sauce or the red wine mignonette; beer-battered Portobello Fries dripping with something sweet and spicy; or, perhaps the Restaurant's signature chowder, smoked pheasant soup, a warm, creamy lusciousness hiding under 'sweet potato hay.' If greens are your fancy, there's the Warm Spinach Salad, a charismatic Caesar, or an aromatic, fruity Gorgonzola pear creation.

Moving on to the main course, true carnivores are in for a treat. Those who prefer tradiional cuts can take on the Colorado rack of lamb, a 20-ounce, dry-aged T-bone steak, BBQ babyback pork ribs, the Double-Cut Pork Chop, or roasted chicken in lemon poultry jus.

Feeling exceptionally ravenous? Chap's offers prime-cut filet mignon or New York steaks in "suit-your-size" cuts ranging from 8 and 12 ounces, respectively, up to a far heftier, Texas-sized 40 ounces in more manageable 4-ounce increments.

What's a chophouse, you ask, without chops of regional game? Well, there's a tender, 16-ounce veal porterhouse or a lean but hearty 12-ounce buffalo ribeye. For a real taste of local bounty, however, one must indulge in the restaurant's signature dish, Chap's Colorado Trio. Featuring thick, delectable medallions of local lamb, elk and venison served with a tri-colored quinoa, parsnips and crisp veal bacon, the platter should satisfy the hunger and curiosity of any downstream diner, as well as the seasoned hunter with a quest for succulent game right off the hoof. Chap's selects only the choicest meats, Craney says, having employed more than two dozen people in blind taste tests before selecting cuts and suppliers. That's one reason the restaurant has been awarded a Four-Diamond rating by AAA, he adds, "the only one in Colorado for steakhouses."

Those with the desire for lighter fare can reel in the juicy Cast Iron Skillet Trout with creamy horseradish; seafood lovers can try Pacific Northwest salmon smothered in Bearnaise, oven-roasted Chilean sea bass in white butter or a pound of Alaskan king crab legs.

Chap's caters to vegetarians, too, with at least five entrees, including wild mushroom ravioli, a grilled vegetable torte and a steamed vegetable quinoa with risotto served in a "beggar's purse." "We've accommodated a vegetarian guest staying at the resort for five days," Craney says. "We try to cater to all dietary needs. That's another reason we received the Four-Diamond rating."

Of course no fine dining establishment is complete without a comprehensive wine collection. That's where the management of Chap's hopes its progressive list created by the resort's director of food and beverage, Ewell Sterner, and including wines from France, Italy, California, Spain and Colorado, distinguishes the chophouse from other restaurants. Independent of price, which can range from $24 to $1,700, milder wines precede the richer, full-bodied vintages. "To further demystify wine," Craney says, a unique, two-tiered, blued-steel wine flight can be brought to the table with samples of four of Chap's 40 house wines." Every waiter on the staff attends weekly Friday tastings, and is considered a true sommelier, ready to offer suggestions for any dining situation. For example, head waiter Luke Callaghan suggests a reasonably priced house wine of Sonoma vintage, the '96 Carmenet Moon Mountain Reserve, as the best wine with which to savor the Colorado Trio.

"Our team came up with the best wines, and our wait staff can recommend the best one for your meal," Craney says. "Talk to them; they know everything."

Dessert anyone? Don't leave the table without sharing the Mud Pie, an enormous offering of Ben & Jerry's mocha-fudge ice cream and macadamia nuts sandwiched between two huge Oreo cookies and topped with a to-die-for chocolate granache. Craney says it's designed so guests of the resort can take any remaining portions upstairs to enjoy later in their refrigerator-equipped rooms.

Of course a full selection of digestifs is available from the Lobby Lounge bar. A nice cognac, perhaps, served "a la Luke," with snifter tilting over a glass of steaming water, is the perfect finale.

Despite the eclectic elegance, one can enjoy dinner at Chap's without jeopardizing his or her credit rating. Prices for entrees range from $19 for the Colorado trout and $22 for ribs to $29 for the 20-ounce T-bone and $36 for the Colorado Trio. Appetizers cost from $6 to $12 (with the Seafood Sampler priced at $18 or $3.50 per piece) while salads range from $6 to $8. Family-style side dishes serving two, including fresh steamed asparagus or broccoli, sauteed garlic mushrooms, green beans and wild rice pilaf, are $5; and desserts "designed to share" are $6 each.

A 12-item children's menu for those under 12 years old includes $6 entrees ranging from make-your-own-pizza and New York Steak to sandwiches of the grilled cheese or "double-decker peanut butter" variety. Valet parking is provided free to Chap's diners, and a 20 percent discount is on offer to owners and guests of the Cascade's condominium properties.

The managers of Chap's say the decision to renovate Alfredo's, the resort's primary restaurant, was part of a multi-year, $18 million capital improvement plan. The Chap's concept was chosen, they add, to fill a void in fine steak and grilled food dining in the Vail Valley. Value, coupled with a superb dining experience, just may be helping give the chophouse quite a reputation beyond just the five-star resort's clientele.

"We're doing quite a lot of local business, too," Craney says, suggesting prospective diners make reservations, especially on weekends. Chap's also serves a buffet breakfast from 7 A.M. to 11 A.M. daily, as well as lunches with a lighter fare of salads, soups and sandwiches from 11:30 A.M. to 5:30 P.M. Dinner is served 5:30 P.M. to 10 P.M. A complete menu can be found online at www.ChapsChophouse.com.

Source: *The Vail Daily*

Activity 2   *Visions of the World*

Most likely, your grandmother and your grandfather had very different dreams and aspirations than you do. Their world was probably quite different from yours, and so were their goals.

Compare the way that your grandmother or your grandfather saw their place in the world and the way that you see yours. If you prefer, you can use your parents instead. Choose fundamental bases of comparison (i.e., educational goals, career plans, role in the family) and fill out the comparison chart below. After you complete the chart, select between structure 1 (direct comparison) and structure 2 (separated structure) to organize your ideas.

Writing Assignment

Write a Comparison Paragraph

Following the comparison chart closely, write a clearly organized paragraph on a separate piece of paper on the topic above that supports your points with specific examples.

Comparison Chart		
Points of Comparison	**Object of Comparison 1:** *Your Grandparent or Parent*	**Object of Comparison 2:** *You*

F. Graded Writing Assignment: Compare and Contrast Two Languages

There are probably many differences between English and another language you know. In a clearly written, well-organized paragraph on a separate piece of paper, compare and contrast the two languages.

G. Part 5 Summary

Based on your work in Part 5, answer and discuss the following questions.

1. Explain the differences between *direct comparison* and *separated structure* in the organization of comparison paragraphs.

2. Analyze the use of descending and ascending order in organizing support for paragraphs of comparison.

3. Review the process by which you arrive at the final bases of comparison.

4. Explain perspective and bias.

H. Reflections on Your Progress

Write your reflections or thoughts below on some of the writing you have done in Part 5.

1. Which were your two favorite journal entries, and why?

2. How did you enjoy the work on poetry?

3. What was the most interesting writing assignment, and why?

4. What was the least interesting writing assignment, and why?

5. What is the most important thing about writing you learned?

6. Were you satisfied with the progress you made in the assignments?

I. Part 5 Assignment Checklist

Assignment	Required or Optional	Grade	Revised	Returned and Filed
Write Comparison Charts (page 151)				
Write Sentences with Connectors (page 161)				
Four-Entry Journal Practice (Journal Activity) (page 168)				
Summarize an Article (page 172)				
Write about Cultural Characteristics (page 175)				
How to Cope with the Loss of a Loved One (page 177)				
Write about a Common Object (page 178)				
Literary Format and Point of View (page 180)				
Write a Restaurant Review (page 180)				
Write a Comparison Paragraph (page 184)				

J. Part 5 Journal Summary

Date of First Journal	Date of Last Journal	Number of Journal Entries Written for Part 5

PART 6

Persuasion Paragraphs

Suggested Journal Topics
for Persuasion Paragraphs

- Your opinion on capital punishment

- Is hunting a harmless sport or should it be banned?

- Should smoking be prohibited in all public places?

- Is it the responsibility of the government to take care of homeless people?

- Should divorce laws be stricter to make it more difficult for couples to separate?

- Does the violence shown on television have an effect on those who watch it?

- Should parents be blamed when their child commits a serious crime?

- Do you think that people should have the right to own guns?

A. Persuasion Paragraphs

The ability to form a definite opinion and to state it clearly, forcefully, and convincingly is the basis of the persuasion paragraph (or, when expanded, of the persuasion essay). This skill is essential in the academic world, because many professors test knowledge through essay questions that require students to state their opinion in an organized manner. Since these questions often must be written in class under time constraints rather than at home, it is particularly important to understand the structure for the persuasion paragraph. Organization probably constitutes the difference between a grade of B and A on the answer.

Opinions carry much more weight and are much more persuasive when they are supported by *objective* proof. Objective proof is generally accepted and seldom subject to discussion and disagreement. It includes statistics and data gathered from literature on a particular subject. For example, if writers wish to substantiate a claim that a particular region, such as the metropolitan area of Atlanta, Georgia, is overcrowded, they should use population data that may be found in an encyclopedia or on a county or state website on the Internet.

Objective proof is the most persuasive, but writers may also use their own experiences as the basis of *subjective* proof. Subjective opinions vary from person to person. For example, two people shopping for a car might have different opinions on price and quality. An affluent person may believe that a $60,000 Mercedes is affordable, whereas others with lower incomes may think that amount is too high. Similarly, two people might taste a particular dish and have different opinions regarding its quality. While one person thinks it is too salty, the other might think it is just right.

Before writing a persuasion paragraph, pause to consider the facts in the particular case. These paragraphs probably require more work in the prewriting phase than the other types of paragraphs considered in this text. It may be necessary to conduct research to find support for your opinion. The steps in writing persuasion paragraphs are:

1. Research the topic in the encyclopedia, on the Internet, in magazines, journals, or newspapers. Take notes.

2. Prepare and analyze a list of points that support your topic sentence (and your opinion).

3. Write an outline that includes any proof considered necessary to strengthen the argument.

4. Finally, and only after these steps, write the paragraph.

STRUCTURE OF THE PERSUASION PARAGRAPH

Verb Tense: Simple present

Order: According to the listing of reasons, advantages, benefits, methods, characteristics, etc.

Discourse Markers: *furthermore, in addition; moreover; first; second; third; one advantage is; another reason is; the third reason is that*

Structure: Below is a typical structure for a persuasion paragraph.

1. **Topic Sentence**

2. **Reason No. 1**

   a. Support (Why? So what?)

   b. Support (Specific examples or facts)

   c. Statistics or personal experience

3. Reason No. 2

    a. Support

    b. Support

4. Reason No. 3

    a. Support

    b. Support

5. Reason No. 4

    a. Support (Reason no. 4 may not be necessary if the first three provide enough material and support)

    b. Support

6. Conclusion

Exercise 1   Read this sample paragraph, and answer the questions that follow.

There are three reasons why I like to eat fast food. First, I am always in a rush, and I never have time to cook. Going to McDonalds or Burger King gives me the chance to have a hot meal without the work. I don't have to make a mess with the pots and pans or wash the dishes. Most people eat fast food once a week. I eat it more often, and my house always stays clean, especially my kitchen. Another reason why I like fast food is the variety. I can eat fast food every day without eating the same thing. For example, last week I went to McDonalds for a hamburger on Monday, pizza on Tuesday, Kentucky Fried Chicken on Wednesday, and Arthur Treacher's Fish and Chips on Thursday. Too many people think that you can only eat hamburgers if you go out to a fast-food restaurant. The third reason why I like fast food is the price. I don't have a lot of money to eat in fancy restaurants, so eating fast food is a good way to get a convenient meal without spending too much money or cooking by myself. I can eat a complete meal for less than $5. I know that the food I am eating is fresh, because they sell so much that it never sits around for too much time. These are the reasons why I like to eat fast food.

1. Trace the structure of the persuasion paragraph, using the outline given on pages 191 and 192.

2. Underline the discourse markers (transition words) used in this paragraph.

3. Analyze the quality of the support. Has the author stated the points clearly and forcefully? Are the reasons valid? Is there anything to question in terms of the support?

Writing Assignment

Write from Another Point of View

Suppose that you were asked to write a paragraph from the *opposite point of view*. Find four reasons why you *hate* fast food, and write a persuasion paragraph that supports your point.

Notice that in the persuasion paragraph, *all the reasons* presented must support your point. Do not introduce points that contradict your point of view. For example, in the paragraph that tells why you do not like fast food, you probably would not say there are health benefits to eating it. You should not allow the reader (or the listener in a persuasive speech) to find weaknesses in the consistency of your support and your argument.

B. Vocabulary Acquisition: Word Clusters

An excellent method to increase vocabulary is to practice word clusters based on a root. Here are three clusters using *-cide* (murder, killing), *-logy* (the study of), and *-archy* (government). Try to figure out the meaning of the words formed by combining the prefix with the suffix or root.

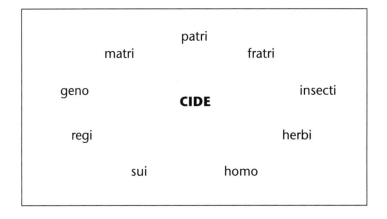

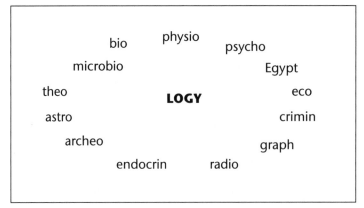

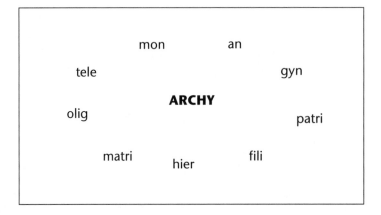

Exercise 2 Construct clusters for the following roots. Find as many words as you can that begin with the root, end with the root, or that have the root in the middle.

Root	Words That Begin with Root	Words That End with Root	Words with Root in the Middle
1. *psych* (mind)			
2. *vis* (to see)			
3. *spec* (to look at, see)			
4. *bio* (life)			
5. *sub* (under)			
6. *gen* (birth)			
7. *bene* (good)			
8. *mal* (bad)			
9. *ped* (foot)			

Root	Words That Begin with Root	Words That End with Root	Words with Root in the Middle
10. *ist* (someone who) [suffix]			
11. *ous* (full of) [adjective suffix]			
12. *intro* (in, inside)			
13. *poly* (many)			
14. *mono* (one)			
15. *gyn* (woman)			
16. *mania* (madness)			
17. *graph* (writing)			
18. *biblio* (book)			
19. *phil* (a lover of)			
20. *chron* (time)			

C. Grammatical Structures

Two common problems with punctuating are **run-on sentences** (where *independent* clauses are joined with only a comma instead of a period or a semicolon with a conjunction), and **sentence fragments** (where periods are used after *dependent* clauses). Fragments are not complete sentences.

Exercise 3   Correct the punctuation mistakes in the following sentences.

1. They exchange some jewelry, after that they are introduced to the family and friends, It is exciting.

2. This event usually takes place in the bride's house, all the relatives of the young couple are invited.

3. The clothes worn by the couple are special, the girl wears a long white dress, the man wears a suit.

4. The parents of the bride and groom are very proud on that day, everyone looks so nice.

5. On the day of the wedding everyone comes to the bride's house, they eat a special breakfast.

6. Sometimes the bride comes 20 minutes late to the church, the groom waits for her.

7. The bride throws a bouquet of flowers to all the women, the one who catches it will marry next.

8. The father of the bride dances with his daughter, this is one of the special moments of the day.

9. The bride and groom are not supposed to see each other on the wedding day before they meet in church, if they do it is supposed to be bad luck.

10. The house looks beautiful with all the flowers, everyone is dressed so nicely, too.

HW

Exercise 4   Correct the punctuation mistakes in the following sentences.

1. When the people come into the house, They immediately give their gifts to the bride and groom.

2. It is a special day, Because the bride and groom have been waiting for a long time, For the ceremony.

3. The first-time bride usually wears white, Because this is the color of purity.

4. She throws the bouquet Far across the room, And the person who catches it, Will get married next.

5. Every time I see a wedding, I remember my own ceremony, When all my friends came.

6. Many people get married when they are in their late twenties, Because they are already working.

7. Because they love each other, They try to do everything to make the ceremony wonderful.

8. It is a special day, And everyone is very excited, Because they love the bride and groom.

9. On the afternoon of the wedding, The mother-in-law dances with the groom. Who is very proud.

10. The music plays. When the bride walks down the aisle, Everyone stands up.

Exercise 5   Make up sentences that compare your car and someone else's car. Use the suggestions for adjectives and sentence structures below.

1. comparative adjective *(-er)*

2. equality *(as + adjective + as)*

3. comparative adjective (*more* + adjective + *than*)

4. *Although* S V , S V.

5. S V ; *on the other hand,* S V.

6. S V *but* S V.

Exercise 6   Find the mistakes in the following sentences and correct them.

1. There are too much cars because most of people think to drive a car is more convenient than take a bus when they want to go any places, so all most every adult has one car.

2. The pollution problem will be lessen if the department of transportation will do something about this.

3. Because it an independent country, Poland tries to build a new economical system, but changes from one system to another cost Poland a very high unemployment, a low productivity, a high prices of goods.

4. The most important of education in my country has not enough school and university.

5. Our country has separated South Korea from North Korea since 1950. It is one of the most serious problem in my country.

6. People drink for many reason but result is always the same. They have some health problem.

7. After they will work ten hours, they go to the movies tomorrow.

8. People not only visiting some places but also spending time at home.

Exercise 7   Circle the correct verb tense in the following sentences.

1. Carlos (has never flown, never flew) in a plane, and he does not plan to do so in the near future either.

2. After I (will finish, finish) my work, I will go to the movies.

3. Before (left, leaving) work, Jim called his mother.

4. Every day I (hope, am hoping) to learn more and more.

5. By the time I got home, my sister (had left, left).

6. When she walked into the room, the child (slept, was sleeping).

7. Whenever I see her, I (will give, give) her a big smile.

8. I (think, am thinking) about her every day.

9. By the time you get to class, the teacher (will leave, will have left).

10. Yesterday, while I (shaved, was shaving), the doorbell rang.

1. Tomorrow when she (wake) ___*wakes*___ up, she (call) ___*will call*___ her friend.

2. While I (study) ___*was studying*___, my brother (call) ___*called*___.

3. I demand that he (be) ___*be*___ fired. *subjunctive*

4. I believe that she (be) ___*is*___ a good friend.

5. Six years ago, I (come) ___*came*___ from Guatemala.

6. The doctor asked me if I (speak) ___*spoke*___ Russian.

7. Guana told him that she (go) ___*had to go*___ home early.

8. I (see, never) ___*have never seen*___ a fish that big.

9. The professor told me (study) ___*to study*___ harder.

10. When I saw the president, I (shake) ___*shook*___ his hand.

D. Writing Skills: Writing Evaluation

This evaluation form on page 202 might be used by instructors and students to quantify the errors encountered. The holistic scoring model (1–6) is used in many standardized entry tests such as the SAT2 Writing.

Writing Evaluation Form

Name: _____

Assignment: _____

Your paper contains errors in the following areas:

SENTENCE STRUCTURE AND USAGE	PARAGRAPH STRUCTURE
____ Subject/verb agreement	____ Clear topic sentence
____ Using articles correctly	____ Arranging sentences in logical order
____ Writing complete sentences that contain independent clauses	____ Using clear transitions
____ Using pronouns that clearly refer to nouns	____ Supplying enough examples, facts, or details
____ Ending sentences with a period or question mark	____ Supplying relevant examples, facts, or details
____ Expressing your ideas in English sentence patterns	____ Writing on the assigned topic
____ Sentence variety	____ Other errors
____ Spelling	
____ Verb tenses	
____ Using verb forms (participles, gerunds, infinitives) correctly	
____ Choosing words that express your ideas clearly	
____ Omitting words	
____ Word order	

SCORE

6 The writing is outstanding, perfect or nearly perfect, and the paper easily passes the exit examination.

5 The writing is very good, and the paper clearly passes the exit examination.

4 The paper passes the exit examination, but it is not outstanding or excellent.

3 The paper comes close but has too many mistakes to pass the exit examination; the writer must do a little better to pass the exam.

2 The paper clearly fails the exit examination; the writer must do much better work to meet passing standards.

1 The paper is on the wrong topic or impossible to understand or evaluate for some reason.

E. Journal Type 6:
The Memorandum Journal

In Jane Austen's novel *Emma* (1816), Mr. George Knightly, a British gentleman, carries a small notebook in which he records all kinds of useful and interesting information, from grain prices to herbal remedies. Today, businesspersons seeking more organization in their life sometimes carry electronic organizers or agendas (palm pilots) that remind them of appointments and that store information about such things as restaurants, hotels, books, and wines.

The memorandum journal (or its electronic counterpart) is an indication that writing is an art of remembering, and the act of writing is an attempt to make fleeting knowledge more permanent. Memorandum journals are particularly useful for recording interesting statistics and other data. When one reads, for example, that the best-selling non-fiction author of all time was Agatha Christie, whose 78 detective novels have sold more than 2 billion copies in 44 languages, it might serve a purpose to write this information down. It is interesting to note that Bollywood (Bombay, the movie center of India) produces more movies in a year (900) than the United States film industry does (300). In order to remember this information better, you might write it down in the memorandum journal.

The memorandum journal should be small enough to fit in the pocket, solid enough to last, and elegant enough to serve as the source of pride. Barnes and Noble and Border's Books both have a wide display of journals, many with beautiful covers. After buying the book, remember to carry it with you at all times. Whenever you come across interesting information— from lectures in school, on television and radio, in newspapers and magazines, and from friends—just write it down in the memorandum journal. After you have done this for a few weeks, take a few minutes to read the journal: it is often quite fascinating.

Journal Activity

Keep a Memorandum Journal

For the next two weeks, carry a memorandum journal with you at all times. When you read something interesting, when someone tells you something you didn't know, when you come across some information on television, the radio, or the Internet, write it down in the memorandum journal. At the end of two weeks, bring your journal to class and compare what you have written with your classmates' entries. Find the five most interesting points of information and explain them to the class.

Building Your Skill in Writing about Literature

Activity 1   *"Honey Boy": Analyzing Characters*

 Read "Honey Boy" and answer the questions about the story in two or three sentences each.

HONEY BOY

A Traditional Story of the American South

The old woman sat on the old couch in the steaming heat of an August afternoon in Bayou, Mississippi, which is about ten miles from the County line. She was all alone, and sat looking around at her old furniture and the frayed rug on the floor. She got up to sweep the dust around a little bit, then settled back into her favorite chair, the one with the faded yellow pillow that her Aunt Ivy had made so many years before. Everything was old and still. Even the flies on the window sill were too lazy to lift themselves from their resting place in the cool shade of the sash.

Everybody called her Mom, although she had only had one child. She got up slowly and moved to the center of the room to turn on her radio. It was a splendid radio, new, shiny, of glistening mahogany wood. It stood out even more because it was the only new thing in the whole house. But Mom didn't like it for that, she worshipped that radio because it had been a present from Honey Boy. She still remembered the day he had brought it two years before, riding down the dusty road with his hot rod, blowing the horn and yelling and singing, with his best friend Big Blue, his sidekick he called him, right by his side. They had made her close her eyes and stand there in the middle of that room while they carried it in, all shiny and bright, all the time laughing like little kids. Then they turned her around and around like ring-around-the-rosy in the second grade until she was all dizzy and faint. After that, they had made her open her eyes. Mom cried and cried and hugged Honey Boy and hugged Big Blue, and they had a celebration with iced tea and molasses cakes, and they sang and danced with Rudy Vallee and Eddie Cantor and laughed with Amos and Andy and Allen's Alley.

They called him Honey Boy because when he was born he had a big birthmark on his right shoulder that looked just like a beehive. Nobody knew his real name. Everybody liked Honey Boy because he was a good friend, a wild, uncontrollable sort in school but so genuine and unaffecting that even his teachers had a hard time scolding him. He was so full of life that he could never sit still. He was always squirming and plotting, he and Big Blue always, making big plans to get rich and take their mamas to live in big houses right in the middle of town.

Mom sat on the old couch that August afternoon watching the radio. She always said she "watched" the radio because she heard the voices and the music, but she saw Honey Boy's face on the front of the radio, with that big smile he always had. But when she heard the words "WANTED DEAD OR ALIVE," and then heard Honey Boy's name, she got up, turned the radio off, and began to wait. She didn't have to wait long. Just a few hours later she heard the car moving very slowly down the dirt road that led to Mom's house. It was moving so slowly that it sounded like it never wanted to get there. Mom knew. Mom waited. And a feeling of deep weariness came over her whole body, as if something was pressing down real hard on her.

The sheriff was the biggest man in the County, and the wooden steps creaked as he ascended. Despite his size, he could have the softest voice, just a little higher than a whisper, but everyone understood him just fine. You just had to look in his eyes to catch his meaning. His eyes told everything. The sheriff knew this, so sometimes he put on a pair of dark sunglasses. He had these on now, but when Mom came to the door, he took them off. His words were orderly:

"Hello, Mrs. Summers. Sorry to bother you. I hate to do this. But it's my job. I have to ask you to take a ride to the station house with me. It's official business. I wish you didn't have to. But it's official business."

Mom understood right away. Her face had no expression at all. She replied:

"All right sheriff. I just have to get my coat."

Now the sheriff didn't tell her that she didn't need a coat, in that great heat in August. Her dress was a little old, and had been mended in a few places. But she had a beautiful pink coat, spotless and new, that Honey Boy had given her one Sunday morning, as he came flying through town, ready to embark on a new adventure, and he promised her that he would come back rich and take her to live in a big house. With her new coat on, she was ready, and she accompanied the sheriff to the car.

On the way, the sheriff remained silent for a long time, and drove so slowly that you could count the weeds along the side of the road. Finally, he coughed a little, and began:

"Ma'am, I hate to have to do this, but I have to. You see, I have a dead body in my office, and they think it's Honey Boy. There was a $100,000 reward to turn in Honey Boy dead or alive, and Big Blue, he come struttin' in this mornin' and he say that he'd shot Honey Boy. For the reward. He wants the $100,000. So we need you to identify Honey Boy. You see, he was shot in the face, and we can't recognize whether it's him or not. So that's why I have to bring you out there. They say a mother always knows her son. I'm awful sorry. But it's official business, you understand."

When they pulled up in front of the station house, there was a big crowd of people, all talking and milling around. On the top step was Big Blue. He was telling a bunch of them what he was going to do with all his money.

Big Blue said:

"I'm going to buy myself a new car, and a house and some land. I'm going to buy myself some new clothes and get myself married, oh yeah."

But when Mom came slowly up the steps he hushed and bowed his head. She walked right up to him and said:

"Big Blue, how've you been. You've not been to the house lately. I've not seen you with my Honey Boy. Don't you like my iced tea anymore?"

Big Blue didn't say a word, but kept his head down.

The sheriff led Mom into the dusty station house. They moved slowly towards a small room in the back where on a table in the corner was a large mass covered with a bright white sheet. The sheriff apologized again:

"Ma'am, I'm terribly sorry to have to make you do this. But you understand. Now, I'm going to show you the body. As soon as you're sure, tell me."

Then the sheriff slowly peeled the sheet from the body, starting at the top of the head and unrolling oh so slowly down, past the disfigured, unrecognizable face to the broad shoulders. It seemed that he lingered a bit in this position, as they both looked at the beehive birthmark on the right shoulder. Mom did not make a sound, did not move. However, if you looked real close you might have been able to perceive a tiny tear welling up in the corner of one eye. Then the sheriff continued, moving down the chest, until Mom said softly:

"That's enough sheriff. I'm sure. I know now. You know that a mother always knows her son. That's not Honey Boy."

There was utter silence in the room. Neither person said anything. They just stood there looking at the whiteness of the sheet covering the body. Finally, the sheriff moved slowly towards her and said:

"Thank you ma'am. I'm real sorry. But you understand. It's official business. Thank you for your help. I'll take you home now. Could you wait in the car a moment?"

As Mom walked out the door, her face without a trace of emotion, the crowd outside hushed. She walked over to Big Blue and touched his face, and said to him:

"So long, Big Blue. Say hello to your Mama for me."

And she moved down to the car, opened the door and sat in the front seat and looked straight ahead at the dusty main street.

When the sheriff came out, the crowd suddenly came to life. Big Blue had a big smile on his face, and an expectant look in his eyes. The sheriff came over and said:

"Big Blue, put out your hand." He said: "Oooo eeee, sheriff. I can't wait to get that reward."

The sheriff continued, as if not hearing, "Big Blue, put out your other hand."

Big Blue went on, "Woooo, it's a powerful lot of money."

Just then the sheriff clapped the handcuffs on his wrist, and looked him right in the eye: "Big Blue, you're under arrest. For murder. Mrs. Summers has identified the body. It's not Honey Boy. You've killed an innocent man."

Big Blue just stared out, his eyes wide in amazement. Then he bellowed out: "What do you mean sheriff? Are you telling me I don't know my best friend? I killed my best friend! I killed Honey Boy!" He was still shouting as the sheriff led him away.

As the car rolled slowly down the dirt road leading to Mom's house neither spoke a word. It wasn't until he had brought Mom to the door, that the sheriff finally spoke: "Thank you ma'am. I'm just doing my job."

The old woman sat down on that old couch and looked around at her old furniture and the frayed rug on the floor. Now, in the calm of her sanctuary she looked at the glistening radio, which she never turned on again in her life, and started to cry very profoundly, to the accompaniment of a moan that sounded like a chant: "Oh, Honey Boy . . . Oh, Honey Boy . . . Oh, Honey Boy."

1. How does the author portray the mother?

2. How does the author portray the sheriff?

3. Give the main characteristics of Big Blue.

4. Did the sheriff act righteously?

5. Did the sheriff fulfill his duty?

6. How did Big Blue act?

7. Was Big Blue's action legal? Why or why not?

8. What is the setting of the story (time, place)?

9. Is the setting important to the story? Is it unique, or can the setting be transferred to other parts of the country and world and to other time periods? For example, could the setting be moved to Los Angeles in the year 2004?

10. Why does the sheriff accept the mother's lie?

Activity 2 *"Honey Boy": The Morality/Legality Matrix*

Fill in the matrix below. Indicate with a check mark whether you feel the action is moral, legal, or both.

Action	Moral?	Legal?
Honey Boys kills someone		
Big Blue kills Honey Boy		
Mom lies		
The sheriff accepts Mom's lie		
The sheriff arrests Big Blue		

Writing Assignment

"Honey Boy": The Moral and Legal Aspects

Based on the matrix, write a paragraph on a separate piece of paper in which you discuss the differences between the moral and legal aspects in "Honey Boy."

Activity 3 *"Honey Boy": The Projection Matrix*

Project the condition and actions of the characters after the end of the story. What are they doing?

Character	Projection of Conditions and Actions
Honey Boy	
Big Blue	
Mom	
The Sheriff (Will he get a promotion, a demotion, or will he remain in basically the same position?)	
Big Blue's Mother (hypothetical—with the premise that Big Blue receives quick capital punishment)	

Writing Assignment

Express an Opinion about the Mother's Actions in Honey Boy

The ending of "Honey Boy" may have come as a surprise. However, the actions of the mother are quite decisive and strong. She performs an act (lying to the sheriff) for several reasons. The results of her act probably will be quite severe. In fact, Big Blue has already been arrested by the time she sits down in the police car for her return trip home. What happens to Big Blue after she leaves is not told in the story. But we can imagine from the setting that he will probably be punished, perhaps even sent to jail for life or given capital punishment.

Write a persuasion paragraph on a separate piece of paper in which you agree or disagree with the mother's actions at the end of the story. State your case clearly, and support your opinions well. You might cite passages from the text to substantiate your beliefs. Begin your paragraph with one of these sentences:

I agree with the mother's actions for the following reasons.

I disagree with the mother's actions for the following reasons.

Building Your Skill in Analyzing Cultural Issues

Activity 1 *Military Service*

Many countries, such as Korea, Israel, and Italy, have mandatory military service in which every citizen of a certain age (usually between 18 and 25) must serve a certain period of time (one or two years) in the army. In Korea and Italy, the service is limited to men, while in Israel both men and women must serve. On the other hand, other countries, such as the United States and Japan, have eliminated compulsory military service and rely exclusively on a volunteer army.

Have you served in the armed forces? If so, talk about your experience; stress both the positive and negative aspects.

Writing Assignment

Should Military Service Be Compulsory?

What do you think about the issue? Do you feel that military service should be compulsory for every citizen? Or do you believe that military service should not be forced on those who do not want to enlist? In a clearly analyzed and well-structured paragraph written on a separate piece of paper, convince the reader of your opinion. Begin your paragraph with one of these sentences:

I feel that military service should be compulsory for the following reasons.

I do not believe that military service should be compulsory for the following reasons.

Activity 2 *Penalties for Drug Traffickers*

Read the passage below, and do the Writing Assignment that follows.

51 Drug Traffickers Executed In China

BEJING—Chinese authorities, struggling to combat a growing drug problem, executed 51 drug traffickers in a single day in the southern province of Guangdong.

Courts Tuesday also announced sentences for 219 other drug offenders, ranging up to a suspended death sentence, the Yancheng Evening News newspaper reported. These sentences can be commuted to life in prison for good behavior.

Mass sentencing rallies were held in 12 cities around the province, which borders the capitalist enclave of Hong Kong.

The execution included 26 people put to death in Canton, Guangdong's capital, among them a Hong Kong resident who bought 31 pounds of a stimulant. A Chinese farmer was executed for producing and selling 2.8 pounds of heroin.

Chinese authorities have admitted that the nation's drug problems are growing despite efforts to curb trafficking and use.

China borders the "Golden Triangle" countries of Thailand, Burma, and Laos, and drug lords increasingly are using southern China as a transport route to the West.

Guangdong's top judge, Mai Congkai, said Guangdong's drug traffickers' links with other provinces and foreign countries are growing, and the problem is spreading from urban centers into remote rural regions.

Source: The Associated Press

Writing Assignment

How Should Drug Traffickers Be Punished?

The penalty for drug trafficking described in the article is death for severe violations and long terms of imprisonment for lesser offenses. Penalties for drug offenders vary from country to country, but most of the punishment is given to those who sell, not buy, drugs. How do you feel about this matter? What penalties should be imposed on drug traffickers? Do you feel that the punishment described in the article is correct or too severe? Write a persuasion paragraph on a separate piece of paper and support your ideas.

VOCABULARY FROM THIS PASSAGE

drug trafficker	execute	transport route
sentence	commuted	urban
life	execution	remote
stimulant	curb	rural
Golden Triangle	drug lord	

Activity 3   *Life Expectancy*

There are many perceived or real differences between men and women, many of which are subject to debate. However, there is one incontrovertible fact: the life expectancy of a woman is longer than that of a man in every country in the world. In most cultures the difference is almost five years. The reasons for this phenomenon, though, are subject to conjecture. The article below introduces one opinion on the subject.

1. Read the article, and write a summary of its main ideas.

2. There are many adjective clauses or phrases in the article; underline them.

3. List any new vocabulary words; identify their part of speech and their meaning.

Writing Assignment

Write a paragraph in which you present your ideas on the topic; provide support for your thesis. Your paragraph might begin with the following sentence:

There are several reasons why women live longer than men.

The Male State of Mind Might Be the Cause of Lower Life Expectancy

Perhaps it is the fact that they smoke and drink more than women. Maybe it is their tendency toward reckless behavior, the dangerous activities they are involved in, the many work-related injuries suffered. Whatever the reason, men live shorter lives than women, both in the United States and in every other country in the world.

Another reason might be that men have a "Superman mentality," which means that they feel invulnerable. They generally hate going to their doctor, and in fact, when they do manage to go, they are reluctant to talk about their problems or ask significant questions.

Some doctors feel that men take better care of their cars or their computers than their bodies. "Many men change the oil in their car engine every three thousand miles. They change computers when they don't have enough power. As for monitoring their health, though, they just don't keep up," said Dr. Mark Schwartz, director of the Tristate Health Group and manager of Bergen Family Practice.

Government statistics indicate that men make 150 million fewer visits to the doctor each year than women do. Dr. Mark Ruttigliano, internist at New York Hospital, believes that men were more likely to wait to see the doctor until a less serious problem becomes severe or even life-threatening.

"When they are in their twenties, they think they are too powerful to require a doctor. In their thirties, they are much too busy. When they get to their forties, they are much too scared," Dr. John Schaeffer, Australian neurologist at the Hospital for Special Surgery pointed out.

Those who believe that the reason for men's shorter life span is linked to a harder working life might be surprised to learn that in the early 1900s, American women and men had the same life expectancy. No one is sure what has happened in the last 100 years to change the situation. Dr. Schwartz, who has tracked men's attitudes toward medical care, stated, "In order for men to gain those same extra years, they would have to change their habits."

Men do not check themselves for the warning signs of prostate cancer in the way women do for breast cancer. In addition, according to Dr. Ruttigliano, women are much more likely to discuss personal matters such as sexual health than are men.

Doctors agree that insurance companies must also pitch in to help all Americans increase their life expectancy by covering more preventive care expenses. In addition, employers might add wellness programs such as organized exercise, meditation and relaxation courses, and screening conducted by physicians and nurses right in the workplace. The idea is that the workplace is the major area where men spend most of their lives. Perhaps the doctors should be brought to the workplace if men will not go to their offices.

Activity 4   *Capital Punishment*

There are more than 20,000 murders every year in the United States, the most violent country in the world. Some people believe that capital punishment for criminals convicted of first-degree murder serves as a deterrent to other murderers who might think twice before committing the act because of the threat of death. On the other hand, others feel that capital punishment is a sign of a barbarian society that uses antiquated methods that are unsuccessful in handling the problem.

Writing Assignment

Write about Capital Punishment

Read the following statement, and write a paragraph on a separate piece of paper in which you agree or disagree with it.

Criminals who murder people should be killed and thus eliminated from society. Capital punishment is necessary in an increasingly violent society.

UNIT 6.3

Building Your Skill in Expressing Personal Opinions

Activity 3   *Machiavelli's Concept of Inherent Evil*

In 1513, Niccolò Machiavelli, an Italian diplomat exiled from his beloved city of Florence, wrote a revolutionary book, *The Prince.* In this work, Machiavelli gives advice to rulers on how to acquire and hold onto power. By separating politics from ethics, Machiavelli seeks to find practical solutions to the problems encountered by political leaders. His advice is based on the assumption that people are inherently selfish, and that if pressed by circumstances, they will show this trait and behave in an evil manner. Read the passage on page 215, and do the Writing Assignment that follows.

The Prince

by Niccolò Machiavelli

FROM CHAPTER XV

It now remains for us to consider what ought to be the conduct and bearing of a Prince in relation to his subjects and friends. And since I know that many have written on this subject, I fear it may be thought presumptuous in me to write of it also; the more so, because in my treatment of it I depart from the views that others have taken.

But since it is my object to write what shall be useful to whosoever understands it, it seems to me better to follow the real truth of things than an imaginary view of them. For many Republics and Princedoms have been imagined that were never seen or known to exist in reality. And the manner in which we live, and that in which we ought to live, are things so wide asunder, that he who quits the one to betake himself to the other is more likely to destroy than to save himself; since anyone who would act up to a perfect standard of goodness in everything, must be ruined among so many who are not good. It is essential, therefore, for a Prince who desires to maintain his position, to have learned how to be other than good, and to use or not to use his goodness as necessity requires.

FROM CHAPTER XVII

And here comes in the question whether it is better to be loved rather than feared, or feared rather than loved. It might perhaps be answered that we should wish to be both; but since love and fear can hardly exist together, if we must choose between them, it is far safer to be feared than loved. For it may be generally said that *people are thankless, fickle, false, eager to avoid danger, devoted to you while you are able to confer benefits upon them, and ready, while danger is distant, to shed their blood and sacrifice their property, their lives, and their children for you; but in the hour of need they turn against you.* The Prince, therefore, who without otherwise securing himself builds wholly on their professions is undone. For the friendships which we buy with a price, and do not gain by greatness and nobility of character, though they be fairly earned are not made good, but fail us when we have occasion to use them.

Moreover, people are less careful how they offend those who make themselves loved than those who make themselves feared. For love is held by the tie of obligation, which, because people are a sorry breed, is broken on every whisper of private interest; but fear is bound by the apprehension of punishment which never relaxes its grasp.

FROM CHAPTER XVIII

But since a Prince should know how to use the beast's nature wisely, he ought of beasts to choose both the lion and the fox; for the lion cannot guard himself from the toils, nor the fox from wolves. He must therefore be a fox to discern toils, and a lion to drive off wolves.

To rely wholly on the lion is unwise; and for this reason a prudent Prince neither can nor ought to keep his word when to keep it is hurtful to him and the causes which led him to pledge it are removed. If all people were good, this would not be good advice, but since they are dishonest and do not keep faith with you, you, in return, need not keep faith with them; and no prince was ever at a loss for plausible reasons to cloak a breach of faith.

. . . It is necessary, indeed, to put a good color on this nature, and to be skillful in simulating and dissembling. But *people are so simple, and governed so absolutely by their present needs, that he who wishes to deceive will never fail in finding willing dupes.*

Writing Assignments

Human Nature and Inherent Evil

1. Summarize Machiavelli's concepts on human nature. List the characteristics that he gives to people, and analyze how these traits affect their behavior.

2. Machiavelli is stating that people are basically inherently evil. Do you agree with this concept? In a clearly written, well-organized paragraph on a separate piece of paper, give your reactions to the ideas set forth by Machiavelli in the three excerpts from *The Prince*. Begin your paragraph with one of these sentences.

   I agree with Machiavelli that people are inherently evil for the following reasons.

   I disagree with Machiavelli that people are inherently evil for the following reasons.

Activity 2   *Desirable and Undesirable Jobs*

When you focus on a particular course of study in college, you choose a major. After you finish your studies and earn your degree, you will begin your career, a series of jobs at which you will work throughout your life. People choose careers for many reasons. Most are deeply interested in the field. Other reasons for the selection of a career are the working conditions, the potential for advancement, the salary, and the prestige attached to it. From the time that you are a small child, people constantly ask you, "What do you want to be when you grow up?" The choice of a career is one of the most important decisions in life.

Writing Assignments

Dream Job/Nightmare Job

Write two paragraphs, one that focuses on your dream job, and the other on what you would consider a nightmare job.

1. In a well-organized paragraph, describe your dream job on a separate piece of paper. Cite the characteristics of the job and the reasons why you think that it is desirable.

2. Describe a nightmare job that you would never do, even if you were paid an excellent salary. Cite the characteristics of the job and the reasons why you think it would be a nightmare.

F. Graded Writing Assignment: Write a Persuasion Paragraph on a Social Issue

According to recent studies, there are as many as 5,500 homeless people who live underground in train, bus, and subway stations in New York City. From data relating to the use of homeless shelters during the winter

months, it is estimated that there are between 25,000 and 30,000 homeless in the city. The sight of homeless people is unfortunately quite common in cities across the United States. Travel to a train station in Denver, a bus station in San Francisco, a park in Boston, or the beaches of Miami, and you will find many homeless people. Finding solutions to the problem is a complex task. Some feel that the government should intervene and offer assistance and alternatives to life on the street, including examining what has led people to live on the street. Others feel that the responsibility lies instead with the homeless people themselves. How do you feel about this situation? Agree or disagree with the following statement in a clearly organized persuasion paragraph on a separate piece of paper in which you take a position and support your decision.

It is the responsibility of the government to take care of the homeless people.

G. Part 6 Summary

Based on your work in Part 6, answer and discuss the following questions.

1. What is the difference between *subjective* and *objective* proof? Which is more effective in supporting a persuasion paragraph?

2. Summarize the structure of a persuasion paragraph.

3. How can outlining skills help to organize the paragraph of persuasion?

4. What is the goal of the persuasion paragraph? How do you achieve this goal?

H. Reflections on Your Progress

Write your reflections or thoughts below on some of the writing you have done in Part 6.

1. Which were your two favorite journal entries, and why?

2. What was the most interesting writing assignment, and why?

3. What was the least interesting writing assignment, and why?

4. What is the most important thing about writing you learned?

5. Were you satisfied with the progress you made in the assignments?

I. Part 6 Assignment Checklist

Assignment	Required or Optional	Grade	Revised	Returned and Filed
Write from Another Point of View (page 193)				
Keep a Memorandum Journal (Journal Activity) (page 203)				
"Honey Boy": The Moral and Legal Aspects (page 208)				
"Honey Boy": The Projection Matrix (page 208)				
Express an Opinion about the Mother's Actions in "Honey Boy" (page 209)				
Should Military Service Be Compulsory? (page 210)				
How Should Drug Traffickers Be Punished? (page 211)				
Why Women Live Longer Than Men (page 212)				
Write about Capital Punishment (page 214)				
Human Nature and Inherent Evil (page 216)				
Dream Job/Nightmare Job (page 216)				
Write a Persuasion Paragraph on a Social Issue (page 217)				

J. Part 6 Journal Summary

Date of First Journal	Date of Last Journal	Number of Journal Entries Written for Part 6

PART 7

The Essay

Suggested Journal Topics for Essay Writing

- Do you feel that space exploration should continue even after the Challenger and Columbia disasters and the profound cost of the program? Are there enough positive benefits to outweigh the negative aspects?

- Some critics have said that violent video games can lead to violent crimes because game players sometimes copy the behavior learned in the game and commit heinous acts. Do you agree with this? Research the topic, and write an essay in response.

- The second amendment to the U.S. Constitution grants every citizen the "right to bear arms." Do you believe that this right is still valid more than 200 years after the ratification of the Constitution?

- College athletes in the United States generate a great deal of money for their schools. Football games, for example, are attended by thousands of spectators, and television rights fees are enormous. Should college athletes be paid a salary in addition to receiving free tuition and free books?

- Discuss the issue of music file sharing and music piracy. Does downloading music files from the Internet and compiling CDs constitute theft?

A. The Essay

An **essay** is a series of paragraphs based on one topic analyzed from the point of view of the writer. While a paragraph develops the main point with supporting sentences, an essay develops the main idea with supporting paragraphs. The essay contains three principal parts: the **introduction**, the **body** or **interior paragraphs**, and the **conclusion.** In a typical essay, the introduction is the first paragraph, the body is composed of several paragraphs, and the conclusion constitutes the last paragraph.

The introductory paragraph attracts the reader with an interesting exposition of the subject. It also has a **thesis statement**, which presents and narrows the main idea of the essay, the central point to be developed. The thesis statement takes a broad topic and narrows or focuses it so that it can be managed in a five-paragraph essay. For example, the subject of the homeless is very broad. Thus, a thesis statement might narrow it to a discussion of the effects of weather on the homeless population in Miami: "The warm winter weather in Miami makes it an attractive place to be homeless."

The **body** or **interior paragraphs** of an essay present the facts, details, ideas, and examples that support the thesis statement expressed in the introductory paragraph. The length of the essay varies according to the topic and the purpose. While the specific number of interior paragraphs in the essay may vary, the standard academic essay in Composition I or Freshman English class has three. Each of these paragraphs has a topic sentence, a main idea, and supporting sentences. The paragraph usually consists of five to seven sentences.

In the **conclusion,** the writer summarizes the thesis statement and the main ideas of each paragraph in a forceful and interesting manner. In the conclusion, the writer tries to leave the reader with a memorable impression.

STRUCTURE OF THE ESSAY

Below is a typical structure for an essay.

1. **Introductory Paragraph**

    a. Attract Interest

    b. Thesis Statement

2. **Interior Paragraph 1**

    a. Topic Sentence

    b. Supporting Information

3. **Interior Paragraph 2**

    a. Topic Sentence

    b. Supporting Information

4. **Interior Paragraph 3**

    a. Topic Sentence

    b. Supporting Information

5. **Conclusion**

FOCUS, UNITY, SUPPORT, AND COHERENCE IN THE ESSAY

The essay must have a specific **focus,** or direction. One of the pitfalls in writing an essay is trying to write about a topic that is too broad. An unfocused essay lacks a common thread. The topic must be sufficiently narrowed for development in a limited space. An essay is not a chapter of a book. It has specific constraints in length.

The **unity** of an essay comes from the fact that all the details, fact, ideas, opinions, and examples presented should be directly related to the central point. Unrelated details and information are excluded. In addition, each paragraph has an internal unity, with a main idea that supports and develops the central point of the essay. Each paragraph also has a topic sentence. The three interior paragraphs of the five-paragraph essay serve as **support** for the central point. It is the goal of these paragraphs to prove the point and to verify the thesis statement.

Finally, there must be a logical progression of sentences and paragraphs in the essay, leading to **coherence.** The role of transitions in establishing coherence and unity is very important.

PROCESS FOR WRITING AN ESSAY

The following is the general process for writing an essay:

1. Prewriting	Think and plan for your writing. Brainstorm, collect information, organize your material, and write outlines for the work as a whole and for the individual paragraphs.
2. Draft	Use the ideas and outlines developed in the prewriting step. Use structures that are appropriate to your purpose.
3. Revision	Read over your draft. Decide what parts have to be improved. See if there are any further details needed.
4. Editing	Check thoroughly in the following areas: grammar, punctuation, and spelling. Use a dictionary, spell check, grammar check, and a grammar/style book.
5. Final Proof	Carefully reread the entire paper to be handed in.

B. Vocabulary Acquisition: Using the Dictionary

Exercise 1

It is important to be able to use the dictionary effectively to find the meaning of a word with several definitions. Use a dictionary and then give the following information about the word in boldface in each sentence: write the word; give the part of speech; indicate whether the word has a positive (+), negative (−), or neutral (=) connotation; choose the number of the correct definition from the dictionary; and write the correct definition in the space provided.

1. I got a flat tire when I hit the speed **bump** too hard.

   word:_____ **a.** part of speech _____

   b. pos/neg/neut_____ **c.** definition no. _____

   definition: _____

2. Don't **blame** me if you fail the test. I told you exactly what to study.

   word:_____ **a.** part of speech _____

   b. pos/neg/neut_____ **c.** definition no. _____

   definition: _____

3. The kids are destroying my beautiful garden. They ran through my bed of roses.

   word:_____ **a.** part of speech _____

   b. pos/neg/neut_____ **c.** definition no. _____

   definition: _____

4. Those apples are **bad.** I found them in the refrigerator. I bought them five months ago.

   word:_____ **a.** part of speech _____

   b. pos/neg/neut_____ **c.** definition no. _____

   definition: _____

5. He **chained** his bicycle to the tree, but the bicycle was stolen anyway.

word: _____   **a.** part of speech _____

b. pos/neg/neut_____   **c.** definition no. _____

definition: _____

6. That math problem was very **challenging**. It took me almost an hour to complete it.

word: _____   **a.** part of speech _____

b. pos/neg/neut_____   **c.** definition no. _____

definition: _____

7. She wore a **delicate** perfume that had the faintest hint of jasmine.

word: _____   **a.** part of speech _____

b. pos/neg/neut_____   **c.** definition no. _____

definition: _____

8. Sometimes my brother is incredibly **dense**. When I explain something, he doesn't understand.

word: _____   **a.** part of speech _____

b. pos/neg/neut_____   **c.** definition no. _____

definition: _____

9. The doctor seemed **cold** when she explained the diagnosis, but in reality she cared a great deal about her patient's condition.

word: _____   **a.** part of speech _____

b. pos/neg/neut_____   **c.** definition no. _____

definition: _____

10. She **fished** around for her keys in her bag, but she couldn't find them.

word: _____   **a.** part of speech _____

b. pos/neg/neut_____   **c.** definition no. _____

definition: _____

11. That restaurant is a success. It was so **packed** that we had to wait an hour to eat.

word:_____ **a.** part of speech _____

b. pos/neg/neut_____ **c.** definition no. _____

definition: _____

12. Alex knows Tommy Hilfiger **personally.**

word:_____ **a.** part of speech _____

b. pos/neg/neut_____ **c.** definition no. _____

definition: _____

13. Farmer Johnson is a rich man. He **raises** livestock and has ten types of cows.

word:_____ **a.** part of speech _____

b. pos/neg/neut_____ **c.** definition no. _____

definition: _____

14. She is **rather** tall for her age. In fact, she is the tallest girl in the third grade.

word:_____ **a.** part of speech _____

b. pos/neg/neut_____ **c.** definition no. _____

definition: _____

15. In the summer, it seems that you can only watch **repeats** on television.

word:_____ **a.** part of speech _____

b. pos/neg/neut_____ **c.** definition no. _____

definition: _____

16. I heard a **report,** and I was so afraid that I ran and called the police.

word:_____ **a.** part of speech _____

b. pos/neg/neut_____ **c.** definition no. _____

definition: _____

17. Please **return** the three books that you borrowed from me.

word:_____ **a.** part of speech _____

b. pos/neg/neut_____ **c.** definition no. _____

definition: _____

18. I have a very bad toothache. My tooth is very **sensitive** when I eat ice cream.

word:_____ **a.** part of speech _____

b. pos/neg/neut_____ **c.** definition no. _____

definition: _____

19. I have read that religious laws are **strictly** interpreted in that country.

word:_____ **a.** part of speech _____

b. pos/neg/neut_____ **c.** definition no. _____

definition: _____

20. The government is **taxing** the citizens too much. There is talk of a revolution.

word:_____ **a.** part of speech _____

b. pos/neg/neut_____ **c.** definition no. _____

definition: _____

21. In the summer, I love to sleep on the **terrace.**

word:_____ **a.** part of speech _____

b. pos/neg/neut_____ **c.** definition no. _____

definition: _____

22. If the Chicago Cubs beat the Yankees in the World Series, it would be an **upset.**

word:_____ **a.** part of speech _____

b. pos/neg/neut_____ **c.** definition no. _____

definition: _____

23. The **youth** was arrested by the police. They also caught his uncle, the ringleader.

word:_____ **a.** part of speech _____

b. pos/neg/neut_____ **c.** definition no. _____

definition: _____

24. Sunday was wonderful. I **zipped** right over the bridge in five minutes.

word:_____ **a.** part of speech _____

b. pos/neg/neut_____ **c.** definition no. _____

definition: _____

25. I would love to **while** away the summer just reading long novels on the beach.

word:_____ **a.** part of speech _____

b. pos/neg/neut_____ **c.** definition no. _____

definition: _____

26. Tom was **dead** after he worked 16 hours at the mall.

word:_____   **a.** part of speech _____

b. pos/neg/neut_____   **c.** definition no. _____

definition: _____

27. They asked Maria to **monitor** her younger brother's activities.

word:_____   **a.** part of speech _____

b. pos/neg/neut_____   **c.** definition no. _____

definition: _____

28. The frustrated man could not **program** his VCR, even after reading
the manual.

word:_____   **a.** part of speech _____

b. pos/neg/neut_____   **c.** definition no. _____

definition: _____

29. That approach to the problem is **novel**. I have never heard anything
like it before.

word:_____   **a.** part of speech _____

b. pos/neg/neut_____   **c.** definition no. _____

definition: _____

30. The coach thought he got a raw **deal** when he was fired after the team
lost the championship game.

word:_____   **a.** part of speech _____

b. pos/neg/neut_____   **c.** definition no. _____

definition: _____

C. Grammatical Structures: Adjective Clauses

If you open a newspaper, you will find that one of the most common grammatical forms used in the **adjective clause.** In the complex sentence, the adjective clause goes immediately after the noun it modifies. Thus, it may be placed after the subject or after the object. Adjective clauses are often introduced by relative pronouns that link the noun to be described with the verb of the adjective clause. In the sentence *Rosa saw a man who was wearing a large Panama hat,* the word **who** is a relative pronoun linking *man* with *was wearing.* The following is a presentation of the forms of adjectives clauses.

FORMS OF ADJECTIVE CLAUSES

Typical Structure of Adjective Clauses	
Structure	Examples
1. **who, that,** (and sometimes **which**) as the subject of the adjective clause	Mary Johnson, who works in a pet store, loves dogs more than people. The cold pizza that I had for breakfast was not very good.
2. **who, whom, that, which** as the object of the adjective clause	He is the man who the dog bit on the leg. The woman whom I dated had a diamond in her navel. The hamburger that Sal ate was very rare. The book, which Catalan bought for class, was the wrong one.
3. **when** followed by subject and verb	I will never forget the day when he stole his mother's wig. That was the year when I started teaching at this college.
4. **where** followed by subject and verb	Paris is the place where lovers whisper in each other's ears. Venezuela is the country where even the cats are beautiful.

Typical Structure of Adjective Clauses *(continued)*	
Structure	**Examples**
5. **whose** followed by a noun	Robert Jons, whose nose is enormous, causes problems when he sneezes.
	I could love a person whose bank account was small.
6. **(quantity word)** + **whom** or **which** (one of whom, several of whom, two of which)	He has read three books, one of which he borrowed from an old woman.
	I have two brothers, one of whom lives in San Francisco.
7. **which** to modify the whole sentence	His cat had seven kittens, which made his one-room studio very crowded.
	Jesse Ventura became governor of Minnesota, which was a happy occasion for wrestling fans.

REDUCING AN ADJECTIVE CLAUSE TO AN ADJECTIVE PHRASE

Structure	**Examples**
1. If there is a **be** verb in the adjective clause, eliminate the subject and the **be** verb.	Jack, who is the president of the club, was arrested yesterday.
	Jack, the president of the club, was arrested yesterday.
2. If there is no **be** verb in the adjective clause, eliminate the subject of the clause and change the verb to **-ing.**	I have an apartment that overlooks the golf course.
	I have an apartment overlooking the golf course.

PUNCTUATING ADJECTIVE CLAUSES

Structure	Examples
1. If the information is necessary for identification, **do not** place a comma in the sentence.	The man who married Jane often invites himself to my house for dinner. The policeman shot the man who had robbed the bank. The elephant that I saw at the zoo yesterday was a filthy mess.
2. If the information is **not** necessary for identification, place a comma in the sentence.	Prof. Meyers, who teaches biology, loves to work late. My cousin is married to Bill Johnson, who has never had a job in his life.
3. Adjective clauses that identify categories of fruits, vegetables, animals, meats, etc., are set off by commas.	Rice, which is grown in China, is a staple food. Ducks, which make loud noises, can fly, swim, and waddle. Boswana cannot eat pork, which comes from a pig.
4. Adjective clauses that identify specific fruits, vegetables, animals, meats, etc., are not set off with commas.	The banana that she ate was brown instead of yellow. The chicken whose neck she twisted tasted wonderful for dinner. The turkey that I will eat for Thanksgiving is now running happily around the barnyard. The alligator that I saw in Florida last year is now part of my mother's shoes.
5. When the adjective clause describes the general idea expressed in the independent clause, a **comma** and **which** are used.	Dick won the lottery, which made him a rich man. The plane was late, which meant that we missed our connecting flight. The movie theatre in Des Moines closed early because of the snow, which meant that we took the 90-minute trip for nothing.

Exercise 2   Place a comma in the following sentences, if necessary.

1. The elk that I ate for dinner last night was very tasty.

2. Dogs which are the most loyal of all animals sniff the bushes.

3. Rice which is the staple food in Korean cooking is rarely eaten in France.

4. The rice that your mother made tasted like glue.

5. Professor Balango whose students dislike him doesn't prepare for class.

6. I have fond memories of my hometown which is located near a waste dump.

7. We took a trip to Brooklyn where they speak very colorful English.

8. The town in which Giacomo lives is quaint and beautiful.

9. Joanna's husband left for good which caused her to celebrate for four days.

10. I fell in love with the woman who was wearing the army uniform.

Exercise 3   Complete the following sentences, using adjective clauses. Punctuate carefully.

1. I would never marry a person _____.

2. My brother, whose _____.

3. President Bush _____.

4. She passed the test _____.

5. I never talk to people _____.

6. I will never forget the time _____.

7. She will always remember the restaurant _____.

8. Jan has three brothers, one of _____.

9. I have two cars, one of _____.

10. The cat _____.

11. The policemen arrested the man _____.

12. I called my sister Joan _____.

13. I will never forget my trip to Hawaii _____.

14. I want to tell you about the place _____.

15. Mosquitoes _____.

Exercise 4   Combine the two sentences into one, using the second as the adjective clause.

   1. In the early 19th century, Venezuela achieved independence. Simon Bolivar was born in Venezuela.

   2. Germany is now a unified country. It had been divided into East and West in 1945.

   3. Sudan is the largest country in Africa. Its population is 121 million.

   4. Thailand has never been ruled by a foreign power. It is located in southeast Asia.

   5. There are six principal dialects of Spanish. Spanish is the official language of 12 South American countries.

   6. Ranjett's mother won two tickets to travel anywhere in the continental United States. This made her very happy.

   7. My brother has never visited a place as exotic as Tahiti. He is a dentist.

IDENTIFYING ADJECTIVE CLAUSES AND PHRASES

A good exercise to practice adjective clauses and phrases is to identify them in newspapers, where they are used at the rate of at least 15 per page.

You should recall that a clause has both a subject and a verb while a phrase is simply a group of words. Adjective phrases are often used in apposition to describe the subject's job or title. In the sentence *Bill Gates, founder of Microsoft, earns more in one month than I will earn in my whole life,* the words following "Bill Gates" and the comma constitute an adjective phrase. If a verb is used in an adjective phrase, it is usually in the gerund *(-ing)* or past participle form *(-ed).*

The following is a list of hints that will help you to identify adjective clauses and phrases.

Adjective Clauses and Phrases	
Hint	**Examples**
1. Look for a **name of a person, place,** or **company followed by a comma** in either the subject or the object position. The words that follow usually indicate the person's job or position. If the word *who* appears after the comma, it will be an *adjective clause.* If instead the words *a* or *the* appear after the comma, it will be an *adjective phrase.* The title may come first, followed by a comma and the person's name.	*Adjective Phrases* **Anthony Trahar, the new chief executive officer of Anglo American, is 63.** **Afeni Shakur, the mother of rapper Tupac Shakur, was a member of the Black Panthers.** **The commission approved a design by the French architect, Jean Nouvel, for a new hotel.** **The stock price of Aetna, the nation's largest health insurer, dropped more than 17 percent.** *Adjective Clauses* **Mia Hamm, who is the world's most famous female soccer player, played in Chicago.** ***Lulu* is a play by Frank Wedekind, who based the story on the life of a dancer.** **Woodstock, New York, where the famous 1969 concert was held, is fighting gentrification.**
2. For **adjective clauses,** look for nouns followed by the relative pronouns *who, that, which, where, when,* and *whose.*	**Officials in Detroit, which has one of the nation's highest homicide rates, are perplexed.** **Kmart has received hundreds of e-mail messages that demand price reductions.** **Senators met at Finnegan's Restaurant, where politicians have met for two generations.** **The Clair Memorial Church was built at a time when the city was rapidly expanding.**

Adjective Clauses and Phrases *(continued)*	
Hint	Examples
3. For **adjective phrases**, look for nouns followed by past or present participles.	Clair Memorial was the first church *built* in Jersey City by a black congregation.
	The lawyer *appearing* on behalf of Ms. Belon said that his client would fight the charge.
	The woman *killed* in the incident was the mother of three.
	The object *stolen* from the museum was found to be a mummy from ancient Egypt.
	A cook *using* hot chili peppers might wish to add oranges to mitigate the spiciness.

Exercise 5 Read the article on pages 237–38 and underline as many adjective clauses or phrases as you can. Then find three articles of interest from the newspaper. Underline as many adjective clauses and phrases as you can from each article. Bring the articles to class, and exchange them with your classmates. See if you can find even more adjective clauses and phrases.

Run DMC DJ Gunned Down in New York

NEW YORK (Oct. 31) -Jam Master Jay, a founding member of the pioneering rap trio Run DMC, was shot and killed at his recording studio near the New York neighborhood where he grew up, police said.

Two men were buzzed into the second-floor studio shortly before shots were fired inside its lounge at 7:30 p.m. on Wednesday, police said. As of early Thursday, police had made no arrests.

The 37-year-old disc jockey, whose real name was Jason Mizell, was shot once in the head in the studio's lounge and died at the scene, said Detective Robert Price, a police spokesman.

Urieco Rincon, 25, who was not a member of Run DMC, was shot in the leg, police said.

About five other people in the studio at the time were not hurt.

"Rest in Peace Jam Master," Run DMC's official Web site read early Thursday, underneath a picture of Mizell.

Mizell served as the platinum-selling group's disc jockey, providing background for singers Joseph Simmons, better known as Run, and Darryl McDaniels, better known as DMC.

The group is widely credited with helping bring hip-hop into music's mainstream, including the group's smash collaboration with Aerosmith on the 1980s standard "Walk This Way" and hits like "My Adidas" and "It's Tricky."

"We always knew rap was for everyone," Mizell said in a 2001 interview with MTV.

"Anyone could rap over all kinds of music."

Mizell is the latest in a line of hip-hop artists to fall victim to violence. Rappers Notorious B.I.G. and Tupac Shakur were murdered within seven months of each other in 1996 and 1997—crimes that some believe were the result of an East Coast–West Coast rap war.

But Run DMC and their songs were never about violence. The group promoted education and unity.

In 1986, the trio said they were outraged by the rise of fatal gang violence in the Los Angeles area. They called for a day of peace between warring street gangs.

"This is the first town where you feel the gangs from the minute you step into town to the time you leave," Mizell said at the time.

Mizell's friends and fans gathered near the studio, located above a restaurant and a check-cashing business. The crowd included many people from the Hollis section of Queens, where the members of Run DMC grew up.

"They're the best. They're the pioneers in hip hop," said Arlene Clark, 39, who grew up in the same neighborhood. "They took it to the highest level it could go."

Chuck D, the founder of the hip-hop group Public Enemy, blamed record companies and the advertising for perpetuating "a climate of violence" in the rap industry. "When it comes to us, we're disposable commodities," he said.

Doctor Dre, a New York radio station DJ who had been friends with Mizell since the mid-1980s, said, "This is not a person who went out looking for trouble. . . . He's known as a person that builds, that creates and is trying to make the right things happen."

Leslie Bell, 33, said the band members often let local musicians record for free at the studio, and had remained in Queens to give back to the community.

"He is one great man," said Bell. "As they say, the good always die young."

Publicist Tracy Miller said Mizell and McDaniels had planned to perform in Washington, D.C., on Thursday at a Washington Wizards basketball game. Mizell had performed on Tuesday in Alabama, she said.

Mizell was married and had three children, she said.

Run DMC released a greatest-hits album earlier this year. In 2001, the rappers produced "Crown Royal," breaking an eight-year silence.

Source: The Associated Press

D. Writing Skills: Symbolism and Figurative Language

Symbols have meaning generally agreed upon by a culture. Colors, characters, objects, and actions sometimes represent something other than their literal value. For example, a flag is a piece of cloth with different colors. However, those colors and that flag represent a specific country, which we may love or fear. When people wave a flag, it has a symbolic meaning. If they burn it, this action has another symbolic meaning. When the flag is placed across the casket of a soldier who has died in battle, it has yet another symbolic meaning.

Exercise 6 Symbols sometimes vary from culture to culture. For example, at funerals in America, people generally wear black to show respect for the dead. Wearing white or bright colors would be a sign of disrespect. On the other hand, people in Korea wear white clothes at funerals. Write your thoughts about the symbolic meaning of the words and phrases below.

Symbolic Colors

yellow _____

black _____

white _____

red _____

blue _____

green _____

purple _____

orange _____

Symbolic Characters

a police officer _____

a postal worker _____

the Pope _____

the President of the United States _____

the Queen of England _____

an old man _____

a soldier _____

a baby _____

Symbolic Objects

a wedding ring _____

a mink coat _____

blood _____

the moon _____

a cross _____

ashes _____

a Christmas tree_____

fire _____

water _____

a heart _____

the sun _____

red roses (white roses) _____

a snake_____

the American flag _____

Symbolic Actions

catching the bouquet at a wedding _____

exchanging rings _____

giving two thumbs up _____

giving the middle finger _____

carrying the bride over the threshold _____

pouring water at a baptism _____

throwing dirt on a coffin _____

breaking a glass at a Jewish wedding _____

offering a seat to another person _____

sitting at the head of the table _____

Writing Assignment

A Personally Meaningful Symbol

On a separate piece of paper, describe the physical nature of some personal symbol so that it becomes real for your reader. Tell how this symbol acquired meaning for you, whether through tradition, culture, competition, marriage, crisis, or traumatic experience. Analyze the values associated with the symbol and why it remains in your mind. Finally, tell whether the symbol has changed meaning over time or if it has retained the same significance for you.

E. Journal Type 7: The Essay as Journal Entry

As you move from one paragraph to the five-paragraph essay, it is important to expand your reading to include writers of essays and editorials. Editorials are found on the last page of the news section of newspapers, as well as the last page of national news magazines such as *Time, Newsweek,* and *U.S. News and World Report.* The essay or treatise presents a personal opinion on a particular topic such as politics, sociology, economics, psychology, or criminology. It may be the result of empirical knowledge (learned through experience or, in science, through trial-and-error) or research.

One of the best-known essayists was Henry David Thoreau, who is most famous for *Walden Pond, or Life in the Woods* (1846). In *Walden* he describes an experiment during which he lived by himself in a small cabin that he built on a New England pond. His celebration of nature, the poetry of the seasons, and the untainted natural world is a last crying out to a nation on the verge of the industrial revolution. His essays are provocative: he commands attention in the form of agreement or disagreement. When he states in his essay "Walking" about those who stay indoors all day to work—"I think that they deserve some credit for not having all committed suicide long ago"—he is offering a challenge. As our lives become increasingly sedentary, Thoreau's message takes on increased force.

Walking

by Henry David Thoreau

I have met with but one or two persons in the course of my life who understood the art of Walking, that is, of taking walks,—who had a genius, so to speak, for *sauntering.*

I think that I cannot preserve my health and spirits, unless I spend four hours a day at least—and it is commonly more than that—sauntering through the woods and over the hills and fields, absolutely free from all worldly engagements. When sometimes I am reminded that the mechanics and shopkeepers stay in their shops not only all the forenoon, but all the afternoon, too, sitting with crossed legs, so many of them—as if the legs were made to sit upon, and not to stand or walk upon—I think that they deserve some credit for not having all committed suicide long ago.

I, who cannot stay in my chamber for a single day without acquiring some rust, and when sometimes I have stolen forth for a walk at the eleventh hour or four o'clock in the afternoon, too late to redeem the day, when the shades of night were already beginning to be mingled with the daylight, have felt as if I had committed some sin to be atoned for,—I confess that I am astonished at the power of endurance, to say nothing of the moral insensibility, of my neighbors who confine themselves to shops and offices the whole day for weeks and months, ay, and years almost together. I know not what manner of stuff they are of—sitting there now at three o'clock in the afternoon, as if it were three o'clock in the morning. I wonder that about this time, or say between four and five o'clock in the afternoon, too late for the morning papers and too early for the evening ones, there is not a general explosion heard up and down the street, scattering a legion of antiquated and housebred notions and whims to the four winds for an airing—and so the evil cure itself.

Source: "Walking" in *Essays English and American*

Journal Activity

The Internet Surfing Journal

The art of *sauntering* as Thoreau describes it implies walking for the sheer enjoyment of the exercise and the joy of wonderful things encountered. In our age, people can saunter in a completely different manner, without venturing into the fields and woods; in fact, they do not even have to leave their homes. Through the Internet, it is now possible to move among wonderful new things. The concept of *surfing* the Internet may be seen as an electronic equivalent to Thoreau's *sauntering.* There are many similarities between the two activities.

Just as Thoreau recorded his observations of nature discovered during his walks, it is possible to keep an Internet Surfing Journal that records the interesting places visited during a session on the World Wide Web. For this Journal Activity, keep this type of journal. You can do it in the form of a memorandum journal as discussed in Part 6 on page 203, which keeps a record of surfing activity, or in the form of essays evolved from a reading of topics found on the Internet.

After you have finished with your Internet Surfing Journal, list the most interesting websites that you have visited in the last few weeks. Did you find any ESL sites? Have you visited the ESL Café? What other sites would you recommend to your classmates? Prepare a list of great websites, and bring it to class. Share the list with your classmates and your teacher.

UNIT 7.1

Building Your Skill in Literary Analysis

Activity 1   *"The Tell-Tale Heart"*

Reading and understanding literature are essential critical-thinking skills. Because literary language is both figurative and literal, sometimes deciphering meaning is a difficult task. To comprehend literature, you must first analyze the components of fiction. *Setting* is the time and place in which the action occurs. The *characters* are the people in the piece. *Style* is the way the author writes, and the *plot* is the sequence of actions that make up the story. The plot should have *complication, surprise,* and a *climax,* the most interesting and exciting part of the story. Finally, there is the *theme* of the piece, what the story is really about. The **plot** of "Honey Boy," for example, involves a man (Big Blue) who shoots his best friend for a reward, the mis-identification of the victim by his mother, and the arrest of Big Blue by the sheriff. The **themes,** on the other hand, are the sweetness of a mother's revenge; the betrayal of trust by a friend; and the concepts of justice, morality, and retribution. In this section of the text, you will read three short stories by famous American writers: Edgar Allan Poe, O. Henry, and Ernest Hemingway. Each passage will be followed by exercises and a text-based writing assignment that requires you to relate to the themes introduced in the stories.

Read "The Tell-Tale Heart." Then answer the questions on pages 247 and 248.

The Tell-Tale Heart

by Edgar Allan Poe

True!—nervous—very, very, dreadfully nervous I had been and am; but why *will* you say that I am mad? The disease had sharpened my senses—not destroyed—not dulled them. Above all was the sense of hearing acute. I heard all things in the heaven and in the earth. I heard many things in hell. How, then, am I mad? Hearken! And observe how healthily—how calmly I can tell you the whole story.

It is impossible to say how first the idea entered my brain; but once conceived, it haunted me day and night. Object there was none. Passion there was none. I loved the old man. He had never wronged me. He had never given me insult. For his gold I had no desire. I think it was his eye! Yes, it was this! He had the eye of a vulture—pale blue eye, with film over it. Whenever it fell upon me, my blood ran cold; and so by degrees—very gradually—I made up my mind to take the life of the old man, and thus rid myself of the eye forever.

Now this is the point. You fancy me mad. Madmen know nothing, but you should have seen me. You should have seen how wisely I proceeded—with what caution—with what foresight—with what dissimulation I went to work! I was never kinder to the old man than during the whole week before I killed him. And every night, about midnight, I turned the latch of his door and opened it—oh so gently! And then, when I had made an opening sufficient for my whole head, I put in a dark lantern, all closed, closed, so that no light shone out, and then I thrust in my head. Oh, you would have laughed to see how cunningly I thrust it in! I moved it slowly—very, very slowly, so that I might not disturb the old man's sleep. It took me an hour to place my whole head within the opening so far that I could see him as he lay upon his bed. Ha!—would a madman have been so wise as this? And then, when my head was full in the room, I undid the lantern cautiously—oh, so cautiously—cautiously (for the hinges creaked)—I undid it just so much that a single thin ray fell upon the vulture eye. And this I did for seven long nights—every night just at midnight—but I found the eye always closed; and so it was impossible to do the work; for it was not the old man, who vexed me, but his Evil Eye. And every morning, when the day broke, I went boldly into the chamber, and spoke courageously to him, calling him by name in a hearty tone, and inquiring how he had passed the night. So you see, he would have been a very profound old man, indeed, to suspect that every night, just at twelve, I looked upon him while he slept.

Upon the eighth night I was more than usually cautious in opening the door. A watch's minute hand moves more quickly than did mine. Never before that night, had I felt the extent of my own powers—of my sagacity. I could scarcely contain my feelings of triumph. To think that there I was, opening the door, little by little, and he not even to dream of my secret deeds or thoughts. I fairly chuckled at the idea; and perhaps he heard me; for he moved on the bed suddenly, as if startled. Now you may think that I drew back—but no. His room was as black as pitch with the thick darkness, (for the shutters were close fastened, through fear of robbers) and so I know that he could not see the opening of the door, and I kept pushing it on steadily, steadily.

I had my head in, and was about to open the lantern, when my thumb slipped upon the tin fastening, and the old man sprang up in bed, crying out—"Who's there?"

I kept quite still and said nothing. For a whole hour I did not move a muscle, and in the meantime I did not hear him lie down. He was still sitting up in the bed listening;—Just as I have done, night after night, hearkening to the death watches in the wall.

Presently I heard a slight groan, and I knew it was the groan of mortal terror. It was not a groan of pain or of grief—oh, no!—it was the low stifled sound that arises from the bottom of the soul when overcharged with awe. I knew the sound well. Many a night, just at midnight, when all the world slept, it has welled up from my own bosom, deepening, with its dreadful echo, the terrors that distracted me. I say I knew it well. I knew what the old man felt, and I pitied him, although I chuckled at heart. I knew that he had been lying awake ever since the first slight noise, when he had turned in the bed. His fears had been ever since growing upon him. He had been trying to fancy them causeless, but could not. He had been saying to himself—"It is nothing but the wind in the chimney—it is only a mouse crossing the floor." Or "it is merely a cricket which has made a single chirp." Yes, he had been trying to comfort himself with these suppositions: but he had found all in vain. All in vain; because Death, in approaching him, had stalked with his black shadow before him, and enveloped the victim. And it was the mournful influence of the unperceived shadow that caused him to feel—although he neither saw nor heard—to feel the presence of my head within the room.

When I had waited a long time, very patiently, without hearing him lie down, I resolved to open a little—a very, very little crevice in the lantern. So I opened it—you cannot imagine how stealthily, stealthily—until, at length a simple dim ray, like the thread of the spider, shot from out the crevice and fell full upon the vulture eye.

It was open—wide, wide open—and I grew furious as I gazed upon it. I saw it with perfect distinctness—all a dull blue, with a hideous veil over it that chilled the very marrow in my bones; but I could see nothing else of the old man's face or person: for I had directed the ray as if by instinct, precisely upon the damned spot.

And have I not told you that what you mistake for madness is but over acuteness of the senses?—now, I say, there came to my ears a low, dull quick sound, such as a watch makes when enveloped in cotton. I knew that sound well, too. It was the beating of the old man's heart. It increased my fury, as the beating of a drum stimulates the soldier into courage.

But even yet I refrained and kept still. I scarcely breathed. I held the lantern motionless. I tried how steadily I could maintain the ray upon the eye. Meantime the hellish tattoo of the heart increased. It grew quicker and quicker, and louder and louder every instant. The old man's terror must have been extreme! It grew louder, I say, louder every moment!—do you mark me well? I have told you that I am nervous: so I am. And now at the dead hour of the night, amid the dreadful silence of that old house, so strange a noise as this excited me to uncontrollable terror. Yet, for some minutes longer I refrained and stood still. But the beating grew louder, Louder! I thought the heart must burst. And now a new anxiety seized me—the sound would be heard by a neighbor! The old man's hour had come! With a loud yell, I threw open the lantern and leaped into the room. He shrieked once—once only. In an instant I dragged him to the floor, and pulled the heavy bed over him. I then smiled gaily, to find the deed so far done. But, for many minutes, the heart beat on with a muffled sound. This, however, did not vex me; it would not be heard through the wall. At length it ceased. The old man was dead. I removed the bed and examined the corpse. Yes, he was stone, stone dead. I placed my hand upon the heart and held it there many minutes. There was no pulsation. He was stone dead. His eye would trouble me no more.

If still you think me mad, you will think so no longer when I describe the wise precautions I took for the concealment of the body. The night waned, and I worked hastily, but in silence. First of all I dismembered the corpse. I cut off the head and the arms and the legs.

I then took up three planks from the flooring of the chamber, and deposited all between the scantlings. I then replaced the boards so cleverly, so cunningly, that no human eye—not even his—could have detected anything wrong. There was nothing to wash out—no stain of any kind—no blood-spot whatever. I had been too wary for that. A tub had caught all—ha! ha!

When I had made an end to these labors, it was four o'clock—still dark as midnight. As the bell sounded the hour, there came a knocking at the street door. I went down to open it with a light heart,—for what had I now to fear? There entered three men, who introduced themselves, with perfect suavity, as officers of the police. A shriek had been heard by a neighbor during the night; suspicion of foul play had been aroused; information had been lodged at the police office, and they (the officers) had been deputed to search the premises.

I smiled,—for what had I to fear? I bade the gentlemen welcome. The shriek, I said, was my own in a dream. The old man, I mentioned, was absent in the country. I took my visitors all over the house. I bade them search—search well. I led them, at length, to his chamber. I showed them his treasures, secure, undisturbed. In the enthusiasm of my confidence, I brought chairs into the room, and desired them here rest from their fatigues, while I myself, in the wild audacity of my perfect triumph, placed my own seat upon the very spot beneath which reposed the corpse of the victim.

The officers were satisfied. My manner had convinced them. I was singularly at ease. They sat, and while I answered cheerily, they chatted of familiar things. But, ere long, I felt myself getting pale and wished them gone. My head ached, and I fancied a ringing in my ears; but still they sat and still chatted. The ringing became more distinct:—it continued and became more distinct: I talked more freely to get rid of the feeling: but it continued and gained definiteness—until, at length, I found that the noise was not within my ears.

No doubt I now grew very pale;—but I talked more fluently, and with a heightened voice. Yet the sound increased—and what could I do? It was a low, dull, quick sound—much such a sound as a watch makes when enveloped in cotton. I gasped for breath—and yet the officers heard it not. I talked more quickly—more vehemently; but the noise steadily increased. I arose and argued about trifles, in a high key and with violent gesticulations; but the noise steadily increased. Why would they not be gone? I paced the floor to and fro with heavy strides, as if excited to fury by the observations of the men—but the noise steadily increased. Oh God! what could I do? I foamed—I raved—I swore! I swung the chair upon which I had been sitting and grated it upon the boards, but the noise arose over all and continually increased. It grew louder—louder—louder! And still the men chatted pleasantly, and smiled. Was it possible they heard not? Almighty God!—no, no! They heard!—they suspected!—they knew!—they were making a mockery of my horror!—this I thought, and this I think. But anything was better than this agony! Anything was more tolerable that this derision! I could bear those hypocritical smiles no longer! I felt that I must scream or die! And now—again!—hark! louder! louder! louder!

"Villains!" I shrieked, "dissemble no more! I admit the deed!—tear up the planks! Here, here!—it is the beating of his hideous heart!

Source: *Complete Stories* by Edgar Allan Poe

1. What is the relationship between the narrator and the old man?

2. Describe the setting of the story.

3. On several occasions in the story, the narrator tries to prove that he is sane. Summarize the reasons why he believes that he is not mad. Do they support his point or not?

4. Near the end of the story, officers of the police arrive at the house where the narrator lives. Why don't they leave right away?

5. If the police arrived at your house at 4:00 A.M., how would you react? Does the narrator react in the same way?

6. In the first sentence of the story, the narrator asks "why *will* you say that I am mad?" Who is the "you" in the sentence? Who is the audience for the story? Give several possibilities for the identity of "you."

7. The first sentence of the story reads: "True!—nervous—very, very, dreadfully nervous I had been and am; but why *will* you say that I am mad?" Analyze the effect of the devices that Poe uses: the exclamation point, the dashes, the italics for the word *will,* the repetition of the word *very,* the combination of past perfect and simple present verbs (had been and am), and the use of the question in the opening of a piece of writing.

Writing Assignment

How Should the Murderer Be Punished?

"The Tell-Tale Heart" presents a confession for a brutal murder, or actually a justification for this act. Since there is no doubt about the narrator's guilt, and no question that the murder was premeditated, the jury will undoubtedly find the killer guilty of first-degree murder. How should he be punished? What is fitting punishment for his actions? In a five-paragraph essay on a separate piece of paper, present the matter (paragraph 1), analyze the possibilities (paragraph 2), choose the possibility that you consider most appropriate (paragraph 3), and provide support for your choice (paragraphs 4 and 5).

Activity 2   *"After Twenty Years"*

Read "After Twenty Years" on pages 249 and 250. Then answer the questions on page 251.

After Twenty Years

by O. Henry

The POLICEMAN on the beat moved up the avenue impressively. The impressiveness was habitual and not for show, for spectators were few. The time was barely 10 o'clock at night, but chilly gusts of wind with a taste of rain in them had well nigh depeopled the streets.

Trying doors as he went, twirling his club with many intricate and artful movements, turning now and then to cast his watchful eye down the pacific thoroughfare, the officer, with his stalwart form and slight swagger, made a fine picture of a guardian of the peace. The vicinity was one that kept early hours. Now and then you might see the lights of a cigar store or of an all-night lunch counter; but the majority of the doors belonged to business places that had long since been closed.

When about midway of a certain block, the policeman suddenly slowed his walk. In the doorway of a darkened hardware store a man leaned, with an unlighted cigar in his mouth. As the policeman walked up to him the man spoke up quickly.

"It's all right, officer," he said, reassuringly. "I'm just waiting for a friend. It's an appointment made twenty years ago. Sounds a little funny to you, doesn't it? Well, I'll explain if you'd like to make certain it's all straight. About that long ago there used to be a restaurant where this store stands—'Big Joe' Brady's restaurant."

"Until five years ago," said the policeman. "It was torn down then."

The man in the doorway struck a match and lit his cigar. The light showed a pale, square-jawed face with keen eyes, and a little white scar near his right eyebrow. His scarfpin was a large diamond, oddly set.

"Twenty years ago tonight," said the man, "I dined here at 'Big Joe' Brady's with Jimmy Wells, my best chum, and the finest chap in the world. He and I were raised here in New York, just like two brothers, together. I was eighteen and Jimmy was twenty. The next morning I was to start for the West to make my fortune. You couldn't have dragged Jimmy out of New York; he thought it was the only place on earth. Well, we agreed that night that we would meet here again exactly twenty years from that date and time, no matter what conditions might be or from what distance we might have to come. We figured that in twenty years each of us ought to have our destiny worked out and our fortunes made, whatever they were going to be."

"It sounds pretty interesting," said the policeman. "Rather a long time between meets, though, it seems to me. Haven't you heard from your friend since you left?"

"Well, yes, for a time we corresponded," said the other. "But after a year or two we lost track of each other. You see, the West is a pretty big proposition, and I kept hustling around over it pretty lively. But I know Jimmy will meet me here if he's alive, for he always was the truest, staunchest old chap in the world. He'll never forget. I came a thousand miles to stand in this door tonight, and it's worth it if my old partner turns up."

The waiting man pulled out a handsome watch, the lids of it set with small diamonds.

"Three minutes to ten," he announced. "It was exactly ten o'clock when we parted here at the restaurant door."

"Did pretty well out West, didn't you?" asked the policeman.

"You bet! I hope Jimmy has done half as well. He was a kind of plodder, though, good fellow as he was. I've had to compete with some of the sharpest wits going to get my pile.

A man gets in a groove in New York. It takes the West to put a razor-edge on him."

The policeman twirled his club and took a step or two.

"I'll be on my way. Hope your friend comes around all right. Going to call time on him sharp?"

"I should say not!" said the other. "I'll give him half an hour at least. If Jimmy is alive on earth he'll be here by that time. So long, officer."

"Good night, sir," said the policeman, passing on along his beat, trying doors as he went.

There was now a fine, cold drizzle falling, and the wind had risen from its uncertain puffs into a steady blow. The few foot passengers astir in that quarter hurried dismally and silently along with coat collars turned high and pocketed hands. And in the door of the hardware store the man who had come a thousand miles to fill an appointment, uncertain almost to absurdity, with the friend of his youth, smoked his cigar and waited.

About twenty minutes he waited, and then a tall man in a long overcoat, with collar turned up to his ears, hurried across from the opposite side of the street. He went directly to the waiting man.

"Is that you, Bob?" he asked, doubtfully.

"Is that you, Jimmy Wells?" cried the man in the door.

"Bless my heart!" exclaimed the new arrival, grasping both the other's hands with his own. "It's Bob, sure as fate. I was certain I'd find you here if you were still in existence. Well, well, well! Twenty years is a long time. The old restaurant's gone, Bob; I wish it had lasted, so we could have had another dinner there. How has the West treated you, old man?"

"Bully; it has given me everything I asked it for. You've changed lots, Jimmy. I never thought you were so tall by two or three inches."

"Oh, I grew a bit after I was twenty."

"Doing well in New York, Jimmy?"

"Moderately. I have a position in one of the city departments. Come on, Bob; we'll go around to a place I know of, and have a good long talk about old times."

The two men started up the street, arm in arm. The man from the West, his egotism enlarged by success, was beginning to outline the history of his career. The other, submerged in his overcoat, listened with interest.

At the corner stood a drug store, brilliant with electric lights. When they came into this glare each of them turned simultaneously to gaze upon the other's face.

The man from the West stopped suddenly and released his arm.

"You're not Jimmy Wells," he snapped. "Twenty years is a long time, but not long enough to change a man's nose from a Roman to a pug."

"It sometimes changes a good man into a bad one," said the tall man. "You've been under arrest about ten minutes, 'Silky' Bob. Chicago thinks you may have dropped over our way and wires us she wants to have a chat with you. Going quietly, are you? That's sensible. Now, before we go to the station here's a note I was asked to hand to you. You may read it here at the window. It's from Patrolman Wells."

The man from the West unfolded the little piece of paper handed him. His hand was steady when he began to read, but it trembled a little by the time he had finished. The note was rather short.

Bob: I was at the appointed place on time. When you struck the match to light your cigar I saw it was the face of the man wanted in Chicago. Somehow I couldn't do it myself, so I went around a got a plainclothes man to do the job.

Jimmy

Source: *The Four Million* by O. Henry

1. Why is the man with the cigar waiting in the doorway of a hardware store?

2. Has the man with the cigar enjoyed success in the twenty year interval? Where has he been? What has he been doing?

3. How does Bob realize that the man with the overcoat is not Jimmy Wells?

4. What has Jimmy Wells done with his life in the twenty years since the last meeting?

5. Why can't Jimmy Wells "do the job?"

6. What is surprising about the end of the story?

7. How is O. Henry's technique similar to the technique used by de Maupassant in "The Diamond Necklace" in Part 3 on page 86?

Writing Assignment

Your Life in 20 Years

Imagine that you have made an appointment with your best friend to meet in twenty years. What will you be like? What job will you have? Will you have a family? A house? Where will you be living? How different will you be? In a clearly written essay on a separate piece of paper, project yourself into the future and present the person that you will be in the year 2024.

Dedicate one paragraph each to a discussion of your career, your family, your achievements, and your activities (hobbies and interests).

Activity 3   *"In Another Country"*

Read "In Another Country." Then do the Writing Assignment on page 255.

In Another Country

by Ernest Hemingway

In the fall the war was always there, but we did not go to it any more. It was cold in the fall in Milan and the dark came very early. Then the electric lights came on, and it was pleasant along the streets looking in the windows. There was much game hanging outside the shops, and the snow powdered in the fur of the foxes and small birds blew in the wind and the wind turned their feathers. It was a cold fall and the wind came down from the mountains.

We were all at the hospital every afternoon, and there were different ways of walking across the town through the dusk to the hospital. Two of the ways were alongside canals, but they were long. Always, though, you crossed a bridge across a canal to enter the hospital. There was a choice of three bridges. On one of them a woman sold roasted chestnuts. It was warm, standing in front of her charcoal fire, and the chestnuts were warm afterward in your pocket. The hospital was very old and very beautiful, and you entered through a gate and walked across a courtyard and out a gate on the other side. There were usually funerals starting from the courtyard. Beyond the old hospital were the new brick pavilions, and there we met every afternoon and were all very polite and interested in what was the matter, and sat in the machines that were to make so much difference.

The doctor came up to the machine where I was sitting and said: "What did you like best to do before the war? Did you practice a sport?"

I said: "Yes, football."

"Good" he said. "You will be able to play football again better than ever."

My knee did not bend and the leg dropped straight from the knee to the ankle without a calf, and the machine was to bend the knee and make it move as in riding a tricycle. But it did not bend yet, and instead the machine lurched when it came to the bending part. The doctor said: "That will all pass. You are a fortunate young man. You will play football again like a champion."

In the next machine was a major who had a little hand like a baby's. He winked at me when the doctor examined his hand, which was between two leather straps that bounced up and down and flapped the stiff fingers, and said: "And will I too play football, captain-doctor?" He had been a very great fencer, and before the war the greatest fencer in Italy.

The doctor went to his office in a back room and brought a photograph which showed a hand that had been withered almost as small as the major's, before it had taken a machine course, and after was a little larger. The major held the photograph and his good hand and looked at it very carefully. "A wound?" he asked.

"An industrial accident," the doctor said.

"Very interesting, very interesting," the major said, and handed it back to the doctor.

"You have confidence?"

"No," said the major.

There were three boys who came each day who were about the same age I was. They were all three from Milan, and one of them was to be a lawyer, and one was to be a painter, and one had intended to be a soldier, and after we were finished with the machines, sometimes we walked back together to the Café Cova, which was next door to the Scala. We walked the short way through the communist quarter because we were four together. The people hated us because we were officers, and from a wineshop some one would call out, *"A basso gli ufficiali!"* as we passed. Another boy who walked with us sometimes and made us five wore a black silk handkerchief across his face because he had no nose then and his face was to be rebuilt. He had gone out to the front from the military academy and been wounded within an hour after he had gone into the front line for the first time. They rebuilt his face, but he came from a very old family and they could never get the nose exactly right. He went to South America and worked in a bank. But this was a long time ago, and then we did not any of us know how it was going to be afterward. We only knew then that there was always the war, but that we were not going to it any more.

We all had the same medals, except the boy with the black silk bandage across his face, and he had not been at the front long enough to get any medals. The tall boy with a very pale face who was to be a lawyer had been a lieutenant of *Arditi* and had three medals of the sort we each had only one of. He had lived

a very long time with death and was a little detached. We were all a little detached, and there was nothing that held us together except that we met every afternoon at the hospital. Although, as we walked to the Cova through the tough part of town, walking in the dark, with light and singing coming out of the wine-shops, and sometimes having to walk into the street where the men and women would crowd together on the sidewalk so that we would have had to jostle them to get by, we felt held together by there being something that had happened that they, the people who disliked us, did not understand.

We ourselves all understood the Cova, where it was rich and warm and not too brightly lighted, and noisy and smoky at certain hours, and there were always girls at the tables and the illustrated papers on a rack on the wall. The girls at the Cova were very patriotic, and I found that the most patriotic people in Italy were the café girls – and I believe they are still patriotic.

The boys at first were very polite about my medals and asked me what I had done to get them. I showed them the papers, which were written in very beautiful language and full of *fratellanza* and *abnegazione,* but which really said, with all the adjectives removed, that I had been given the medals because I was an American. After that their manner changed a little towards me, although I was their friend against outsiders. I was a friend, but I was never really one of them after they had read the citations, because it had been different with them and they had done very different things to get their medals. I had been wounded, it was true; but we all knew that being wounded, after all, was really an accident. I was never ashamed of the ribbons, though, and sometimes, after the cocktail hour, I would imagine myself having done all the things they had done to get their medals; but walking home at night through the empty streets with the cold wind and all the shops closed, trying to keep near the street lights, I knew that I would never have done such things, and I was very much afraid to die, and often lay in bed at night by myself, afraid to die and wondering how I would be when I went back to the front again.

The three with the medals were like hunting hawks; and I was not a hawk, although I might seem a hawk to those who had never hunted; they, the three, knew better and so we drifted apart. But I stayed good friends with the boy who had been wounded his first day at the front, because he would never know now how he would have turned out; so he could never be accepted either, and I liked him because I thought perhaps he would not have turned out to be a hawk either.

The major, who had been the great fencer, did not believe in bravery, and spent much time while we sat in the machines correcting my grammar. He had complimented me on how I spoke Italian, and we talked together very easily. One day I had said that Italian seemed such an easy language to me that I could not take a great interest in it; everything was so easy to say. "Ah, yes," the major said. "Why, then, do you not take up the use of grammar?" So we took up the use of grammar, and soon Italian was such a difficult language that I was afraid to talk to him until I had the grammar straight in my mind.

The major came very regularly to the hospital. I do not think he ever missed a day, although I am sure he did not believe in the machines. There was a time when none of us believed in the machines, and one day the major said it was all nonsense. The machines were new then and it was we who were to prove them. It was an idiotic idea, he said, "a theory, like another." I had not learned my grammar, and he said I was a stupid impossible disgrace, and he was a fool to have bothered with me. He was a small man and he sat straight up in his chair with his right hand thrust into the machine and looked straight ahead at the wall while the straps thumped up and down with his fingers in them.

"What will you do when the war is over if it is over?" he asked me. "Speak grammatically!"

"I will go to the States."

"Are you married?"

"No, but I hope to be."

"The more of a fool you are," he said. He seemed very angry. "A man must not marry."

"Why, Signor Maggiore?"

"Don't call me 'Signor Maggiore.'"

"Why must not a man marry?"

"He cannot marry. He cannot marry," he said angrily. "If he is to lose everything, he should not place himself in a position to lose that. He should not place himself in a position to lose. He should find things he cannot lose."

He spoke very angrily and bitterly, and looked straight ahead while he talked.

"But why should he necessarily lose it?"

"He'll lose it," the major said. He was looking at the wall. Then he looked down at the machine and jerked his little hand out from between the straps and slapped it hard against his thigh. "He'll lose it," he almost shouted. "Don't argue with me!" Then he called to the attendant who ran the machines. "Come and turn this damned thing off."

He went back into the other room for the light treatment and the massage. Then I heard him ask the doctor if he might use his telephone and he shut the door. When he came back into the room, I was sitting in another machine. He was wearing his cape and had his cap on, and he came directly toward my machine and put his arm on my shoulder.

"I am so sorry," he said, and patted me on the shoulder with his good hand. "I would not be rude. My wife has just died. You must forgive me."

"Oh —" I said, feeling sick for him. "I am *so* sorry."

He stood there biting his lower lip. "It is very difficult," he said. "I cannot resign myself."

He looked straight past me and out through the window. Then he began to cry. "I am utterly unable to resign myself," he said and choked. And then crying, his head up looking at nothing, carrying himself straight and soldierly, with tears on both his cheeks and biting his lips, he walked past the machines and out the door.

The doctor told me that the major's wife, who was very young and whom he had not married until he was definitely invalided out of the war, had died of pneumonia. She had been sick only a few days. No one expected her to die. The major did not come to the hospital for three days. Then he came at the usual hour, wearing a black band on the sleeve of his uniform. When he came back, there were large framed photographs around the wall, of all sorts of wounds before and after they had been cured by the machines. In front of the machine the major used were three photographs of hands like his that were completely restored. I do not know where the doctor got them. I always understood we were the first to use the machines. The photographs did not make much difference to the major because he only looked out the window.

Source: *The Complete Works of Ernest Hemingway,* ©1987

Writing Assignment

Confronting a Personal Problem

In "In Another Country," Hemingway describes a personal tragedy: serious war injuries. Personal problems, when overcome, may serve as a way to make people stronger, giving confidence in the ability to survive and to face difficulties with fortitude and confidence. In a well-organized essay on a separate piece of paper, present a personal problem that has confronted you. Tell how you managed to overcome this problem, and whether it has changed your behavior or attitude. What did you learn from the experience? Will you have the ability to confront problems of this nature better in the future?

Building Your Skill in Writing Personal Journals

<u>**Activity 1**</u> *"The Truth about Lying"*

Read "The Truth about Lying" and do the assignments on pages 260–62.

The Truth about Lying

by Allison Kornet

Has Lying Gotten A Bad Rap?

We do it as often as we brush our teeth, yet until recently lying received little attention from psychologists. Could we really get through life without it?

If, as the cliché has it, the 1980's was the decade of greed, then the quintessential sin of the 1990's might just be lying. After all, think of the accusations of deceit leveled at politicians like Bob Packwood, Marion Barry, Dan Rostenkowski, Newt Gingrich, and Bill Clinton.

And consider the top-level Texaco executives who initially denied making racist comments at board meetings; the young monk who falsely accused Cardinal Bernadin of molestation; Susan Smith, the white woman who killed her young boys and blamed a black man for it; and Joe Klein, the *Newsweek* columnist who adamantly swore for months that he had nothing to do with his anonymously-published novel *Primary Colors.* Even Hollywood has noticed our apparent deception obsession: witness recent films like *Quiz Show, True Lies, The Crucible, Secrets & Lies,* and comedian Jim Carrey's latest release, *Liar, Liar.*

What's going on here? Nothing out of the ordinary, insists Leonard Saxe, Ph.D., a polygraph expert, and professor of psychology at Brandeis University. "Lying has long been a part of everyday life," he says. "We couldn't get through the day without being deceptive." Yet until recently lying was almost entirely ignored by psychologists, leaving serious discussion of the topic in the hands of ethicists and theologians. Freud wrote next to nothing about deception; even the 1500-page *Encyclopedia of Psychology,* published in 1984, mentions lies only in a brief entry on detecting them. But as psychologists delve deeper into the details of deception, they're finding that lying is a surprisingly common and complex phenomenon.

For starters, recent work by Bella DePaulo, Ph.D., a psychologist at the University of Virginia, confirms Nietzsche's assertion that the lie is a condition of life. In a 1996 study, DePaulo and her colleagues had 147 people between the ages of 18 and 71 keep a diary of all the falsehoods they told over the course of a week. Most people, she found, lie once or twice a day—almost as often as they snack from the refrigerator or brush their teeth. Both men and women lie in approximately a fifth of their social exchanges lasting 10 or more minutes; over the course of a week they deceive about 30 percent of those with whom they interact one-on-one. Furthermore, some types of relationships, such as those between parents and teens, are virtual magnets for deception: "College students lie to their mothers in one out of two conversations," reports DePaulo. (Incidentally, when researchers refer to lying, they don't include the mindless pleasantries or polite equivocations we offer each other in passing, such as "I'm fine, thanks" or "No trouble at all." An "official" lie actually misleads, deliberately conveying a false impression. So complimenting a friend's awful haircut or telling a creditor that the check is in the mail both qualify.)

Saxe points out that most of us receive conflicting messages about lying. Although we're socialized from the time we can speak to believe that it's always better to tell the truth, in reality society often encourages and even rewards deception. Show up late for an early morning meeting at work and it's best not to admit that you overslept. "You're punished far more than you would be if you lie and say you were stuck in traffic," Saxe notes. Moreover, lying is integral to most occupations. Think how often we see lawyers constructing far-fetched theories on behalf of their clients or reporters misrepresenting themselves in order to gain access to good stories.

OF COURSE I LOVE YOU

Dishonesty also pervades our romantic relationships, as you might expect from the titles of books like *101 Lies Men Tell Women* (HarperCollins), by Missouri psychologist Dory Hollander, Ph.D. (Hollander's nomination for the #1 spot: "I'll call you.") Eighty-five percent of the couples interviewed in a 1990 study of college students reported that one or both partners had lied about past relationships or recent indiscretions. And DePaulo finds that

dating couples lie to each other in about a third of their interactions—perhaps even more often than they deceive other people.

Fortunately, marriage seems to offer some protection against deception: Spouses lie to each other in "only" about 10 percent of their major conversations. The bad news? That 10 percent just refers to the typically minor lies of everyday life. DePaulo recently began looking at the less frequent "big" lies that involve deep betrayals of trust, and she's finding that the vast majority of them occur between people in intimate relationships. "You save your really big lies," she says, "for the person that you're closest to."

SWEET LITTLE LIES

Though some lies produce interpersonal friction, others may actually serve as a kind of harmless social lubricant. "They make it easier for people to get along," says DePaulo, noting that in the diary study one in every four of the participants' lies were told solely for the benefit of another person. In fact, "fake positive" lies—those in which people pretend to like someone or something more than they actually do ("Your muffins are the best ever")— are about 10 to 20 times more common than "false negative" lies in which people pretend to like someone or something *less* ("That two-faced rat will never get my vote.").

Certain cultures may place special importance on these "kind" lies. A survey of residents at 31 senior citizen centers in Los Angeles recently revealed that only about half of elderly Korean Americans believe that patients diagnosed with life-threatening metastatic cancer should be told the truth about their condition. In contrast, nearly 90 percent of Americans of European or African descent felt that the terminally ill should be confronted with the truth.

Not surprisingly, research also confirms that the closer we are to someone, the more likely it is that the lies we tell them will be altruistic ones. This is particularly true of women: although the sexes lie with equal frequency, women are especially likely to stretch the truth in order to protect someone else's feelings, DePaulo reports. Men, on the other hand, are more prone to lying about themselves—the typical conversation between two guys contains about eight times as many self-oriented lies as it does falsehoods about other people.

Men and women may also differ in their ability to deceive their friends. In a University of Virginia study, psychologists asked pairs of same-sex friends to try to detect lies told by the other person. Six months later the researchers repeated the experiment with the same participants. While women had become slightly better at detecting their friends' lies over time, men didn't show any improvement—evidence, perhaps, that women are particularly good at learning to read their friends more accurately as a relationship deepens.

WHO LIES?

Saxe believes that anyone under enough pressure, or given enough incentive, will lie. But in a study published in the *Journal of Personality and Social Psychology,* DePaulo and Deborah A. Kashy, Ph.D., of Texas A&M University, report that frequent liars tend to be manipulative and Machiavellian, not to mention overly concerned with the impression they make on others. Still, DePaulo warns that liars "don't always fit the stereotype of caring only about themselves." Further research reveals that extroverted, sociable people are slightly more likely to lie, and that some personality and physical traits—notably self-confidence and physical attractiveness—have been linked to an individual's skill at lying when under pressure.

On the other hand, the people *least* likely to lie are those who score high on psychological scales of responsibility and those with meaningful same-sex friendships. In his book *Lies!*

Lies!! Lies!! The Psychology of Deceit (American Psychiatric Press, Inc.), psychiatrist Charles Ford, M.D. adds depressed people to that list. He suggests that individuals in the throes of depression seldom deceive others—or are deceived themselves—because they seem to perceive and describe reality with greater accuracy than others. Several studies show that depressed people delude themselves far less than their nondepressed peers about the amount of control they have over situations, and also about the effect they have on other people. Researchers such as UCLA psychologist Shelley Taylor, Ph.D., have even cited findings as evidence that a certain amount of self-delusion—basically, lying to yourself—is essential to good mental health. (Many playwrights, including Arthur Miller and Eugene O'Neill, seem to share the same view about truth-telling. In *Death of a Salesman* and *The Iceman Cometh,* for example, lies are life sustaining. The heroes become tragic figures when their lies are stripped away.)

DETECTING LIES

Anyone who has played cards with a poker-faced opponent can appreciate how difficult it is to detect a liar. Surprisingly, technology doesn't help very much. Few experts display much confidence in the deception-detecting abilities of the polygraph, or lie detector. Geoffrey C. Bunn, Ph.D., a psychologist and polygraph historian at Canada's York University, goes so far as to describe the lie detector as "an entertainment device" rather than a scientific instrument. Created around 1921 during one of the first collaborations between scientists and police, the device was quickly popularized by enthusiastic newspaper headlines and by the element of drama it bestowed in movies and novels.

But mass appeal doesn't confer legitimacy. The problem with the polygraph, say experts like Bunn, is that it detects fear, not lying; the physiological responses that it measures—most often heart rate, skin conductivity, and rate of respiration—don't necessarily accompany dishonesty.

"The premise of a lie detector is that a smoke alarm goes off in the brain when we lie because we're doing something wrong," explains Saxe. "But sometimes we're completely comfortable with our lies." Thus a criminal's lie can easily go undetected if he has no fear of telling it. Similarly, a true statement by an innocent individual could be misinterpreted if the person is sufficiently afraid of the examination circumstances. According to Saxe, the best-controlled research suggests that lie detectors err at a rate anywhere from 25 to 75 percent. Perhaps this is why most state and federal courts won't allow polygraph "evidence."

Some studies suggest that lies can be detected by means other than a polygraph—by tracking speech hesitations or changes in the vocal pitch, for example, or by identifying various nervous adaptive habits like scratching, blinking, or fidgeting. But most psychologists agree that lie detection is destined to be imperfect. Still, researchers continue to investigate new ways of picking up lies. While studying how language patterns are associated with improvements in physical health, James W. Pennebaker, Ph.D., a professor of psychology at Southern Methodist University, also began to explore whether a person's choice of words were a sign of deception. Examining data gathered from a text analysis program, Pennebaker and SMU colleague Diane Berry, Ph.D., determined that there are certain language patterns that predict when someone is being less than honest. For example, liars tend to use fewer first person words like *I* or *my* in both speech and writing. They are also less apt to use emotional words, such as *hurt* or *angry*, cognitive words, like *understand* or *realize*, and so-called exclusive words, such as *but* or *without*, that distinguish between what is and isn't in a category.

NOT GUILTY

While the picture of lying that has emerged in recent years is far more favorable than that suggested by its biblical "thou shalt not" status, most liars remain at least somewhat conflicted about their behavior. In DePaulo's studies, participants described conversations in which they lied as less intimate and pleasant than truthful encounters, suggesting that people are not entirely at ease with their deceptions. That may explain why falsehoods are more likely to be told over the telephone, which provides more anonymity than a face-to-face conversation. In most cases, however, any mental distress that results from telling an everyday lie quickly dissipates. Those who took part in the diary study said they would tell about 75 percent of their lies again if given a second chance—a position no doubt bolstered by their generally high success rate. Only about a fifth of their falsehoods were discovered during the one-week study period.

Certainly anyone who insists on condemning all lies should ponder what would happen if we could reliably tell when our family, friends, colleagues, and government leaders were deceiving us. It's tempting to think that the world would become a better place when purged of the deceptions that seem to interfere without attempts at genuine communication or intimacy. On the other hand, perhaps our social lives would collapse under the weight of relentless honesty, with unveiled truths destroying our ability to connect with others. The ubiquity of lying is clearly a problem, but would we want to will away all of our lies? Let's be honest.

Source: *Psychology Today*, May/June 1997

Journal Activity

Keep A Lying Journal

The article from *Psychology Today* states that most people lie two to three times each day. Do you think that you do the same? For the next two weeks, keep a lying journal in which you will record the lies you told each day.

Right before you go to sleep every night for two weeks, make a quick list of the number of lies that you told that day. Indicate what type of lie it was, using the categories established in the article (sweet lie, lying on the job, in relationships, in school, exaggeration of your abilities, about your age). Also indicate whether the lies were told in person, on the telephone, or in Internet chat rooms. Keep a running record of the total number of lies told over a two-week span.

You might also keep track of the lies told by the people around you. Who is the biggest liar you know? Who tells the most lies in your class? At your job? In your family? Among your friends? Pay close attention to lying in all its forms during the next two weeks.

Exercise 1

Think about the last two weeks in which you monitored your lying habits. Circle the letter indicating your response or write your answer in the blank.

1. What is your nationality and gender?_____

2. How many times did you lie on the average every day?

    a. more than 20

    b. 10–29

    c. 5–10

    d. 2–4

    e. 0–1

3. Did you lie in school?   a. yes   b. no

4. Did you lie to your friends?   a. yes   b. no

5. Did you lie to your family?   a. yes   b. no

6. Did you lie on your job?   a. yes   b. no

7. Did you lie in dating or with your spouse?   a. yes   b. no

8. In which situation did you lie the most? _____

9. Did the number of lies you told every day surprise you?   a. yes   b. no

Analyze the type of lies that you told.

10. Good lies? (sweet lies as discussed in the article; these are sometimes called white lies)   a. yes   b. no

11. Exaggeration of your abilities?   a. yes   b. no

12. Deception in terms of age?   a. yes   b. no

13. Deception in terms of nationality?   a. yes   b. no

14. Lies in romantic relationships?   a. yes   b. no

15. What is the most common type of lie that you told? _____

16. Did you lie more on the telephone or in speaking directly with another person?
   a. telephone
   b. in person

17. As a result of this two-week study on lying, because you are more aware of your behavior, do you think that in the future you will:
   a. lie less often
   b. lie the same amount

18. Do you consider yourself a basically honest person?   a. yes   b. not really

19. Do you think that lying is:
   a. always bad
   b. usually bad
   c. sometimes necessary
   d. a normal part of life

20. Did you lie on this survey?   a. yes   b. no

Writing Assignment

Personal Lying Habits

Write a five-paragraph essay on a separate piece of paper resulting from your experience with the two-week analysis of your personal lying habits. Use your lying journal and the survey to organize your thoughts. Structure your essay in the following manner. Each paragraph will be five to six sentences long.

1. **Paragraph 1.** Provide an introduction to lying with a very general topic sentence (or sentences) such as "Lying is a very common activity. . . ." or "On television or radio news or in newspapers, people are confronted with reports of lying every day. . . ." Continue in this paragraph by introducing the fact that you kept a lying journal and analyzed your lying habits for a week.

2. **Paragraph 2.** In this paragraph, present your general attitude about lying, whether you consider it really bad, somewhat bad, or something that is common or even necessary. Tell about what you thought your lying habits might be *before* you kept the journal and closely monitored your lying habits. You might bring in what you were taught about lying, who taught you, and if you really paid attention to this training. You might also bring in your *lying history,* that is, the situations in which you normally lied in the past.

3. **Paragraph 3.** Begin with a time transition ("During the last two weeks . . ."). In this paragraph present the results of the survey (which reflect your journal). Tell how often you lied on an average every day, the situations in which you lied the most, and what type of lies you told (use the categories presented in the article).

4. **Paragraph 4.** Get more specific about the most common area in which you lied. Analyze one specific lie (or a series of lies). Write about why you told the lie(s), what the motivation was, what the result of the lie was, if you felt sorry later about telling the lie, and whether you would tell the lie again in the future under the same circumstances.

5. **Paragraph 5.** In the concluding paragraph, discuss whether you were surprised at your behavior, and whether this experience of keeping the journal and analyzing your habits will change your behavior in terms of lying. Do you think that you will lie less in the future? Has your opinion about lying changed?

Activity 2   *The Self-Improvement Plan and Journal*

Benjamin Franklin, one of the most important of America's founding fathers, led a rich and varied life centered around the city of Philadelphia. He was a writer, politician, statesman, publisher, editor, scientist, and inventor. He was also an excellent problem-solver. For example, when he saw several houses burn down in his city, he helped establish the first permanent fire department in the colonies. He also helped found the public library, the medical school at the University of Pennsylvania, and the police department. He was an important contributor to the Constitution of the United States and played a primary role in the fight for independence against England.

Throughout his life Franklin continually tried to improve himself. His strategies are described in detail in Chapter IX of his *Autobiography,* written in 1771, which he calls "My Catalogue of Moral Virtues." His attempt at self-improvement is as valid today as it was more than 200 years ago.

Read "My Catalogue of Moral Virtues." Then do the Journal Activity and Writing Assignment on page 266.

My Catalogue of Moral Virtues

by Benjamin Franklin

In the various enumerations of the moral virtues I had met with in my reading, I found the catalogue more or less numerous, as different writers included more or fewer ideas under the same name. *Temperance,* for example, was by some confined to eating and drinking, while by others it was extended to mean moderating every other pleasure, appetite, inclination, or passion, bodily or mental, even to our avarice and ambition. I proposed to myself, for the sake of clearness, to use rather more names, with fewer ideas annexed to each, than a few names with more ideas; and I included under thirteen names of virtues all that at that time occurred to me as necessary or desirable, and annexed to each a short precept, which fully expressed the extent I gave to its meaning.

These names of virtues, with their precepts, were:

Benjamin Franklin: Statesman and Philospher. Courtesy of The Library of Congress.

1. *Temperance.* Eat not to dullness; drink not to elevation.
2. *Silence.* Speak not but what may benefit others or yourself; avoid trifling conversation.
3. *Order.* Let all your things have their places; let each part of your business have its time.
4. *Resolution.* Resolve to perform what you ought; perform without fail what you resolve.
5. *Frugality.* Make no expense but to do good to others or yourself; i.e., waste nothing.
6. *Industry.* Lose no time; be always employ'd in something useful; cut off all unnecessary actions.
7. *Sincerity.* Use no hurtful deceit; think innocently and justly, and, if you speak, speak accordingly.
8. *Justice.* Wrong none by doing injuries, or omitting the benefits that are your duty.
9. *Moderation.* Avoid extremes; forbear resenting injuries so much as you think they deserve.
10. *Cleanliness.* Tolerate no uncleanliness in body, clothes, or habitation.
11. *Tranquillity.* Be not disturbed at trifles, or at accidents common or unavoidable.
12. *Chastity.* Rarely use venery but for health or offspring, never to dullness, weakness, or the injury of your own or another's peace or reputation.
13. *Humility.* Imitate Jesus and Socrates.

My intention being to acquire the habitude of all these virtues, I judged it would be well not to distract my attention by attempting the whole at once, but to **fix it on one of them at a time;** and, when I should be master of that, then to proceed to another, and so on, till I should have gone through the thirteen; and, as the previous acquisition of some might facilitate the acquisition of certain others, I arranged them with that view, as they stand above. Temperance first, as it tends to procure that coolness and clearness of head, which is so necessary where constant vigilance was to be kept up, and guard maintained against the unremitting attraction of ancient habits, and the force of perpetual temptations. This being acquired and established, *Silence* would be more easy; and my desire being to gain knowledge at the same time that I improved in virtue, and considering that in conversation it was obtained rather by the use of the ears than of the tongue, and therefore wishing to break a habit I was getting into of prattling, punning, and joking, which only made me acceptable to trifling company, I gave *Silence* the second place. This and the next, *Order,* I expected would allow me more time for attending to my project and my studies. *Resolution,* once become habitual, would keep me firm in my endeavors to obtain all the subsequent virtues; *Frugality* and *Industry* freeing me from my remaining debt, and producing affluence and independence, would make more easy the practice of *Sincerity* and *Justice,* etc., etc. Conceiving then, that, agreeably to the advice of Pythagoras in his Golden Verses, daily examination would be necessary, I contrived the following method for conducting that examination.

I made a little book, in which I allotted a page for each of the virtues. I ruled each page with red ink, so as to have seven columns, one for each day of the week, marking each column with a letter for the day. I crossed these columns with thirteen red lines, marking the be-

ginning of each line with the first letter of one of the virtues, on which line, and in its proper column, I might mark, by a little black spot, every fault I found upon examination to have been committed respecting that virtue upon that day.

I determined to give a week's strict attention to each of the virtues successively. Thus, in the first week, my great guard was to avoid every the least offence against *Temperance,* leaving the other virtues to their ordinary chance, only marking every evening the faults of the day. Thus, if in the first week I could keep my first line, marked T, clear of spots, I supposed the habit of that virtue so much strengthen'd, and its opposite weakened, that I might venture extending my attention to include the next, and for the following week keep both lines clear of spots. Proceeding thus to the last, I could go through a complete course in thirteen weeks, and four courses in a year. And like him who, having a garden to weed, does not attempt to eradicate all the bad herbs at once, which would exceed his reach and his strength, but works on one of the beds at a time, and having accomplish'd the first, proceeds to a second, so I should have, I hoped, the encouraging pleasure of seeing on my pages the progress I made in virtue, by clearing successively my lines of their spots, till in the end, by a number of courses, I should be happy in viewing a clean book, after a thirteen weeks' daily examination.

I entered upon the execution of this plan for self-examination, and continued it with occasional intermissions for some time. I was surprised to find myself so much fuller of faults than I had imagined; but I had the satisfaction of seeing them diminish. To avoid the trouble of renewing now and then my little book, which, by scraping out the marks on the paper of old faults to make room for new ones in a new course, became full of holes, I transferred my tables and precepts to the ivory leaves of a memorandum book, on which the lines were drawn with red ink, that made a durable stain, and on those lines I marked my faults with a black-lead pencil, which marks I could easily wipe out with a wet sponge. After a while I went thro' one course only in a year, and afterward only one in several years, till at length I omitted them entirely, being employed in voyages and business abroad, with a multiplicity of affairs that interfered; but I always carried my little book with me.

In truth, I found myself incorrigible with respect to Order; and now I am grown old, and my memory bad, I feel very sensibly the want of it. But, on the whole, although I never arrived at the perfection I had been so ambitious of obtaining, but fell far short of it, yet I was, by the endeavour, a better and a happier man than I otherwise should have been if I had not attempted it; as those who aim at perfect writing by imitating the engraved copies, though they never reach the wished-for excellence of those copies, their hand is mended by the endeavor, and is tolerable while it continues fair and legible.

It may be well my posterity should be informed that to this little artifice, with the blessing of God, their ancestor owed the constant felicity of his life, down to his 79th year, in which this is written. What reverses may attend the remainder is in the hand of Providence; but, if they arrive, the reflection on past happiness enjoyed ought to help his bearing them with more resignation. To Temperance he ascribes his long-continued health, and what is still left to him of a good constitution; to Industry and Frugality, the early easiness of his circumstances and acquisition of his fortune, with all that knowledge that enabled him to be a useful citizen, and obtained for him some degree of reputation among the learned; to Sincerity and Justice, the confidence of his country, and the honorable employs it conferred upon him; and to the joint influence of the whole mass of the virtues, even in the imperfect state he was able to acquire them, all that evenness of temper, and that cheerfulness in conversation, which makes his company still sought for, and agreeable even to his younger acquaintance. I hope, therefore, that some of my descendants may follow the example and reap the benefit.

Personal Self-Improvement Plan							
Virtue	Sun	Mon	Tues	Wed	Thurs	Fri	Sat
Temperance	x	x		x		x	
Silence							
Order							
Resolution							
Frugality							
Industry							
Sincerity							
Justice							
Moderation							
Cleanliness							
Tranquility							
Chastity							
Humility							

Source: *The Autobiography of Benjamin Franklin*

Journal Activity

Create a Personal Self-Improvement Plan

For the next month try to follow Benjamin Franklin's model for a self-improvement plan. Since you will be working over a four-week period, you will not need all 13 virtues described in the excerpt from the *Autobiography*. Instead, concentrate on the four that you consider most important for you personally. Follow these steps.

1. From Benjamin Franklin's list of 13 qualities, choose the 4 that are most important to you.

2. List the four virtues that you have chosen in order of importance.

3. Write the first virtue in the chart on page 267 for Week 1.

4. During Week 1 concentrate on the first virtue only. Try to achieve this virtue for an entire day. If you succeed, mark an X in the box.

5. Continue for the other days of the week; place an X in the box if you are successful.

6. At the end of Week 1, analyze your progress. Write a journal entry in which you describe your experiences with the self-improvement plan. How many days were you successful? Was it difficult to follow?

7. During Week 2, continue with the same virtue you concentrated on in Week 1, and add a second virtue. Try to achieve both virtues. Mark an X in the box for the days that you succeed.

8. At the end of Week 2, analyze your progress again, noting any reactions in your journal.

9. During Week 3, continue with the first two virtues and add a third. Mark an X in the box for the days that you succeed. Write a journal at the end of the week.

10. During Week 4, continue with the first three virtues and add a fourth. Mark an X in the box for the days that you succeed.

Writing Assignment

Your Experience with the Personal Self-Improvement Plan

At the end of Week 4, write an essay on a separate piece of paper in which you relate your month-long experience with the personal self-improvement plan.

Personal Self-Improvement Plan, Week 1							
Virtue	Sun	Mon	Tues	Wed	Thurs	Fri	Sat

Personal Self-Improvement Plan, Week 2							
Virtue	Sun	Mon	Tues	Wed	Thurs	Fri	Sat

Personal Self-Improvement Plan, Week 3							
Virtue	Sun	Mon	Tues	Wed	Thurs	Fri	Sat

Personal Self-Improvement Plan, Week 4							
Virtue	Sun	Mon	Tues	Wed	Thurs	Fri	Sat

Activity 3 *The Advice Journal*

One of the fundamental characteristics of human beings is that they love to give advice, perhaps to friends who ask their opinion or to family members who seek consolation and direction. However, people often give advice even when no one asks for it. If you listen to your local sports radio program, you know that callers often offer advice on what they think the coaches or managers should do so that their team wins more. Americans love to give advice to the president on how to conduct domestic and international affairs. They offer advice at work ("If I were the President of this company. . . .") and at school ("If I were the President of this college. . . .").

Journal Activities

Offer Advice/Analyze a Mistake

1. For the next two weeks, write advice in your journal to any individual, company, club, team, or country. Make your advice as practical as possible. Use modals and imperatives as verb forms, and organize your writing by listing steps to follow to achieve the goal.

2. Analyze a big mistake that you have made in your life. Because you are writing about something that has already happened, use the following modal structures in this order:

   I should never have

   I should really have

   I might have

   I could have

   As a result of that mistake, I had to

   The next time this situation arises, I should

   In the future, I must

   In the future, I will certainly

Writing Assignment

Write an Essay Offering Advice

Write essays on the following topics, offering advice to improve the situation.

1. If you are married, you have probably received a great deal of advice from your mother-in-law. However, you know that she is not perfect. In fact, she probably makes as many mistakes as you do. Give advice to your mother-in-law to help her to improve the quality of her life. Do so in letter format on a separate piece of paper. For example: "My dearest mother-in-law, I know that you care so much about me that you give me advice on everything. I would like to return the favor."

2. Your parents constantly give you advice and have done so your whole life. Now is the time to give advice to them. Help them solve their problems and improve their life by giving them advice in letter format on a separate piece of paper. For example: "Dear Mom and Dad, I would like to give you some advice."

Exercise 2 These questions should be answered and compared with the answers written by other members of the class. Write one or two reasons for each answer. These questions may also serve as the basis for essays.

1. If you went to a desert island and could take only one person with you, who would it be?

2. If you went to a desert island, which one CD would you take with you?

3. If you went to a desert island, which one book would you take with you?

4. If you could improve one thing about your personality, what would it be?

5. In your opinion, what is the most important invention in the history of the world?

6. What place in the world do you most want to visit?

7. As a child, what was your favorite free-time activity?

8. What is your favorite color? Why do you like it so much?

9. What would you do if you won $2 million in the lottery?

10. What kind of person would you like your son or daughter to marry?

11. After you finish studying English, what language would you like to study next?

12. If you could have dinner with any famous person in the world, who would it be? What questions would you ask this person?

13. As a child, what was your favorite subject?

14. What is the most important characteristic of a good teacher?

15. What is the most important characteristic of a good friend?

16. If you could meet one political leader in the world, who would it be? What would you talk about?

Building Your Skill in Problem Solving

Actvity 1   *The Problem-Solving Model*

The problem-solving model is a process used in the academic and business world to define and find solutions for a particular problem. It includes the following steps:

1. State the problem clearly.
2. Make a list of possible solutions.
3. Gather and examine information.
4. Choose the solution that seems best.
5. Test the chosen solution to find out if it really solves the problem.

1. **State the problem clearly.** A clear understanding of the problem is an essential step in finding a correct solution. Try to make a provisional statement of the problem. Raise questions about the details of the problem. Are any concepts unclear? What kind of facts do we need? How can we find these facts? Is anything being evaluated? If so, what are the standards for evaluation? We should continue to analyze the problem until we can answer the following questions:

♦ What, exactly, is wrong?

♦ What happens in the situation?

♦ Why is this bad?

♦ What causes this to happen?

♦ Who and what are involved?

♦ How do the other people involved see the problem?

♦ What other problems are related to this problem, and how?

2. **Make a list of possible solutions.** Reflect on the final formulation of the problem, and answer the following questions:

♦ What would each person involved consider necessary to solve the problem?

♦ How will we know when we have solved the problem?

♦ What further facts do we need to know to formulate solutions?

Brainstorm a list of possible solutions to the problem. Remember that during the first phase of brainstorming, we do not fully test the validity of the solution. Instead, we simply list possibilities. The analytical phase will follow.

3. **Gather and examine information.** Now it is time to analyze the solutions listed during the brainstorming activity. Find out how others have tried to solve similar problems. What were the effects of their solutions? Would any of these solutions satisfy everyone involved in the problem?

   The problem-solving technique is based on the analysis of facts, not simply opinions. During this stage, all the information necessary to solve the problem will be gathered.

4. **Choose the solution that seems best.** It is important to remember that in group work there should be no contest among solutions. Rather, we should look for a solution, or a combination of solutions, that minimizes bad consequences and maximizes relief from the problem.

5. **Test the chosen solution to find out if it really solves the problem.** Make sure that the choice made was the correct one. Implement the solution. Monitor the results. This phase, which unfortunately is often omitted because the problem-solvers believe that their task is completed with the identification of the solution, is among the most important. Make sure that the solution has actually fixed the problem. If it has, the problem-solving activity has been successful. However, if the problem persists, another solution must be found.

Writing Assignment

Solve This Problem

There is a problem at the school cafeteria. At the peak lunch periods, from 11:45 A.M. to 1:15 P.M., the line is out the door. There are only three food stations, and at each one customers have to make their order and wait for the food service worker to hand them the food. After customers get their food, they must move to another line to pay. The food is very good, but there is not much variety. Most of the food is cooked to order instead of being prepared in advance. The problem with slow service is having a negative effect. Students, staff, and faculty members are becoming frustrated; some are avoiding the cafeteria and buying food from the machines in the school lobby. Most are satisfied with the atmosphere of the cafeteria, but they want greater variety of food and much faster service. They don't want to spend most of their time waiting for food instead of relaxing at the tables with their friends. How could this problem be fixed?

1. Form groups of four.

2. Choose a leader and a scribe for your group. The leader's task is to make sure that everyone in the group participates. The scribe's task is to record the work done.

3. Follow the five steps in problem solving presented above.

4. At the conclusion of the activity, your group should have solutions to the problem of slow service in the cafeteria.

5. The solutions should be discussed by the entire class.

6. Each student should then write an essay on a separate piece of paper presenting the problem, defining the possible solutions, and choosing the correct one.

Activity 2   *Enhancement Surgery*

The person in this drawing has a very large nose, crooked teeth, a protruding chin, and a serious skin problem. Perhaps his self-image is suffering as a result. He has an alternative, though: enhancement surgery. In a few short months, he could become a very handsome man, with an improved opinion of his personal worth.

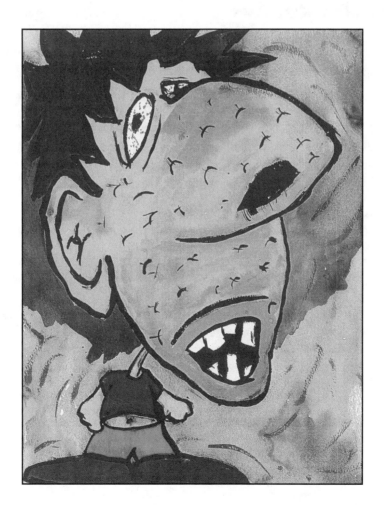

Writing Assignment

Should People Have Cosmetic Surgery

This assignment asks you to analyze yourself. Assume that you meet a cosmetic surgeon who is willing to perform enhancement surgery on any aspect of your appearance that you would like to improve. She will not charge a fee because your photographs will be used for promotional purposes. Would you change anything? Do you think that having enhancement surgery changes people's self-image? Or do you feel that people should never alter their personal appearance just because of vanity? In a clearly organized essay on a separate piece of paper, present your opinion on this matter.

F. Graded Writing Assignment: Who Am I Really?

In analyzing who we are and what makes up the basis of our personality, there are natural determiners and external determiners. Natural determiners are what we receive from birth: gender, race, ethnic background, and social class. For example, a person might have a certain personality because she is a woman, African-American, half-Jamaican and half-Dominican, and has parents who own a small restaurant and are middle class. Another might be a Hispanic man whose mother is Cuban and whose father is part-Irish and part-Italian, and whose family is lower middle class.

You are going to write a five-paragraph essay on a separate piece of paper entitled "Who Am I Really?" Each paragraph of your essay should be six to eight sentences long.

1. **Paragraph 1.** In the first paragraph, you will describe yourself and the natural determiners that make you who you are. Include gender, race, ethnic background, and social class. These are factors that you cannot control, that you are handed at birth.

2. **Paragraphs 2, 3, and 4.** In the second, third, and fourth paragraph, you will analyze which three of these factors are most important in the way you see yourself and identify yourself. Is the most important aspect of your personality that you are Italian, or a woman, or Asian, or that you are a member of the Lee Family? Discuss one aspect in each paragraph.

3. **Paragraph 5.** In the fifth paragraph you will answer the following question: Is it important for you to stay as close as possible to your natural determiners when you choose a mate? That is, might you cross race, ethnic background, social class, or gender in choosing someone to date or to marry?

G. Student Essay: What I Have Learned in This Course

In the final writing assignment, discuss what you have learned in this course. What were the most valuable experiences that you had? In a clearly written essay on a separate piece of paper, present your ideas on this course, your teachers, textbooks, classmates, the information that you gathered, and the techniques that you learned.

H. Part 7 Summary

Based on your work in Part 7, answer and discuss the following questions.

1. Summarize the essay writing process.

2. What are the two functions of the *thesis statement*

3. How is the essay organized?

4. What activities are done during the *editing* phase?

5. How is the *body* of the essay organized and structured?

6. What is the function of the *conclusion* in the essay?

7. Where can you find essays to serve as models?

I. Reflections on Your Progress

Write your reflections or thoughts below on some of the writing you have done in Part 7.

1. Which were your two favorite journal entries, and why?

2. How do you plan to improve your journal writing skills?

3. What was the most interesting writing assignment, and why?

4. What was the least interesting writing assignment, and why?

5. What is the most important thing about writing you learned?

6. Were you satisfied with the progress you made in the assignments?

J. Part 7 Assignment Checklist

Assignment	Required or Optional	Grade	Revised	Returned and Filed
A Personally Meaningful Symbol (page 241)				
The Internet Surfing Journal (Journal Activity) (page 242)				
How Should the Murderer Be Punished? (page 248)				
Your Life in 20 Years (page 251)				
Confronting a Personal Problem (page 255)				
Keep a Lying Journal (Journal Activity) (page 260)				
Personal Lying Habits (page 261)				
Create a Personal Self-Improvement Plan (Journal Activity) (page 266)				
Your Experience with the Personal Self-Improvement Plan (page 266)				
Offer Advice/Analyze a Mistake (Journal Activities) (page 268)				
Write an Essay Offering Advice (page 268)				
Solve This Problem (page 272)				
Should People Have Cosmetic Surgery? (page 274)				
Who Am I Really? (page 274)				
What I Have Learned in This Course (page 275)				

K. Journal Summary

Date of First Journal	Date of Last Journal	Number of Journal Entries Written for Part 7

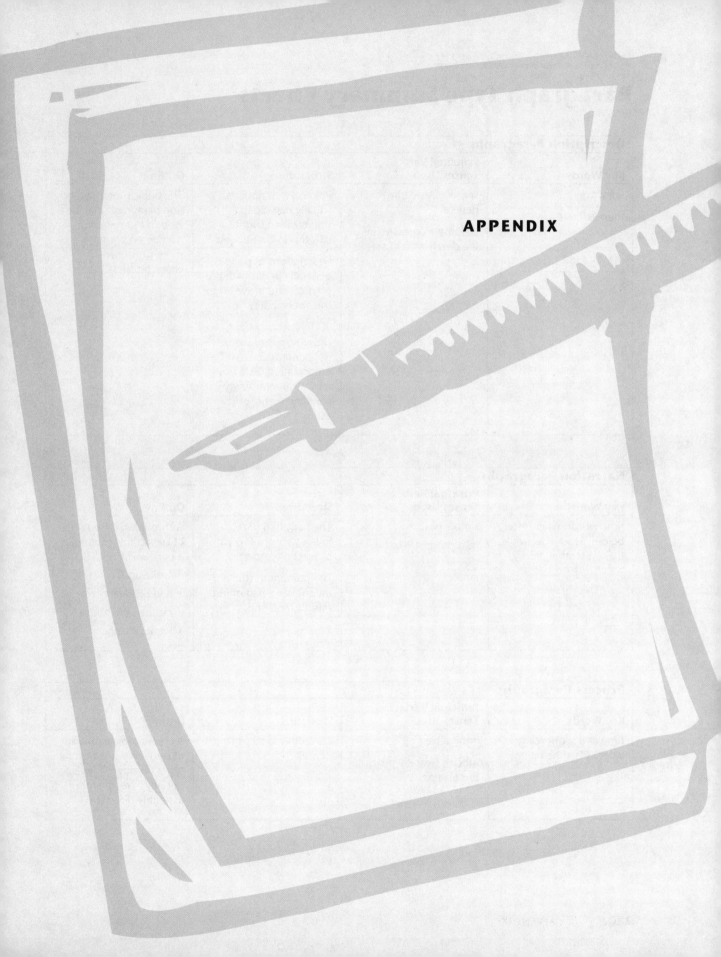

APPENDIX

Paragraph Type Summary Charts

Description Paragraphs

Key Words	Principal Verb Tenses Used	Structure	Outline
adjectives there is/there are	simple present in general present progressive in the description of scenes	Physical descriptions usually have spatial organization (right to left, top to bottom, etc.). Descriptions of people generally begin with the physical and move on to their personality or nature. Descriptions of scenes use *panoramic* organization (as if a movie camera slowly pans the scene) and action verbs.	The outline for a description paragraph may be a web (mindmap) or a numbered list of the three strongest characteristics.

Narration Paragraphs

Key Words	Principal Verb Tenses Used	Structure	Outline
time words: when, after, before, as soon as, while, then, after that, finally	simple past past progressive	The narration paragraph follows **chronological** order (time order). The paragraph (the narration) has a beginning, middle, and end.	A chronological outline of key actions resembles a bulleted list: • woke up • had breakfast • cleaned the house • went to work

Process Paragraphs

Key Words	Principal Verb Tenses Used	Structure	Outline
time and sequencing words (as in narration)	imperatives modals (usually present, but also past)	according to steps or phases	A chronological outline of steps or phases, sometimes numbered (especially in recipes and assembly directions)

Comparison and Contrast Paragraphs

Key Words	Principal Verb Tenses Used	Structure	Outline
contrast words: although, while, whereas, but, yet, nevertheless, nonetheless, however, on the other hand, on the contrary	simple present	There are two structures: • **direct structure,** which focuses on a *point of comparison* (difference) and then alternates between the two *objects of comparison* • **separated structure,** which analyzes one *object of comparison* first, going through three or four *points of comparison,* then moving on to the second point of comparison, going through the same three or four points in the same order	The outline for the two structures is the same: a Comparison Chart with individual boxes for the three–four points of comparison and the two objects of comparison.

Points of comparison	Object 1	Object 2
Point 1		
Point 2		
Point 3		
Point 4		

Persuasion Paragraphs

Key Words	Principal Verb Tenses Used	Structure	Outline
first, second, third, the first reason is, I think, I feel, I believe information and result words such as in addition, furthermore, moreover, as a result, thus hence, finally	simple present, sometimes followed by noun clauses Example: I believe that people should try to live in peace.	The persuasion paragraph is organized by reasons (proof), either in descending order (the best reason first) or ascending order (leading up to the strongest reason). The support should be *objective* if possible, but personal examples as *subjective* support are possible. The persuasion paragraph should lead to a strong conclusion.	A list of reasons and support. There should be 3–4 reasons and major and minor support, presented in bulleted form.

The Essay

Key Words	Principal Verb Tenses Used	Structure	Outline
first, second, third, the first reason is, I think, I feel, I believe adding information and result words such as in addition, furthermore, moreover, as a result, thus hence, finally	simple present, sometimes followed by noun clauses Example: I believe that people should try to live in peace.	The essay generally has five paragraphs, but it may be longer. The first paragraph serves as an introduction. The second, third, and fourth present the reasons (proof) in a persuasion essay, the steps in a process essay, the sequence of events in a narration essay, the differences in comparison writing, or the various aspects or characteristics in a description essay. The last paragraph serves as a conclusion. The paragraphs should be 5–6 sentences each.	Working from a series of notecards or computer files containing research notes, prepare an outline for each individual paragraph. The outlines will vary according to the type of paragraph: description, narration, process, comparison and contrast, and persuasion.

Journal Types and Additional Entry Suggestions

Journal 1: *The Personal Journal (Part 2)*
(Describe and analyze the concepts and events that form your personality.)

- Describe the best gifts that you ever gave others.

- Discuss your most prized possession.

- Describe the person who had the most influence on your life.

- If you could visit any country or city, where would you go? Why?

- Describe your personal religious beliefs.

Journal 2: *The Creative Listings Journal (Part 2)*

(Consider the topic, and write thoughtful lists.)

- List all the jobs that you have had in your life.

- List your favorite sports stars (present and past).

- List the best meals that you have ever eaten.

- List the five best days in your life.

- List your least favorite relatives.

Journal 3: *The Dream Journal (Part 3)*

(Narrate your most powerful dreams.)

- Describe the best dream that you have ever had.

- Describe the worst dream that you have ever had.

- Ask classmates to describe their most powerful dreams.

- Ask friends and relatives to describe their most powerful dreams.

- Try to analyze your most interesting dreams: find deeper significance.

Journal 4: *The Double-Entry Journal (Part 4)*

(Write a summary in the first column, and present your reaction in the second column.)

◆ Research and summarize the life of Abraham Lincoln (column 1), and then indicate your thoughts on the 16th president (column 2).

◆ Read about the September 11, 2001, attack, and present your thoughts.

◆ Read the *Bill of Rights* of the U.S. Constitution, and then analyze them.

◆ Read a significant poem, and discuss it in the second column.

◆ Find an interesting article about a place to visit, and discuss it.

Journal 5: *The Four-Entry Journal (Part 5)*

(Present your opinion, and then share it with your classmates.)

◆ Present your opinion on the most evil person who ever lived.

◆ Present your opinion on the most important invention in the history of the world.

◆ What was the most important event in history?

◆ What was the worst event in history?

◆ Time travel: If you could go anywhere at anytime, where would you go?

Journal 6: *The Memorandum Journal (Part 6)*

◆ Find statistics on life expectancy in various countries around the world.

◆ Research and analyze population data.

◆ Find statistics on capital punishment around the world.

◆ Research and analyze data on violent crimes in various countries.

◆ Conduct research on religion in the United States.

Journal 7: *The Essay as Journal (Part 7)*

(Write editorials on significant and large issues; practice how to narrow them to a dimension that can be treated in a 500-word essay.)

- Analyze the effect of U.S. fast-food franchises that are opening in other countries.

- What is your opinion of malls, with the same stores, the same design, and the same foods?

- How do you feel about new and increased security at the airport? Does it make you feel safer? Is it really necessary? Present your opinion on the matter.

- Present your opinion on the rights of animals. Are they equal to the rights of human beings? Should we eat meat? Wear furs? Hunt?

- Present your opinion on tipping. Do you tip every time you eat out? Do you tip even when the service is bad? Do you add extra to the tip when the service is excellent? Does it bother you that no one tips you in your job?

Journal 8: *The Lying Journal (Part 7)*

(Analyze your habits of dishonesty and those of your friends, relatives, and classmates.)

- Write a journal on the best liar that you have ever met.

- Who is the best liar among your family members?

- Why do you think that people lie so much?

- If you are late for work because you have overslept, would you tell your boss the truth? Can you find other situations in which telling the truth might be dangerous?

- Are you frank or blunt with your friends, classmates, or relatives, or do you tell sweet lies?

Journal 9: *The Personal Improvement Journal (Part 7)*

(Take control of your life by writing down significant actions and goals.)

◆ Analyze your eating habits by listing all the foods that you eat in a week. Before you go to bed at night, write down everything you have eaten that day.

◆ Write down all the good things that you have done in a day.

◆ Make a list of your goals. What do you want to achieve in a given day, week, or month? Analyze whether you have met those goals.

◆ Make a plan to learn something new in a three-month period. Set a schedule of activities to really learn.

◆ Choose one physical space that you would like to keep cleaner and more organized such as your desk, your room, or your car. Set about keeping that space more in order.

Journal 10: *The Advice Journal (Part 7)*

(Give advice [even though you haven't been asked] in various situations.)

◆ How can your favorite sports team improve? What players should they trade? What players should they acquire? Should they keep or fire the coach?

◆ If you were the president of the college that you attend, what changes would you make?

◆ If you were the mayor of the city where you live, what would you do to improve the quality of life there?

◆ Give past-tense advice citing the mistakes that your brothers and sisters have made (use *should have, could have,* and *might have*).

◆ How can students with test anxiety learn to relax so that they can perform better?

Student Paragraphs

The following were written by students in the advanced writing class at Bergen Community College in Paramus, New Jersey.

Student Samples from Part 2

Personal Ad

by Rebecca Lee, China

A beautiful, young woman, 26 years old, black hair, SAF, 5'5, likes going out, dancing, and spending a lot of time reading poems, but dislikes long novels and hiking. Her hobbies are swimming, dancing, cooking, and driving a car. She is an honest, sincere, romantic, and humorous person. She is interested in everything about business. Right now, she is studying English and business and wants to be a good business-woman. She dreams of living in a comfortable house with a loving husband and children, traveling with her family, and having good times until the children grow up. Then she would like to go to the countryside with her husband and live the rest of her life there happily. She seeks a professional man with a similar way of thinking. He must be healthy, outgoing, a good worker, and like animals. She seeks a SW/AM, 26–35, honest, humorous, who knows the rules of etiquette. He should be someone who is studying or has already finished his master's degree and has rich dreams for the future.

My Best Friend

by Iryna Tsyvova, Russia

There must be somebody in your life, whom you can trust and who can trust you. That person can help you in the hardest moments, give you advice, and you can do the same. I am lucky to have a person like this in my life. Her name is Yvonne. I have known her since I was two years old. We grew up together, and I can say that I know her as well as I know myself. We were always together, but I had to leave my native city and country. I wish that she were here now. I could tell her everything that is on my mind and in my soul. Yvonne is an excellent talker, and an even better listener. She can make fun of anything, and we always laugh together. She doesn't care too much about her looks. Yvonne has natural beauty, and her beauty is much stronger because of her sensitive and helpful soul. I really miss her.

The Cascade Village Hotel

by Makiko Imai, Japan

I am at the Cascade Village Hotel. The rooms are spacious and luxurious, but the prices are moderate. It is located in the Rocky Mountains in Colorado, near Durango. I can enjoy skiing in the winter. Of course, this place is located at a high altitude, so I can see mountaintops covered with snow even in the summer. The scenery is breathtaking. I can ride train from Durango which goes through the mountains. The scenery you can see from the train is beautiful, too. If I am tired of skiing or staying in the mountains, I can go to Durango. It is about 15 minutes by car from the Cascade Village Hotel. Durango is an isolated small town, but it has a lot of shops and restaurants. It is an immaculate town. I can go shopping at up-to-date shops and eat delicious food at several rustic restaurants. The restaurants are very good. Why don't they open branches in my area? Then I will be able to eat there once in a while. Spending time at the Cascade Village Hotel is not boring at all. I am having a memorable time.

My Country

by Frida Pertonceli, Slovenia

I used to live in a beautiful country called Slovenia. It is a small country in the middle of Europe, with only two million people. Slovenia borders on Italy in the west, Austria in the north, Hungary in the northeast, and Croatia in the east. In the northern part of Slovenia there is a beautiful mountain range called the Alps, and in the southern part there is the Adriatic Sea. Slovenia has a long history. First it was part of the Hapsburg Empire and the woman who ruled it was Maria Theresa. After World War I, it was part of Yugoslavia and was ruled by King Peter, who escaped to Switzerland at the beginning of World War II. After a four-year war, Slovenia became part of the Socialist Federal Republic of Yugoslavia. In 1991, Slovenia separated from Yugoslavia and became independent. Now it is ruled by Parliament and every four years there is an election for President. Thinking about cultural life in Slovenia, I can say that it is mostly concentrated in the capital city, Ljubljana, and in Maribor. There are operas, ballets, galleries, museums, and most people come to these cities to see performances and exhibitions. Because Slovenia is small, everyone can reach these cities within two hours. Finally, I would like to express my wish that Slovenia would be accepted into the European Union and that its economy continues to develop.

My Hometown

by Hanna Jawinska

I grew up in a small village called Mojki in the eastern part of Poland. The village has only 10 houses and just 70 people live there. Mojki is a very beautiful village, and there is one small food store, one pond in the middle of the village, and only one street. All the houses are new because there was a big fire ten years ago and almost everything burned down. After the fire, people built new houses. The village is located between Kierki and Ktoski. My school was only two miles from Mojki. I spent my childhood in this lovely village. The people are very kind and polite there. They really help each other, and it is like one big family. We know everything about each other because it is difficult to keep secrets in such a small place. My grandmother still lives there, and I can't wait to go back to visit her and all my other neighbors in Mojki.

Someone That I Admired as a Child

by Tatiana Runjka, Uzbekistan

Not everyone had a teacher as I had in my elementary school. Mrs. Yvavya started to work as a teacher the year that I started school. She was a really kind person who always helped her students with love and understanding. We really liked her because of her open soul and deep gray eyes. I could always tell her about my problems though they were not so serious. She listened and tried to help. She even helped students' parents to be closer to their children. Mrs. Yvavya was not like some teachers. She didn't think that teaching was her only task; she was like a second mother for her students. That's why she had love and respect for her little angels and their parents. I visited her as often as I could. It was a pleasure to talk with my first grade teacher. I think I learned to love and care about children from her. I wish all young students could have a teacher like her.

Student Samples from Part 3

My First Month in the United States

by Hanna Huang, China

I was a teenager when I came to America. When I arrived at JFK Airport, my grandmother was there waiting for me. We took a yellow cab to her house. It was hard for me to adapt to the new culture and, at the same time, to keep my own culture. I felt that I was in a strange land, that I did not belong here. People looked strange to me, and I spent most of my time alone and wondering who I really was. The new language seemed so difficult for me to learn. I was not making quick progress in learning, and I felt miserable. After a few months, I began to feel more comfortable and relaxed. Even though everything was strange for me, I started to adapt to the new culture gradually. Life became interesting and, at last, it was a good experience to be living in the United States.

The Bear and the Tiger

by Jae Won Lee, Korea

A long time ago, a bear and a tiger lived together in Korea. They were friends and always envied people and hoped to be human beings, so they decided to talk to God. They said, "God, Holy God. We really want to be human beings. Please help us." God told them, "If you really want to, I will make you into human beings, but to be human beings, you have to take two tests. First of all, you have to live in a dark cave. You can't go out for one month. Second, you must only eat garlic and onions. Can you do these two things?" They told him that they could if they could become human beings. Two weeks later, the tiger couldn't endure the pain of darkness, so he ran out of the cave. The tiger gave up being a human being, but the bear endured the pain until the last day. One month later, the bear changed into a beautiful girl and married a god. One year later, she gave birth to a son. The son was named 'Dan-Goon', the founder of the first nation on the Korean peninsula.

Mouse Hunt

by Doris Pava-Ruiz, Colombia

I always remember the day when my husband went to a restaurant. After he finished eating and left the restaurant, he went to the parking lot. While he was walking to his car, he saw a little mouse inside the car looking through the window. After that, he began to hunt for the mouse, but he couldn't find him. After that, my husband bought different kinds of mousetraps, but we couldn't catch this tricky mouse, even though we put cheese on them. After a few days, we decided to see our mechanic. We told him the story about the mouse, but Luis wasn't surprised because he had had the same experience with other customers. The mechanic was not busy, so he started to look for the mouse. He spent all day long trying to catch the mouse, because he was inside the car's panels. Finally, he found the little mouse and released him into the street in front of the garage. We had to pay $80 to the mechanic because he had to change some electric cables in the car, plus the two or three hours labor to catch the mouse. I always laugh when I remember this situation, especially when I think of my husband's face when the mechanic gave him the bill.

How I Got My Scar

by Andrej Dombrowski, Poland

It is fun to play soccer, but at the right time and in the right place. When I was in grammar school, I love to play soccer. During the winter vacation, I was at home with my brother. It was really bad weather outside, and we were very bored. We were thinking about what to do, and we started to play soccer. We were playing in the living room because it was the biggest room in our house. I kicked the ball, a really good shot, but it hit the chandelier. As soon as the ball struck it, the chandelier fell down. I tried to save it, but the glass fell apart and cut my hand. Later we cleaned the living room as much as possible. By the time my parents came home, the room had been cleaned. We didn't say anything, but they immediately noticed that the chandelier was missing. They started to scream, but then they saw that my hand was wrapped in a towel, full of blood. My parents took me to the emergency room of the local hospital, where a doctor put eleven stitches in my hand. We returned home, and I don't know who was crying more, my brother or I. We told the story to my parents, but they really didn't go as crazy as I thought they would. I do remember, though, that we spent the entire vacation cleaning out the garage, the basement, and the attic. By the time vacation was over, we were sure ready to go back to school. After that, we never played soccer in the house again. Every time I look at my hand, I think of my high shot in the living room.

Identical Twins?

by Manuel Morales, Cuba

This incredible story happened in eastern Russia many years ago. In this part of the country, there is always a lot of snow, and because the mountains are high, the snow never completely melts. There was a 23-year-old man, who was very handsome, with blond hair and blue eyes. He had a wife and a one-year-old son. He loved to go skiing and since he lived in a mountain town, he went almost every day after he finished work. One very cold day he went to the top of the mountain. While he was skiing, the weather changed: the temperature got lower and lower, and it started to snow. pretty hard. While he was going down a difficult part of the course, with a sharp curve, he could not make the turn because of the ice, and he crashed into a tree, and died almost immediately. After an hour when he did not return, rescuers went looking for him. However, the snow continued to fall for three days, and they never found the body.

Twenty-two years later, his son grew up, with blond hair and blue eyes. He liked to ski as his father had done. One day in March the weather was very warm, probably the warmest March in history in that part of Russia. Despite the warm weather, he went skiing on a Sunday afternoon, on the same course where his father had disappeared. The son was skiing down the hill, with all the melting snow, when he crashed into some object and fell down to the ground. He was sure that his leg was broken. He moved over to see what he hit, and noticed a leg uncovered. He brushed the snow off the rest of a human body, which was facing down into the snow. Despite the pain in his leg, he managed to roll the body over, and realized that the man had a face that was identical to his. The rescuers arrived and took to young man to the hospital, and the dead body, too. The young man's mother went to the hospital, and she almost went into shock when she looked at her son, and the man who had been her husband and who had died twenty-two years before. Because the body was perfectly frozen all these years, it was in perfect condition. The frozen body and the young man were identical, and you could say that they were both twenty-three years old. They were almost like identical twins. In that part of Russia, on cold winter nights, people still tell this story of how a son found his father, who really looked like himself.

A Very Embarrassing Experience

by Alyssa Wai, Taiwan

I had one embarrassing experience in the subway of Philadelphia. In Philadelphia, many people take subways and buses to move around the city. Therefore, bus stops and subway stations are very crowded, especially during rush hours. One day around 5:00, I had just finished working in Chinatown, and I went to a supermarket to buy some food for the week. When I was on my way to the subway station, I was carrying some heavy bags filled with groceries. It was hard to walk down the stairs to the station. While I was entering the station, the subway doors were closing and train left, so I had to wait a few minutes for the next one. Inside the station, the air had a bad smell, and I was getting upset because I missed the train and I would probably miss the next bus to King of Prussia, where I lived. After a few minutes the train came, and I jumped fast into the car and a lot of people were already inside standing and sitting. I was standing in the middle of the car, when suddenly a passenger left a seat empty for me to sit down. In that moment I felt lucky, but next to me there was a guy who was such a terrible person. He looked very tired and even though the train was noisy, he was able to sleep. When the train started moving, he fell asleep on my shoulder, and even when I tried to move his head, he didn't wake up. I was feeling very embarrassed, and I was trying to move my body away. He opened his eyes to look around for a second, but then he just went back to sleep. I was very upset, stood up, went to the nearest door, and ran out. After this trouble, I usually don't like to sit down on the subway anymore. Even if I am tired, I just stand near the door.

Student Samples from Part 4

Advice on How to Get High Grades

by Juan Murillo, Mexico

I know how hard it is to get high grades in English language courses, but I will try to help you. First of all, you should go to the bookstore and buy all the course books right away. These books will help you to improve your grades. You should read the whole book throughout the semester and do as many exercises as you can, not just the exercises that the teacher assigns. If there are charts about gerunds and infinitives, or the past tense of irregular verbs, you should memorize this information. In your free time, look at the book to review what you have studied in class. Second, you should go to your English teachers and talk to them about your problems and your goals. Your teachers will be able to give you extra work on the specific area that needs improvement. After you talk to them, you can prepare a program of extra study, with additional exercises and readings for practice. You should also ask your teachers about extra help. Most teachers are available during their office hours, three or four hours a week. Don't be afraid to ask them; if you ask, you will get additional help. Teachers are our friends. I will give you a personal example to convince you. A year after I came to the United States, I took a computer class in high school. In the first marking period my average was 40. I went to the teacher and asked for extra help. She was very happy that I came to her. She gave me extra help twice a week. Guess what? In the last marking period my average was 82. So go to your teacher. If you follow my advice, you can get better grades in your English courses.

Dinner in Afghanistan

by Olga Levit, Israel

If you are invited to dinner by a family in Afghanistan and you want to make a good impression, follow these steps. First, be on time because it is considered impolite to make several people wait for you. If you come very late, they might start dinner without you. Second, you should bring some flowers or fruit, but the hosts will not be angry if you don't bring anything because for them the important thing is to see you, and not receive your gift. Never bring liquor to a Afghani house since they cannot drink it because of their religion. Third, you should take off your shoes when you enter because people, especially in villages, set the tablecloth on the floor. Then the hostess will bring you tea with some sweets. During this time, the hostess will set the table and you have the chance to talk to the other guests or with the host. Before you start eating, you should wash your hands, but do not dry them with a towel. After that, you should say "Bismalah" with the hosts and only then start to eat. This is their custom, and it would be impolite not to follow it. Most people in Afghanistan usually eat with their hands, so you should also try this. Dinner usually takes at least an hour. Afghanis usually say "The more dishes, the more respect for the guests." After dinner they pray and relax with some fruit, tea, and sweets. If you follow these steps, you will make a good impression on the hosts.

Having Dinner in Jordan

by Jadwiga Stefinska, Poland

There are many countries in the world, and each country has a set of customs. While some customs many be similar, other customs differ greatly from country to country. My friend Mather is from Jordan. I asked him what people in his country do when they are invited to dinner. He gave me a great deal of information. He told me that when you are invited to dinner, you should come on time. In this way the hosts will know that you have respect for them. They will know that you are a person that they can depend on. You shouldn't come too early or too late because this will not say anything good about you. You won't make a good impression on them. The next important thing is that you should bring a little gift with you. This gift may be flowers or a little something for the house. Again, it will show respect for your hosts. After you give the present, you should greet all the people in the house. The next point that Mather told me was that the dinner will be special. There will be a great variety of food. During the dinner you may eat as much as you can. When you want more, don't be shy. In Jordan you never ask for food; you just take whatever you want. The hosts feel happy when they see that their guests feel comfortable and free in their homes. They also want to see that you like their food. After everything is eaten, you should thank the hosts for the dinner. Then you will usually have fun talking, joking, looking at pictures, and sharing different experiences. One more important thing: you shouldn't leave too early. Stay as long as you want. If you live far away, they will usually ask you to stay for a night. It is always a pleasure to have guests stay over for the night. They will usually take the best care of you. Guests are always very welcome in Jordan. When you are leaving, you should thank them again, and invite them to your house for the next time. If you do this, they will feel that you have enjoyed the dinner.

Advice If You Are too Nervous to Speak English

by Tipavan Sinisgalesh, Thailand

If you are too nervous to speak English, I think that you should follow my advice. I know your situation. Please do not feel depressed because all foreign students have the same problem. If you feel nervous when you try to speak, you should breathe deeply before you speak. Since you breathe fresh air and calm down, this act will help you relax. Second, you should go to church because many people there who usually speak English would love to talk to you, and they are very nice, too. Sometimes, if you don't speak English very well, they would like to help you improve your language abilities. Moreover, this help is absolutely free. Third, you should try to find a part-time job, especially in a supermarket. Since many English words come from our daily lives, you will learn a lot of vocabulary, and you can talk to many different kinds of people. Sometimes you can even make friends in this way, and this will help you improve your skills. Finally, I am going to give you the most important piece of advice. Don't worry and feel ashamed about what people think about you when you are speaking English since English is your second language. You already speak one language perfectly. Remember that most Americans only know English. Moreover, learning another language is not easy. Many successful people say that if you want to become a successful person, you should always try and not give up. I hope this advice will help you.

Advice to Lonely

by Gladys Arguello, Nicaragua

I read your letter in which you ask me to advise you on how to meet people from your country. First of all, if you not only miss the people but also the food from your native country, you should go to find information in the yellow pages of the phone book about where you can find some restaurants from your country and go there. I suggest this because in these places you should meet someone, either the owner, the waiters and waitresses, or other customers who can talk to you. Also, you should go to the library and look in books about the population and the place where the people from your country are concentrated. Many counties have a concentration of people from different countries. For example, in Orange County, New York there are many Nicaraguans in the small city of Sloatsburg. I went there and found grocery stores, restaurants, even video stores for people from Nicaragua. I felt at home in this little place. Another thing that you can do is to join the international club at your school. It is important to understand that you are not the only one who is in the same situation. There are many other students just like you who miss their native countries and feel lonely in the United States. Sometimes it is good to talk about problems that you have in common. I hope the best for you and I want to tell you finally not to give up.

How to Cook Bulgogi

by Yoojin Yoon, Korea

Bulgogi is one of the most traditional Korean dishes cooked at the table on a bulgogi grill or hibachi over charcoal. The unique aspect of bulgogi is the flavor which comes from the seasonings. Traditionally, in Korea, cooks do not follow precise recipes which ask for exact measurements as in western cooking, so the amount of seasonings can be changed according to one's tastes. Bulgogi is a communal dish, with the warmth of the fire and the aroma of the special sauce bringing people into conversation and happiness.

Ingredients: **(4 servings)**
2 lbs sliced sirloin beef

Seasonings:
5 tb soy sauce
4 tb sugar
1 tb sesame oil
1 tb garlic (minced)
4 tb scallions (coarsely chopped)
1/4 tb black pepper

Cooking method:
1. Make the sauce by mixing together all the ingredients listed under seasonings. Pour the sauce over the beef. Mix the meat and the sauce thoroughly. Let the meat marinate for at least 1 hour.
2. Heat the bulgogi grill over a charcoal fire. Barbecue the beef over a hot fire for approximately 3 minutes. The beef will cook very quickly. Use a frying pan or an oven broiler if you don't have a bulgogi grill.
3. Bulgogi is usually served with white rice and traditional Korean kimchee and pickled vegetables as side dishes.

Student Samples from Part 5

Waiting On Line

by Giuliana Maraini, Italy

One aspect of American behavior that I really like and that I find very different from the behavior of the people in my country is their way of standing in line. Wherever it might be, in a bank, a supermarket, a movie theatre, a bus stop, you always see Americans standing politely and calmly. They seem to respect each other and I rarely see people try to cut the line. For example, I went to Six Flags for Fright Fest last Halloween. The line for the Haunted Hayride was really long, more than one and a half hours. However, you didn't see anyone trying to get in front of other people. In fact, at Six Flags, if people are caught cutting the line, they are thrown out of the park. Unfortunately, in my country, it is common to see a different situation when people wait on line. When you watch the lines at a bus stop, for example, you will see that people are angry, and they push and pull and scream at each other, "I was here before you!" Going to the bank is sometimes an exhausting experience because there is no order, just gigantic chaos. You have to elbow your way to the front of the line, and the strongest one gets served first. This is a great difference in the behavior of Americans and people from my country.

Ideas vs. Reality: Visions of America

by Sojita Ghanshyman, India

Before I came to the United States, I had some ideas about what America would be like. When I got here, I found out that there are some things that I didn't expect. First of all, before I came here, I thought that American way of life was very expensive compared to India. When I came to America, I found out that American life wasn't so expensive. I always go to the store to buy clothes, groceries, and other items, and they cost less than in my country, where everything is expensive. This is because in America there are stores for rich people and stores for regular people. I can't buy my clothes in Nordstrom's or Sacks Fifth Avenue, but there is a great choice in discount stores and outlets. In the United States, almost everyone has a car; in India, it is still very difficult to afford a car. I also thought that the educational system would be more difficult in America. On the contrary, it is much harder in India. In my country, we have to remember everything that we study in each class for the whole year. At the end of each year, we have a final exam for everything. If we fail any subject on the final exam, we fail for the whole year and we can't go forward to the next semester. In America, if students fail a course, they can continue. They only have to repeat that one course. In conclusion, everything is not the same as I thought about America before I came here. I guess it is the same with all countries in the world.

Student Samples from Part 6

Odelia College

by Usha Patel, India

I decided to attend Odelia College because it has many advantages that I could not find anywhere else. For example, the location is very good and the area is safe. It is bordered by two golf courses and a county park. It takes only fifteen minutes to get to school from my house. When I finish classes, if I have some free time, I like to take a walk in the park. There is a duck pond where I can see ducks and geese of many colors. Odelia also has many excellent professors. They like teaching and sharing their knowledge with students. Whenever I have a question or a problem, I can meet with them. They are never in too much of a rush to talk to me. In class they use very interesting materials, in addition to the textbook. My Reading professor, for example, always brings in articles from newspapers and magazines. The other advantage of Odelia College is its student body. There are people from so many different countries that I have learned about different customs, different educational systems, and different languages. Although we do not look alike or even think alike sometimes, we have one common goal: to learn English. Also, I am forced to speak English with many of the students because they cannot speak my native language. Many of the exercises in the Writing book encourage us to learn more about the customs of other countries. This has been a very interesting experience. For all of these advantages, I think that Odelia College is the right place for me to study English, and my major, which will probably be international business.

Mom's Actions

by Roberto Fracaviglia, Italy

After reading this story about Honey Boy I have mixed feelings about the mother's actions. I believe that Big Blue did something immoral by killing his best friend for a payoff. He could have taken him alive by reporting his whereabouts to the proper authorities and still claimed the reward. He could have let the judicial process find Honey Boy guilty or innocent. Big Blue obviously had deeper problems with his relationship with Honey Boy in order to shoot him in the face. This act alone is horrid because now you cannot tell who the dead body is by sight. When Mom looked at her son lying on the table with his face blown off, she knew it was Honey Boy, but probably also thought that Big Blue betrayed his friendship. On the other hand, what the mother did was immoral. She should have identified her son. Now her son will be buried in an unmarked grave and Big Blue will be punished. Like mother like son: I guess immoral acts run in the family.

The Dangers of Living in a Large City

by Patrick Onwubu, Nigeria

There are several reasons why I feel that large cities are terrible and horrible places. First of all, there are a lot of crimes like murder, rape, and robbery. For example, in Chicago in 1998 there were more than 900 murders, and in New York there were 850, almost three people killed every day. You can see crime all the time in the newspaper and on television. People in large cities must lock the doors of their apartments, sometimes with two or three locks in order to protect themselves. Moreover, large cities are usually dirty and noisy. The streets are full of trash and loud noises like sirens and fire trucks. Drivers, especially taxi drivers, sound their horns constantly; therefore, you have to talk loudly for your friends to understand you. But the most important reason why I do not like large cities is the traffic. There are simply too many cars on the roads, so you are always stuck in heavy traffic. Although you can take the subway, it is usually not safe and clean. The noise, pollution, and anger caused by the heavy traffic make me feel depressed. For all these reasons, I feel that large cities are not good places to live. I prefer the calm and beauty of the suburbs.

Violence and Sex on Television

by Manuala Rojao, Portugal

I feel that television programs predominantly show violence and sex, and that tv is not really an educational tool for the following reasons. First, there are a lot of violent shows on tv, which affect us in a negative way. Sometimes we want to act like the hero on tv, without keeping in mind that people can get hurt. Then we see violent crimes committed by kids, who were probably influenced by violent television programs. Second, there is also a lot of sex on television, which plays a negative role in our lives. This situation gets even worse when our children watch these shows. The movies on HBO, Encore, and Cinemax may be R-rated, and it is difficult to control what our children watch. When they start watching this kind of program, their period of innocence finishes in their lives. Third, the news shown on tv desensitizes people. There are so many crimes reported on the news that we don't really get as outraged as we should because we have become accustomed to watching them. In my opinion, these programs do not educate us, but instead fill our brains with non-useful things. They make us afraid to leave the house because we might be the victims of violence. They only show negative things. I think that television should be more positive and not rely so much on violence and sex.

The Job That I Would Never Do

by Claudio Aponte, Colombia

I would never be a garbage collector for several reasons. First, the hours of the job are not very convenient for me. You start the job very early in the morning and finish late. Next, you work outside. Even though it may be very hot in the summer or very cold in the winter, you have to stay outside all the time. When it rains or snows, when the wind is blowing, you still have to work. Also, it isn't a clean job. You have to pick up many dirty things. Some people put the trash in bags and tie them, but other people just throw the trash away loose in the garbage cans without bags. Sometimes small animals or the wind spread the trash on the ground and you have to collect it again. When the trash stands for a long time, it smells very bad. It's very unpleasant and makes the workers smell, too. Moreover, there are many germs which can cause many different diseases. Finally, this is a hard job. You have to be able to carry heavy things. The garbage bags are sometimes very heavy. Some people put big objects like mattresses, bookshelves or other pieces of furniture for collection. It requires great power to lift these things and put them in the garbage truck. These are the major reasons why I would never work as a garbage collector.

PART 1.   THE BASICS

Exercise 1   (page 11)

Sentence 1:

in = *preposition*
the = *article*
soap opera = *noun (object of preposition)*
the = *article*
doctor = *noun (subject)*
loves = *verb (simple present, singular, active)*
the = *article*
shy = *adjective*

nurse = *noun (object of verb love)*
but = *conjunction*
the = *article*
nurse = *noun (subject)*
loves = *verb (simple present, singular, active)*
the = *article*
doctor's = *possessive noun*
wife = *noun (object of verb loves)*

Sentence 2:

I = *pronoun*
have met = *verb (present perfect, singular, active)*
never = *adverb*
a = *article*
person = *noun (object of verb met)*
from = *preposition*
Colorado = *noun (object of preposition)*
who = *relative pronoun*

did like = *verb*
not = *adverb*
to = *preposition*
ski = *verb (infinitive)*
and = *conjunction*
climb = *verb (infinitive)*
mountains = *noun (object of verb climb)*

Sentence 3:

my = *possessive adjective*
mysterious = *adjective*
neighbor = *noun (subject)*
who = *relative pronoun*
works = *verb (simple present, singular, active)*
the = *article*
night shift = *noun (object of verb)*

goes = *verb (simple present, singular, active)*
to = *article*
sleep = *verb (infinitive)*
in = *preposition*
the = *article*
morning = *noun (object of preposition)*

Sentence 4:

the = *article*
man = *noun (subject)*
with = *preposition*
the = *article*
dreadlocks = *noun (object of preposition)*
is drying = *verb (present progressive, singular, active)*
himself = *pronoun*

with = *preposition*
a = *article*
colorful = *adjective*
towel = *noun (object of preposition)*
on = *preposition*
the = *article*
beach = *noun (object of preposition)*

Sentence 5: sometimes = *adverb*
Jimena = *noun (subject)*
drinks = *verb (simple present, singular, active)*
four = *adjective*
cups = *noun (object of verb)*

of = *preposition*
tea = *noun (object of preposition)*
in order to = *prepositions*
be = *verb (infinitive)*
social = *adjective*

Sentence 6: people = *noun (subject)*
travel = *verb (simple present, plural, active)*
great = *adjective*
distances = *noun (object of verb)*

to = *preposition*
return = *verb (infinitive)*
home = *noun (object of verb)*

Sentence 7: my = *adjective*
paternal = *adjective*
grandfather = *noun (subject)*
never = *adverb*
flew = *verb (simple past, singular, active)*
in = *preposition*
a = *article*
four-seat = *adjective*

plane = *noun (object of preposition)*
but = *conjunction*
my = *adjective*
intrepid = *adjective*
father = *noun (subject)*
has = *verb (simple present, singular, active)*
several = *adjective*
times = *noun*

Sentence 8: the = *article*
Houston Astrodome = *noun (subject)*
the = *article*
first = *adjective*
indoor = *adjective*

baseball = *adjective*
stadium = *noun (subject of preposition)*
was built = *verb (passive) (simple past)*
in = *preposition*
1963 = *noun (object of preposition)*

Sentence 9: while = *conjunction*
she = *pronoun*
was reading = *verb (past progressive, singular, active)*
the = *article*
end = *noun (object of verb)*
of = *preposition*
the = *article*

fascinating = *adjective*
novel = *noun (object of preposition)*
she = *pronoun*
did stop = *verb (simple past, singular, active)*
not = *adverb*
to = *preposition*
make = *verb (infinitive)*
coffee = *noun (object of verb)*

Sentence 10: I = *pronoun*
saw = *verb (simple past, singular, active)*
several = *adjective*
very = *adverb*
beautiful = *adjective*
shells = *noun (object of verb)*

on = *preposition*
the = *article*
beach = *noun (object of preposition)*
on = *preposition*
Marco Island = *noun (object of preposition)*
Florida = *noun (object of preposition)*

Sentence 11: the = *article*
lovely = *adjective*
child = *noun (subject)*
bit = *verb (simple past, singular, active)*
the = *article*

hairy = *adjective*
man = *noun (object of verb)*
on = *preposition*
the = *article*
cheek = *noun (object of preposition)*

Sentence 12:   the = *article*   he = *pronoun*
                 mammoth = *adjective*   ate = *verb (simple past, singular, active)*
                 soldier = *noun (subject)*   the = *article*
                 was = *verb (simple past, singular, active)*   cookies = *noun (object of verb)*
                 very = *adverb*   and = *conjunction*
                 hungry = *adjective*   the = *article*
                 so = *conjunction*   box = *noun (object of verb)*

Exercise 2   **(page 12)**

Sentence 1:   First blank = *an adjective with a positive connotation (happy, elated, satisfied, excellent)*
                Second blank = *an adverb with a positive connotation (quickly, happily, swiftly)*

Sentence 2:   First blank: *noun (man, woman, editor, student)*
                Second blank: *adjective (famous, wonderful, tired, depressed)*

Sentence 3:   First blank: *verb (sang, played)*
                Second blank: *adjective or two-word noun (famous, sweet, happy, or love)*
                Third blank: *adverb (softly, carefully, smoothly)*

Sentence 4:   First blank: *noun (summer, afternoon)*
                Second blank: *noun (men, women, lifeguards, beachgoers, swimmers)*
                Third blank: *noun (men, women, swimmers, strollers)*
                Fourth blank: *adjective (short, tight, colorful, baggy)*

Sentence 5:   First blank: *preposition (of)*
                Second blank: *noun (rain, weather, storm)*
                Third blank: *noun (game, concert, picnic)*
                Fourth blank: *verb [past participle to form passive] (cancelled, postponed)*

Sentence 6:   First blank: *article (the)*
                Second blank: *verb (talked, walked, conversed, fought)*
                Third blank: *noun (sister, cousin, mother)*

Sentence 7:   First blank: *preposition (after)*
                Second blank: *noun (streets, roads, houses)*
                Third blank: *noun (water, leaves, debris, dirt, mud)*

Sentence 8:   First blank: *verb (was singing, sang)*
                Second blank: *noun (cat, children, people, woman)*
                Third blank: *adverb (hungrily [for the cat], closely, quietly, carefully)*

Sentence 9:   First blank: *adjective (hungry, happy)*
                Second blank: *verb (went, hurried, walked)*
                Third blank: *adjective (fast, quick)*
                Fourth blank: *conjunction (but)*
                Fifth blank: *verb (eat)*
                Sixth blank: *adjective (closed)*

Sentence 10:   First blank: *conjunction (when)*

Second blank: *adverb of frequency (always, sometimes, often)*

Third blank: *noun (shoes, sneakers, pants).*

Exercise 3   **(page 15)**

   1. She is always angry, but her brother is a calm guy. (3)
   2. Because John is rich, he always has many people in his dining room. (1)
   3. I love her so much since she has a well-paying job. (2)
   4. My brother cannot swim; however, he is not afraid to go on a small boat in the ocean. (5)
   5. Although he never gives flowers to his mother, she still loves him. (1)
   6. John's face is disfigured; in addition, his teeth are not straight. (5)
   7. My uncle and aunt sing duets. They have no talent. (4)
   8. I have never eaten food from Somalia; nevertheless, I have heard that it is excellent. (5)
   9. The hungry man ate two cheeseburgers; furthermore, he ate two orders of fries. (5)
  10. Because she is a skilled manager, Maria has received two promotions this year. (1)
  11. Professor Jackson speaks Chinese; however, he does not speak Russian. (5)
  12. In the morning I always cook breakfast. My kids seldom eat with me. (4)
  13. Whenever I see a full moon, I think of all my long-lost loves. (1)
  14. In the winter, snows falls. In the summer, the weather is warm and sunny. (4)
  15. Before I ate dinner with my mother-in-law for the first time, I drank a double martini. (1)

Exercise 4   **(page 16)**

   1. On July 4, my brother always has a big barbecue. I bring the food, and he cooks it. (4)
   2. My mother made tv dinners every Thursday for ten years. They were delicious. (4)
   3. Since he came to the United States, he has had six jobs. (1)
   4. In the summer, my sister sits in the backyard trying to get a tan. I go to Aruba. (4)
   5. She cried when her boyfriend lost $19,000 in Atlantic City. (2)
   6. The bus driver fell asleep in the bus station, so the bus was two hours late. (3)
   7. My car is so old that I might have to buy a new one this year. (2)
   8. While I was driving to Philadelphia, I saw many polluted rivers. (1)
   9. Last night a mouse walked into my bedroom. My cat enjoyed it a great deal. (4)
  10. Because you are so cheap, no one ever invites you to go away for the weekend. (1)
  11. Marco has a big mole on his nose, and several long hairs come out of it. (3)
  12. Mrs. Jackson hates Mr. Jackson. She loves his money though. (4)
  13. The professor doesn't understand his subject; however, he never stops talking. (5)
  14. You smell as if you had been working in a fish store your whole life. (2)
  15. If I had met you two years earlier, we would be married now. (1)

Exercise 5   **(page 17)**

1. I would marry you if you promised to stop smoking. (2)
2. She married her dance teacher. Now they go to clubs every Saturday night. (4)
3. After I saw her bank balance, I immediately fell in love. (1)
4. He is such a dedicated worker that he never leaves before 11:00 P.M. (2)
5. His wife works the graveyard shift, so she never sees her husband. (3)
6. Tomorrow after I get home, I will write a letter to my brother in jail. (1)
7. Whenever she cooks, I notify the fire department in advance. (1)
8. My mother is not Turkish, but her coffee is very thick and strong. (3)
9. Olivia's sister works for an international company. She is a programmer. (4)
10. The coach screamed at his players; in addition, he yelled at the referee. (5)
11. Although he yelled during the whole game, the team still lost. (1)
12. I was cheering for Germany, yet Brazil won the World Cup. (3)
13. Olga never loses anything. She just misplaces things. (4)
14. Hae Soo makes excellent kimchi; nevertheless, some people call it too spicy. (5)
15. I did not fully understand the punctuation of clauses before; however, I think I do now. (5)

PART 2.   DESCRIPTION PARAGRAPHS

Exercise 3   **(page 32)**

1. punctual—positive
2. passionate—positive
3. mugged—negative
4. fanatic—negative (overly zealous)
5. notorious—negative
6. compassion—positive
7. bellicose—negative
8. famous—positive
9. moldy—negative

Exercise 4   **(page 33)**

1. *Buried* is figurative and means that she has a lot of homework. *Ton* is also figurative, and means a great deal. In the second sentence *buried* has a figurative meaning.
2. In sentence one, *sick* is figurative and means tired or fed up. In the second sentence, sick is literal, that is, ill.
3. *Hooked* in sentence one is figurative and means in love with. Hooking a fish in sentence two is literal. It means to catch because the hook is in the fish's mouth.
4. *Thirsty* has a figurative meaning and means inquisitive.
5. *Whipped* is figurative and means beat by a large margin in a sporting event. Similarly, *crushed* is figurative and means really depressed.
6. Enrico's *crush* is figurative and means infatuated (this occurs a little before one is "hooked" on a person).

Exericse 5   **(page 34)**

1. is / is	6. do	11. is	16. are
2. are	7. is	12. is	17. isn't
3. are	8. is	13. come	18. have
4. is	9. drink	14. is	19. drink
5. have	10. consists	15. is	20. is

Exericse 6   **(page 36)**

1. are	**6.** are	**11.** drink	**16.** is
2. comes	**7.** work	**12.** was	**17.** come
3. is	**8.** live	**13.** has	**18.** is
4. are	**9.** is	**14.** is	**19.** drive
5. contains	**10.** was	**15.** is	**20.** consists

Exericse 7   **(page 37)**

1. are	**7.** was	**13.** has	**17.** was
2. are	**8.** have	**14.** works	**18.** comes
3. are	**9.** is	(work)	**19.** live
4. is	**10.** is	**15.** have	**20.** is
5. is	**11.** is	**16.** It was	
6. drink	**12.** is		

Exercise 8   **(page 39)**

1. toe	**5.** toe	**8.** body
2. toe	**6.** body	**9.** body
3. toe	**7.** body	**10.** body
4. toe		

Unit 2.1, Activity 4, Sherlock Holmes

Exercise 1   **(page 51)**

1. Sherlock Holmes had a "cold, precise, but admirably balanced mind," so romance (which is warm, imprecise, and often unbalanced) would be contrary to his nature.
2. He uses cocaine to combat the boring life that he leads when he has no cases and when there is nothing interesting in the newspaper.
3. Sherlock Holmes is lazy when he is not working, but when an interesting case presents itself, he has incredible energy.
4. He mocked people who fell in love ("a gibe") and also felt himself above them ("a sneer").
5. Watson is very interested in studying Sherlock Holmes and his personality. He respects him a great deal, is in awe of his abilities, and even defends his use of drugs.

Exercise 2   **(page 51)**

1. abhorrent: completely unacceptable because it seems morally wrong
2. cold: lacking normal human feelings such as sympathy, pity, humor, etc.
3. precise: very careful about small details
4. balanced: not giving too much importance to one thing
5. perfect: of the best possible type
6. false: untrue, not completely honest
7. softer: more subtle, weaker
8. admirable: to be revered
9. excellent: fantastic, wonderful
10. trained: well-educated and practiced
11. mental: related to the mind
12. sensitive: precise, to be dealt with carefully
13. high-power: very exact, able to enlarge or focus precisely

14. disturbing: bothersome

15. dubious: questionable, doubtful

16. questionable: not uncertain or possibly not true

17. greater: comparative form of great (good)

18. muscular: powerful, full of muscles

19. finest: best

20. aimless: without specific purpose

21. bodily: related to the body

22. professional: well-trained

23. untiring: continuous, never stopping because of fatigue

24. indefatigable: untiring, never stopping because of fatigue

25. remarkable: unusual or surprising

26. sparest: requiring little in the way of food, drink, clothing

27. simple: basic, no frills

28. occasional: once in a while

29. scanty: not big enough for a particular purpose

30. uninteresting: boring

Unit 2.2, Activity 1, Accommodations

Exercise 1   **(page 53)**

1. The food at the Proto Inn is bland and uninteresting, sort of like the food served in most school cafeterias.

2. Because it has a private beach, three swimming pools, nightly entertainment, and breathtaking views of the water, the Hotel Splendor is probably worth its high price.

3. "People watching" from the outdoor café means that patrons can sit and watch people stroll by. Usually these people look interesting, handsome or beautiful, and varied.

4. The advantages of the White Water Inn are that it is very clean, close to the beach, and has an excellent restaurant. However, the prices are high, and patrons do not have a private bathroom.

5. The evaluator rates the Blue Lagoon Hotel as "fair." The restaurant serves decent, but not fantastic food, and the prices are moderate.

6. Either answer is correct. I would stay at the Proto Inn because I don't stay in my room a great deal on vacation, and I prefer to spend my money on restaurants and attractions rather than hotel rooms. Or else, I would not stay in the Proto Inn because I have great memories of beautiful hotels that I have stayed in. I hate to stay in ugly, boring, cheap hotels.

7. At the White Water Inn, you would probably meet "locals," especially at the restaurant. Locals are people who live in the resort town all year round.

Exercise 2   **(page 54)**

(f)	**1.** up-to-date	a.	ultra-modern
(h)	**2.** spacious	b.	moderate
(a)	**3.** rustic	c.	very simple
(g)	**4.** immaculate	d.	concentrated
(c)	**5.** deluxe	e.	forgettable
(d)	**6.** scattered	f.	outdated
(j)	**7.** luxurious	g.	dirty

(i)	**8.** breathtaking	h. cramped
(e)	**9.** memorable	i. boring
(b)	**10.** exorbitant	j. without extras

Unit 2.3, Activity 1, Description of Mall Activities at Lloyd's Center in Portland, Oregon

Exercise 1   **(page 59)**

1. is turning	**9.** want no	**17.** are really catching
2. are enjoying and	progressive	**18.** no change
forgetting	**10.** are coming	**19.** no change
3. is filling	**11.** no change	**20.** are stopping
4. are racing	**12.** is playing	**21.** are buying
5. are moving	**13.** are wearing	**22.** no change
6. are enjoying	**14.** are gazing	**23.** no change
7. are leading	**15.** is moving	**24.** is complaining
8. are tugging	**16.** no change	**25.** no change

Exercise 2   **(page 59)**

1–2	Every Saturday afternoon, Lloyd's Center in Portland, Oregon turns into a big circus where people enjoy themselves and forget about their problems.
5–6	Other shoppers move leisurely because they enjoy the art of window shopping.
7–8–9	Parents lead small children by the hand, but the children tug in a different direction because they want to visit the nearest toy store to see the new Harry Potter figures.
10–11	Teenagers come to the mall to hang out, but they are not really interested in shopping. [or because they are not . . .]
13–14	They wear baggy pants and baseball hats turned around backward, so the shoppers gaze at them curiously.
15–16	The spinner on the twin turntables moves his hands at lightning speed, and there are three break-dancers in front of the band.
19–20	There are Chinese, Italian, Greek, Japanese, and Mexican stands, and (but) many people stop at McDonald's to buy hamburgers and fries.
21–22	Others buy freshly baked cookies because the aroma is enticing.
23–24	The mall is very crowded, but no one complains.

Part 2 Summary (page 64)

1. Writing a journal every day allows us to develop fluency and ease in writing. It makes it easier to get our ideas on paper because we do not have to worry about grades and mistakes.

2. Topics come from everyday life, the newspaper, television, the movies, and also from the first page of each Part where some topics are suggested.

3. The topic sentence introduces the paragraph, tells its type (description, narration, etc.), and indicates the direction the paragraph will take.

4. There are two types of topic sentence: the toe (standard, clear, concise), and the body (outrageous, interesting, eye-catching).

5. Literal meaning is the first dictionary meaning. Figurative meaning involves the connotation of the word. **Dead,** for example, means no longer in life in the literal meaning, and really exhausted in the figurative meaning. **"I will kill you if you tell this secret to anyone"** is probably intended figuratively, and means "It would really bother me."

6. The **adjective** is the most important part of speech in description because it paints a vivid picture of the person, place, or object for the reader/listener.

7. The best way to check subject/verb agreement is to underline all the verbs and check them against the subject which comes immediately before. Looking only at the verbs in the sentence is called **isolation** and is the most effective way of concentrating on this sticky problem.

8. The most common tense in paragraphs of description is **simple present.** Simple past is possible, especially to describe a place you visited or lived in a long time ago or a person you met in the distant past. The present progressive is possible to describe activities happening right now.

PART 3.   NARRATION PARAGRAPHS

Exercise 1   (page 73)

1. I have read that article. It is very clear and concise.
2. Mary decided to stay home. She wanted to prepare for the test.
3. I opened the front door right away, but no one was there.
4. Marcus never comes to class on time. He sleeps late every day.
5. We arrived at the movie theatre early, but the movie had started.
6. The storm was raging outside. We were warm and dry in the cabin.
7. Last week we went camping. It rained every day and night.
8. A very common bird in Pennsylvania is the bluejay. It has bright colors, but it sometimes eats baby birds from nests.
9. I hurried to answer the telephone. I thought it was my mother.
10. I opened the window, and the fresh air came right in.
11. I have not studied at all. I have to stay home tonight.
12. No one believed that he would pass, but he got a good grade.
13. English is difficult to read aloud. The words do not always sound like they look.
14. Jack works in a department store on Saturdays, and she works in an office during the week.

Exercise 2   (page 74)

1. Because he works nine hours every night, he is very tired when he gets to school in the morning.
2. She studied French for three years in high school, and she is studying German now.
3. John works 60 hours per week, but he never has money.
4. Although he is 6 feet 11 inches tall, he has never played basketball.
5. She always comes on time because she believes that punctuality is important.
6. He comes from a country where people speak Portuguese; nevertheless, his Spanish is excellent.
7. Max has never been to Egypt; as a result, he cannot discuss the pyramids from first-hand experience.
8. Sicily is an island located between Italy and Africa; consequently, it produces many types of citrus fruits.
9. Due to the fact that the rain was very heavy last night, the grass was all wet this morning.
10. Because of the fact that in Vietnam the monsoon season lasts four months, there is sometimes flooding in the lowlands.

Exercise 3 **(page 76)**

1. She is very tall. He is short.
2. I have never seen Paris, but I am going later this year.
3. I love her so much because she is rich.
4. My brother lives in an apartment. My sister lives in an old house.
5. Brock never gives flowers to his wife. He gives flowers to his mistress.
6. Brock's mistress has another lover. His name is Ridge.
7. My uncle and aunt live in New York and work in New Jersey.
8. I have never eaten food from Thailand, but I have heard that it is spicy.
9. The woman talked to the man, and he whispered in her ear.
10. Because she is an excellent speaker, I always stay awake when she talks.
11. Professor Balongi speaks Chinese and French. Professor Jones speaks only English.
12. In the morning, I always look at the clouds. This way I can predict the weather.
13. Whenever I hear her voice, I start to cry.
14. In the late afternoon it becomes difficult to play baseball. The sun is in your eyes.
15. After I saw his face, I wanted to run away.
16. On Halloween, my brother doesn't wear a mask. He just walks around with a smile.
17. My mother cooks Thanksgiving turkeys for everyone in the neighborhood. She is nice.
18. My father works in a restaurant. He is a chef.
19. In the summer, I go to the beach. My sister stays home.
20. He died. She cried.
21. The intelligent doctor married the wise nurse. The nurse was very happy.
22. My car broke down, so I had to take a taxi.
23. While I was driving to school, I saw two cats and three dogs.
24. Last night a bird came into my house. My cat ate it.
25. I will never go to Siberia. It is too cold.
26. In the morning, she makes coffee and drinks three cups.
27. Mrs. Jackson hates Mr. Jackson's dog, but she loves his cat.
28. The professor gave a lot of homework. No one could finish it.
29. You should take a shower. You smell.
30. I take a shower in the morning and a bath in the evening.
31. She married her high school sweetheart. He is a lawyer.
32. She married her first cousin. This custom is against the law in 38 states.
33. When I came home, I watched tv.
34. I watched tv when I came home.
35. While I was eating dinner, I watched tv.
36. Tomorrow I will study all night. After that, I will take a shower.
37. When she cooks, I eat out.
38. My mother is an excellent cook. She knows how to make everything.
39. The teacher prepared the test. Her husband cooked pasta.
40. This exercise is too long. I hate it.

Exercise 4   "The Tortoise and the Hare" (page 78)

One day a hare made fun of the short feet and slow pace of the tortoise, who answered laughing, "You might be fast, but I can certainly beat you in a race." Hare said, "Are you kidding? I will make a bet with you. Whoever gets to the big yellow tree on the other side of the river wins the race. The winner gets free food for a month, and the loser has to pay for it and prepare it." The next day all the animals assembled in the forest, and the race began. Hare bounded into the lead, but Tortoise kept moving steadily, without stopping. After a little while Hare was far ahead, and decided to stop for a snack, so he ate eight carrots. He was tired after eating and, seeing the Tortoise still far behind, stretched out on the ground and took a nap. The Tortoise passed him and swam across the river, and started up the final hill leading to the yellow tree. Just then, Hare woke up and saw that the sun had moved to the other side of the sky. He started to run as fast as he could, but he had some trouble crossing at the river because he could not swim very well. As he ran toward the finish line, Tortoise reached the tree and won the race.

Slow but steady wins the race.

Unit 3.2, Activity 2, "The Diamond Necklace" (page 91)

1. Matilda is unhappy because she has dreams of a beautiful life, with admirers, sumptuous dinners, nice jewelry, fancy tablecloths, and delicious food. Instead, she is married to a clerk in the Ministry of Education, and her life is boring and repetitious.
2. When she learns of the invitation to the ball, she immediately thinks that she has nothing to wear. After she and her husband solve that problem, she decides that she has no jewelry fitting for the occasion.
3. She now has to work very hard, cooking, cleaning, and shopping. It destroys her beauty and makes her an old woman.
4. We learn that she had a maid who shopped, cooked, and cleaned the house for her. She really didn't have any physical work to do in the house, so she really wasn't poor at all, just unhappy.

Part 3 Summary (page 99)

1. Chronological or time order organizes the paragraph of narration in precise steps. By following the sequence of events, the writer can reconstruct narrative (as in "The Tortoise and the Hare" story) or set the order for original narrations.
2. The chronological outline should be easy to follow. Use time words and transitions (*when, after, before, next, after that*) to connect one sentence in the outline with the next.
3. The most common topic sentence uses the words *remember* or *forget*: i.e., I will always remember the most embarrassing experience in my life. Or, "I will never forget the first time that I met my future husband."
4. "We live life in narration" means that in many of our conversations during a typical day, we recount events; narrate the plot of books, television programs, or movies; and tell what other people said in telephone or face-to-face conversations.
5. **While** = *past progressive, simple past*
   While I *was sleeping,* the phone *rang.*

By the time = *simple past, past perfect.*
By the time I *got* to the theatre, the movie *had* already *started.*

After = *simple past, simple past*
After I arrived in San Francisco, I took a tour of Alcatraz Prison.

Since = *present perfect, simple past.*
I *have loved* you since I first *met* you.

Precisely = *either past progressive or simple past.*
At precisely 9:00 A.M., I was eating dinner.
At precisely 9:00 A.M., my sister called.

6. In paragraphs of narration, the most common tenses are *simple past* and *past progressive.*

PART 4. PROCESS PARAGRAPHS

Exercise 2   (page 111)

1. Students must never cheat on tests.
2. Teachers don't have to study for examinations.
3. When you go to Dallas, you should see a Cowboys football game.
4. Grandma used to say, "You ought to eat everything on your plate."
5. When you want someone to check the oil you say, "Could you please check the oil?"
6. When I was six years old, I used to hate to go to school
7. The doctor told the heavy smoker, "You had better smoke less or quit smoking."
8. I get nervous every time that I'm stuck in traffic. I should try to relax because I cannot control the situation.
9. Married people are never supposed to accept diamond rings from admirers.
10. To make a delicious meal, you should follow the recipe carefully.

Exercise 6   (page 114)

I would like to give some advice to those who are taking the exit examination next week. First, students should take their time during the test. The test lasts 70 minutes, so there is no need to rush. Second, I believe that students should be creative because this impresses those who read the test. Third, students should be on time since they will not get nervous if they come early. In addition, students should bring an English-English dictionary to check the spelling of words. It is important to do this because most readers stress correct spelling and students should care about this, too. There is another piece of advice that I want to give. Do not worry. Those students who have done well all semester will certainly pass the exit examination. If they will not get nervous, they will surely do well. In conclusion, come on time, bring a pencil and a dictionary, don't worry, and be creative. The exit test is just like any other writing assignment.

Unit 4.2, Activity 1, Brainteaser

Solution to "The Basket of Cabbages, the Goat, and the Wolf" (page 129)

The key to the solution is that the boatman does not have to come back across the river empty each time when he returns to the first side. Here is the solution. The boatman must 1. Bring the goat across the river and return with an empty boat. 2.

Bring the wolf across and carry the goat back. 3. Bring the cabbage over and leave it on the other side with the wolf, returning with an empty boat. 4. Bring the goat back over.

Activity 2   **Mystery Mathematics (page 129)**

No. 2: You should choose to take the penny and double its value each day. By day 10, you would have $5.12. By day 20, the figure is $5263.36. By day 28 you would pass $1,000,000 ($1,347,420). At the end of 31 days, you would have $10,779,361.28.

Part 4 Summary (page 144)

1. Process paragraphs follow steps in their organization, a similar structure to the chronological outline for paragraphs of narration. In recipes, the steps are numbered. In other process paragraphs, discourse markers such as *first, second, third, then, after that,* and *finally* are used.

2. The two most common verb forms in process paragraphs are *modals* (especially should) and *imperatives.*

3. In the self-improvement program, we select the areas to be improved and work on them **one-by-one.** It is very difficult to change ourselves completely all at one time. In selecting one area for improvement and working on it for a few weeks, we give ourselves the chance to succeed.

4. In proofreading, *verbs* are the most important aspect because many of our mistakes involve them. Check for subject–verb agreement and verb tenses. Another common problem is *punctuation.* Sometimes commas are used instead of periods; other times periods are inserted incorrectly.

5. Giving advice to someone after the fact is useless because we cannot change the past. If a friend of yours ate in a bad restaurant, saw a terrible movie, or even married the wrong person, telling her so will not help her. By saying, "You shouldn't have married Omar Johnson," we don't help the situation.

PART 5. COMPARISON AND CONTRAST PARAGRAPHS

Exercise 1   **(page 155)**

1. Discourse markers: so, as a result, on the other hand, so, on the contrary, however, though, because.

2. The points of comparison are mixed, two in favor of Miami and one for Hallendale. In general, strong paragraphs should provide almost unanimous support for one point of view.

3. There is sufficient example and explanation. On the second point (safety), though, the proof against Miami is entirely subjective. Perhaps statistics should be used.

4. By choosing two of three points of comparison in favor of Miami, the writer makes a choice.

5. To prove that it is better to live in the suburbs, stress the relaxing atmosphere, the abundance of trees, grass, flowers, and shrubs, the convenient shopping malls, and the fact that people may be friendlier and it is easier to meet your neighbors.

Exercise 2   **(page 160)**

Adding Information	Contrast	Result
in addition	yet	as a result
also	but	consequently
moreover	however	therefore
furthermore	on the other hand	for this reason
and	nevertheless	since
	on the contrary	in conclusion
	although	thus
	while	inasmuch as
	whereas	so
	nonetheless	because
		hence

Exercise 3   **(page 161)**

1. While some people enjoy jogging, others prefer to sit on the couch watching tv.
2. My sister is an extrovert; on the other hand, my brother is an introvert.
3. Mario was well qualified for that job; however, he didn't get it.
4. Although we live very close to Los Angeles, we only go there once a month.
5. That Indian restaurant has fair prices; in addition, the food is very good.
6. We have never been to Singapore, but we would love to go there.
7. The Chileans are proud of their wine, and their cheese is excellent, too.
8. She is the vice-president of that company; nevertheless, she doesn't make as much as some managers.
9. Keiko lives far away from her friend Nabuko; as a result, she only sees her once a year.
10. Joseph cannot keep a secret; however, he has many friends.

Exercise 5   **(page 163)**

1. in fact
2. however
3. while
4. but
5. in order to
6. though
7. for example
8. so
9. therefore
10. thus
11. on the other hand
12. and
13. despite
14. both

Unit 5.2, Activity 1, "Lament" (page 176)

1. The mood is somber. The poet has just lost her husband and the father of her children and is trying to come to grips with the situation.
2. The poet cannot understand why someone so dear to her and so young should die. She is trying to understand the logic of life, but doesn't find any. The old saying "Life must go on" does not have any meaning for her.
3. The poet tries to cope by making use of her husband's things, such as making little trousers from his pants and saving his pennies in her son's piggybank.

Activity 2   **"To a Poor Old Woman" (page 178)**

1. In one way the poem is happy. The old woman, although poor, is enjoying a bit of life to the fullest. She is experiencing great joy from a simple object: a plum. On the other hand, she is poor and has little. She is also eating the plum from a paper bag on the street and not at a cozy table in her home or a restaurant.

2. By repeating the lines and breaking them up in different ways, Williams emphasizes the restorative effect that the plums have on the old woman. She is happy, even if only for a brief time.
   3. Plums might represent *life.* Follow the old maxim *carpe diem* (seize the day) and make *everything,* even the simplest thing, special.

Activity 3   **"Good-Bye My Fancy" (page 179)**

   1. The poet seems to be restless, ready for a change, and eager to explore new things. This is not clearly stated, but it generally fits the mood that Walt Whitman sets in many of his poems.
   2. It appears that he will leave. He has prepared his beloved, and most of all, prepared himself for the parting and the departure. Some critics interpret "My Fancy" as poetic inspiration. In this sense, the poet is about to die and thanks his fancy for a life of inspiration.

Part 5 Summary (page 185)

   1. In the *direct comparison method,* you choose points of comparison and then compare the two objects of comparison. For example, one difference between a Toyota Corolla and a Ford Taurus is gas mileage. First, introduce the difference. Then write about Toyota and Ford. After you have finished writing about gas mileage, move on to the next difference. In the *separated structure,* you write six to seven sentences only about Toyota, moving through all the points of comparison. Then you do the same for Ford, with the points of comparison discussed in exactly the same order.
   2. *Descending order* means starting with the most important difference and moving toward less well-defined ones. *Ascending order* is exactly the opposite; it means progressing toward the last difference, which is the strongest.
   3. First you brainstorm and find ten differences, without analysis. Then you analyze the quality of the differences, eliminating some and combining others. Finally, you come to the top four. Three differences will be used in the paragraph, with the fourth saved in case you have not written enough.
   4. *Perspective* is the way of looking at something. Tall and short people have different ways of looking at a doorway. Conservatives and liberals have different perspectives on political issues. *Bias* is a preconception and is the opposite of fairness. When people's views are biased, they cannot see a clear picture. For example, those who have a bias against city life might tend to look primarily at the negative aspects of the urban scene.

PART 6.   PERSUASION PARAGRAPHS

Exercise 3   **(page 197)**

   1. They exchange some jewelry. After that, they are introduced to the family and friends. It is exciting.
   2. This event usually takes place in the bride's house. All the relatives of the young couple are invited.
   3. The clothes worn by the couple are special. The girl wears a long white dress. The man wears a suit.
   4. The parents of the bride and groom are very proud on that day. Everyone looks so nice.
   5. On the day of the wedding everyone comes to the bride's house. They eat a special breakfast.

6. Sometimes the bride comes 20 minutes late to the church. The groom waits for her.
7. The bride throws a bouquet of flowers to all the women. The one who catches it will marry next.
8. The father of the bride dances with his daughter. This is one of the special moments of the day.
9. The bride and groom are not supposed to see each other on the wedding day before they meet in church. If they do it is supposed to be bad luck.
10. The house looks beautiful with all the flowers. Everyone is dressed so nicely, too.

Exercise 4   **(page 198)**

1. When the people come into the house, they immediately give their gifts to the bride and groom.
2. It is a special day because the bride and groom have been waiting for a long time for the ceremony.
3. The first-time bride usually wears white because this is the color of purity.
4. She throws the bouquet far across the room, and the person who catches it will get married next.
5. Every time I see a wedding, I remember my own ceremony when all my friends came.
6. Many people get married when they are in their late twenties because they are already working.
7. Because they love each other, they try to do everything to make the ceremony wonderful.
8. It is a special day, and everyone is very excited because they love the bride and groom.
9. On the afternoon of the wedding, the mother-in-law dances with the groom, who is very proud.
10. The music plays. When the bride walks down the aisle, everyone stands up.

Exercise 6   **(page 199)**

1. There are too many cars because most people think that driving a car is more convenient than taking a bus when they want to go places, so almost every adult has a car.
2. The pollution problem will decrease if the department of transportation does something about it.
3. Because it is an independent country, Poland is trying to build a new economic system; however, the change from one system to another has caused very high unemployment, low productivity, and high prices of goods in Poland.
4. The most negative aspect of education in my country is that there are not enough schools and universities.
5. South Korea has been separated from North Korea since 1950. It is one of the most serious problems in my country.
6. People drink for many reasons, but the result is always the same. They have some health problems.
7. After they work ten hours, they will go to the movies tomorrow.
8. People not only visit some places but also spend time at home.

Exercise 7   **(page 200)**

1. Carlos has never flown in a plane, and he does not plan to do so in the near future either.
2. After I finish my work, I will go to the movies.
3. Before leaving work, Jim called his mother.
4. Every day I hope to learn more and more.
5. By the time I got home, my sister had left.
6. When she walked into the room, the child was sleeping.
7. Whenever I see her, I give her a big smile.
8. I think about her every day.
9. By the time you get to class, the teacher will have left.
10. Yesterday, while I was shaving, the doorbell rang.

Exercise 8   **(page 201)**

1. Tomorrow when she wakes up, she will call her friend.
2. While I was studying, my brother called.
3. I demand that he be fired.
4. I believe that she is a good friend.
5. Six years ago, I came from Guatemala.
6. The doctor asked me if I spoke Russian.
7. Guana told him that she had to go home early.
8. I have never seen a fish that big.
9. The professor told me to study harder.
10. When I saw the president, I shook his hand.

Unit 6.1, Activity 1, "Honey Boy": Analyzing Characters (page 207)

1. The mother may be seen as nurturing (she serves iced tea to her son and his friend) and kind, and worthy of respect (from the sheriff). However, she also accepts stolen goods (from her son) and gets revenge on Big Blue by lying.
2. The sheriff acts according to the stereotype: respectful toward senior citizens and tough toward the youth (Big Blue). He accepts the mother's lie, which is an interesting decision.
3. Big Blue is certainly not a loyal friend. He is greedy for money and would do anything to get it, even kill his best friend.
4. If we accept the mother's actions as good, then the sheriff acted righteously because Big Blue will be punished. Big Blue's betrayal of friendship must be particularly bothersome for the sheriff.
5. He accepted the mother's lie and probably does not carry out his duty as a law enforcement professional, which is to catch the criminal (Honey Boy) and close the case.
6. Big Blue acted in a very selfish manner, killing his best friend for the money.
7. Because the ad said "Wanted Dead or Alive," Big Blue acted in a completely legal manner in killing Honey Boy.
8. The setting of the story is the Deep South (Bayou, Mississippi) in the early 1930s. The time could not be the 1920s because the radio was not invented until 1925 and would not have arrived in Honey Boy's house until later. Similarly, the setting could not be the 1940s because Honey Boy and Big Blue would have been called to the army to fight in World War II.

9. The setting is important because the sheriff relies on the mother's word to identify Honey Boy. There is no forensic evidence such as fingerprints, dental records, or DNA. Also, sheriffs in the South typically have more power and discretion than their counterparts in other parts of the country.

10. This is a complicated question. The sheriff is outraged at Big Blue's betrayal of friendship to Honey Boy and is willing to help the mother get revenge on him. He was probably also happy to get rid of someone like Big Blue.

Unit 6.1, Activity 2, "Honey Boy": The Morality/Legality Matrix (page 208)

Action	Moral?	Legal?
Honey Boys kills someone	No	No
Big Blue kills Honey Boy	No	Yes
Mom lies	No (But this may be acceptable if you accept her right to revenge.)	No (However, she had not taken an oath to tell the truth.)
The sheriff accepts Mom's lie	No (But this action is necessary to make the mother's action effective.)	No. He is not fulfilling his duty as a law enforcement professional.
The sheriff arrests Big Blue	No (He knows that he has committed a crime.)	No. Arresting an innocent man goes against his job duties.

Unit 6.1, Activity 3, "Honey Boy": The Projection Matrix (page 209)

Honey Boy	Honey Boy is dead. He has been shot by Big Blue. However, because he has not been identified, he is buried in an unmarked grave. Of course, according to the law he is not dead, so he is still "wanted dead or alive."
Big Blue	Big Blue will probably get capital punishment (and quickly) for killing an innocent man.
Mom	Mom cannot go to the cemetery to visit Honey Boy because she did not identify his body. She must sit at home, all alone, and she will not even listen to the radio because it reminds her of Honey Boy. In addition, she cannot accept condolence visits because her son is not officially dead.
The Sheriff (Will he get a promotion, a demotion, or will he remain in the same position?)	By accepting the mother's lie, the sheriff has placed himself in a precarious situation. He has not done anything to further his career. Honey Boy is still wanted dead or alive. Big Blue has been arrested and will be killed for murdering someone else (who the sheriff cannot even identify). Furthermore, Honey Boy killed someone, whose murder has not been solved. There are many dead bodies and no legal solutions.
Big Blue's Mother (hypothetical—with the premise that Big Blue receives quick capital punishment)	The difference between Big Blue's mother and Honey Boy's mother is that if Big Blue receives capital punishment, at least his mother can participate in all the healing ceremonies surrounding death (visits from relatives and friends, receiving condolences, and trips to the cemetery to see her son's grave).

Unit 6.2, Activity 3, Life Expectancy (page 212)

1. the dangerous activities (P)
2. they are involved in (C)
3. suffered (P)
4. which means that they feel invulnerable (C)
5. director of the Tristate Health Group (P)
6. manager of Bergen Family Practice (P)
7. internist at New York Hospital (P)
8. Australian neurologist (P)
9. who believe (C)
10. who has tracked men's attitudes toward medical care (C)
11. conducted by physicians and nurses (P)

Part 6 Summary (page 218)

1. *Subjective proof* includes personal opinion and reaction (I think the dish is too salty. I feel that this car is too expensive). *Objective proof* includes statistics, articles, columns, and other data that support an opinion. Because objective proof is much more widely accepted and less subject to debate, it is more effective as support in a persuasion paragraph.
2. The structure of a persuasion paragraph is according to reasons to support the main opinion. The topic sentence states the opinion clearly and concisely. Each reason must be accompanied by proof, either objective or subjective. Three or four reasons are probably sufficient. The last sentence in the paragraph should be a conclusion.
3. The outline should contain the four reasons and the support, written in brief phrases. Full sentences are not required. To write the paragraph, just follow the reasons and the support.
4. The goal of the persuasion paragraph is not simply to state an opinion. It is to *change the mind of the readers* so that they agree with your opinion. If you can succeed in modifying their view of the subject, you have *persuaded* them to come over to your side.

PART 7.   THE ESSAY

Exercise 1   (page 225)

1. **bump:** noun, negative, def. no. 2: *a small raised area on a surface*
2. **blame:** verb, negative, def. no. 1: *to say or think that someone or something is responsible for something bad*
3. **bed:** noun, positive, def. no. 6: *an area of a garden, park, etc. that has been prepared for plants to grow in*
4. **bad:** adjective, negative, def. no. 8: *food that is bad is not safe to eat because it has decayed*
5. **chained:** verb, negative, def. no. 1: *to fasten someone or something to something else using a chain, especially in order to prevent it from escaping or being stolen*
6. **challenging:** adjective, positive, def. no. 1: *difficult in an interesting or enjoyable way*
7. **delicate:** adjective, positive, def. no. 5: *a taste, smell, or color that is pleasant and not strong*
8. **dense:** adjective, negative, def. no. 3: *informal: not able to understand things easily; stupid*

9. cold: adjective, negative, def. no. 5: *lacking normal human feelings such as sympathy, pity, humor, etc.*

10. fished: verb, negative, def. no. 2: *to search through a bag, pocket, container, etc., trying to find something*

11. packed: adjective, negative (or positive if you own the business or like crowds), def. no. 1: *extremely full of people*

12. personally: adverb, positive, def. no. 4: *as a friend or someone you have met*

13. raises: verb, neutral, def. no. 5: *to grow plants or keep cows, pigs, etc. so that they can be sold or used as food*

14. rather: adverb, neutral (depending on the adjective that follows—here it is somewhat positive), def. no. 3: *fairly or to some degree*

15. repeats: noun, negative, def. no. 3: *a television or radio program that is broadcast again*

16. report: noun, negative, def. no. 5: *formal: the noise of an explosion or shot*

17. return: verb, neutral, def. no. 2a: *to give something back to its owner, or to put something back in its place*

18. sensitive: adjective, negative, def. no. 3: *able to feel physical sensations, especially pain, more than usual*

19. strictly: adverb, positive (if you are very religious) or negative (if you are not), def. no. 4: *in a way that must be obeyed*

20. taxing: verb, negative, def. no. 1b: *to charge someone a tax for their income, property, etc.*

21. terrace: noun, positive, def. no. 1: *a flat outdoor area next to a building or on a roof, where you can sit outside to eat, relax, etc.*

22. upset: noun, positive (if you like the team), or negative (if you don't), def. no. 2: *an occasion when a person or team that is not expected to win beats a stronger opponent in a competition*

23. youth: noun, neutral, def. no. 2: *a word meaning a teenage boy, used especially in newspapers*

24. zipped: verb, positive, def. no. 2: *to do something or go somewhere very quickly*

25. while: verb, positive, def. no. 1: *to spend time in a pleasant and lazy way*

26. dead: adjective, negative, def. no. 5: *spoken: very tired*

27. monitor: verb, positive, def. no. 1: *to carefully watch, listen to, or examine something over a period of time; to check for any changes or developments*

28. program: verb, neutral, def. no. 1: *to set a machine to operate in a particular way*

29. novel: adjective, positive, def. no. 1: *new, different, and unusual*

30. deal: noun, negative, def. no. 3: *treatment, the way that someone is treated in a particular situation*

Exercise 2 (page 234)

1. The elk that I ate for dinner last night was very tasty.
2. Dogs, which are the most loyal of all animals, sniff the bushes.
3. Rice, which is the staple food in Korean cooking, is rarely eaten in France.
4. The rice that your mother made tasted like glue.
5. Professor Balango, whose students dislike him, doesn't prepare for class.
6. I have fond memories of my hometown, which is located near a waste dump.
7. We took a trip to Brooklyn, where they speak very colorful English.
8. The town in which Giacomo lives is quaint and beautiful.
9. Joanna's husband left for good, which caused her to celebrate for four days.
10. I fell in love with the woman who was wearing the army uniform.

Exercise 3   **(page 234)**

1. I would never marry a person who is lazy.
2. My brother, whose wife works in a bank, is a pediatrician.
3. President Clinton, who finished his term in 2000, is now a consultant.
4. She passed the test that she took last week.
5. I never talk to people who look unfriendly.
6. I will never forget the time when I lost my favorite necklace.
7. She will always remember the restaurant where she met her husband..
8. Jan has three brothers, one of whom lives in Afghanistan.
9. I have two cars, one of which does run very well.
10. The cat that is sleeping on the couch is a Calico.
11. The policemen arrested the man who had stolen the car.
12. I called my sister Joan, who lives in Oklahoma.
13. I will never forget my trip to Hawaii, where I saw the most incredible flowers.
14. I want to tell you about the place where we saw a volcano.
15. Mosquitoes, which bite once and then die, thrive in humid areas.

Exercise 4   **(page 235)**

1. In the early 19th century, Venezuela, where Simon Bolivar was born, achieved independence.
2. Germany, which had been divided into East and West in 1945, is now a unified country.
3. Sudan, whose population is 121 million, is the largest country in Africa.
4. Thailand, which is located in southeast Asia, has never been ruled by a foreign power.
5. There are six principal dialects of Spanish, which is the official language of 12 South American countries.
6. Ranjett's mother won two tickets to travel anywhere in the continental United States, which made her very happy.
7. My brother, a dentist, has never visited a place as exotic as Tahiti.

Exercise 5   **(page 237)**

1. a founding member of the pioneering rap trio (P)
2. Run DMC (P)
3. where he grew up (C)
4. whose real name was Jason Mizell (C)
5. a police spokesman (P)
6. 25 (P)
7. who was not a member of RUN DMC (C)
8. better known as Run (P)
9. better known as DMC (P)
10. that some believe were the result of an East Coast–West Coast rap war (C)
11. where you feel the gangs from the minute you step into town to the time you leave (C)
12. located above a restaurant (P)
13. where the members of Run DMC grew up (C)
14. 39 (P)
15. who grew up (C)
16. the founder of the hip-hop group Public Enemy (P)
17. a New York radio station DJ (P)

18. who had been friends (C)
19. who went out looking for trouble (C)
20. that builds (C)
21. that creates (C)
22. 33 (P)

Unit 7.1, Activity 1, "The Tell-Tale Heart" (page 247)

1. The relationship is not clearly stated. It could be tenant–landlord, nephew–uncle, son–father, or caretaker–sick person.
2. The setting is also not clear. It is an apartment. Poe does not tell us when the story is taking place or where. This is typical of his writing.
3. First, he says that madmen know nothing. He, though, proceeds cautiously, with a clear goal in mind. He then talks about being in such control of his emotions and movements that it took him more than an hour to move his head into the old man's room. He also describes the wise precautions taken for the concealment of the body. Finally, he invites the policemen into the apartment. All these actions, which are supposed to show the reader that he is not mad, instead show that he is.
4. The police officers don't leave because the narrator is behaving strangely. Also, and most importantly, he invites the officers into the old man's bedroom, a very odd place to sit and talk.
5. Most innocent people would be very nervous and would probably not invite the police officers to inspect their houses.
6. The "you" could be a psychiatrist, a lawyer, a police officer, a judge, or the reader. Or, the narrator could be speaking to himself.
7. The odd grammar and punctuation in the first sentences heighten the effect that the narrator is very nervous, possibly insane, and filled with guilt over his crime.

Unit 7.1, Activity 2, "After Twenty Years" (page 251)

1. He is waiting for his friend Jimmy Wells, with whom he made an appointment to meet 20 years before.
2. He has made money. This is shown by the large diamond in his scarf pin. He has been working in the West, probably doing something illegal.
3. He can tell it is not his friend because of his nose. Jimmy Wells had a large Roman nose, not a small pug nose.
4. Jimmy Wells has been a police officer in New York.
5. Jimmy can't arrest his friend because they were too close.
6. The surprise is that the second man to meet Bob is not Jimmy Wells, but a plainclothes police officer, who arrests Bob.
7. Both have surprise endings, but leave a great deal unexplained.

Part 7 Summary (page 276)

1. The essay writing process involves five steps: prewriting, draft, revision, editing, and final proof.
2. The thesis statement presents the main topic of the essay. It also takes a broad topic and narrows or focuses it so that it can be managed in a five-paragraph essay

3. The essay is organized according to an introductory paragraph, three interior paragraphs, and a concluding paragraph.
4. In the editing phase, you check the following areas thoroughly: grammar, punctuation, and spelling.
5. The body of the essay usually consists of three paragraphs. Each of these paragraphs has a topic sentence, a main idea, and supporting sentences. The paragraph usually consists of five to seven sentences.
6. In the conclusion, the writer summarizes the thesis statement and the main ideas of each paragraph in a forceful and interesting manner. The conclusion is where the writer tries to leave the reader with a memorable impression.
7. Essays, in the form of editorials, may be found on the last two pages of the news section of most newspapers. They are also found on the last page of news magazines such as *Time, Newsweek,* or *U.S. News and World Report.*